The Dread Plague and the Cow Killers

Between 1947 and 1954, the Mexican and US governments waged a massive campaign against a devastating livestock plague, *aftosa* or foot-and-mouth disease. Absorbing over half of US economic aid to Latin America and involving thousands of veterinarians and ranchers from both countries, battalions of Mexican troops, and scientists from Europe and the Americas, the campaign against *aftosa* was unprecedented in size. Despite daunting obstacles and entrenched opposition, it successfully eradicated the virus in Mexico, and reshaped policies, institutions, and knowledge around the world. Using untapped sources from local, national, and international archives, Thomas Rath provides a comprehensive history of this campaign, the forces that shaped it – from presidents to peasants, scientists to journalists, *pistoleros* to priests, mountains to mules – and the complicated legacy it left. More broadly, he uses the campaign to explore the formation of the Mexican state, changing ideas of development and security, and the history of human–animal relations.

Thomas Rath is Associate Professor of History at University College London. He is the author of *Myths of Demilitarization in Postrevolutionary Mexico, 1920–60* and numerous articles, chapters, and reviews on Mexico's political and social history.

CAMBRIDGE LATIN AMERICAN STUDIES

General Editors

KRIS LANE, Tulane University
MATTHEW RESTALL, Pennsylvania State University

Editor Emeritus

HERBERT S. KLEIN
Gouverneur Morris Emeritus Professor of History, Columbia University and Hoover
Research Fellow, Stanford University

Other Books in the Series

(Continued after the Index)

The Dread Plague and the Cow Killers

The Politics of Animal Disease in Mexico and the World

THOMAS RATH

University College London

CAMBRIDGE
UNIVERSITY PRESS

CAMBRIDGE
UNIVERSITY PRESS

University Printing House, Cambridge CB2 8BS, United Kingdom

One Liberty Plaza, 20th Floor, New York, NY 10006, USA

477 Williamstown Road, Port Melbourne, VIC 3207, Australia

314–321, 3rd Floor, Plot 3, Splendor Forum, Jasola District Centre,
New Delhi – 110025, India

103 Penang Road, #05-06/07, Visioncrest Commercial, Singapore 238467

Cambridge University Press is part of the University of Cambridge.

It furthers the University's mission by disseminating knowledge in the pursuit of
education, learning, and research at the highest international levels of excellence.

www.cambridge.org
Information on this title: www.cambridge.org/9781108844482
DOI: 10.1017/9781108951357

First published 2022

Printed in the United Kingdom by TJ Books Limited, Padstow Cornwall

A catalogue record for this publication is available from the British Library.

Library of Congress Cataloging-in-Publication Data
NAMES: Rath, Thomas, 1978- author.
TITLE: The dread plague and the cow killers : the politics of animal disease in Mexico and
the world / Thomas Rath, University College London.
DESCRIPTION: Cambridge, United Kingdom ; New York, NY : Cambridge University Press,
2022. | Series: Cambridge Latin American studies | Includes bibliographical references
and index.
IDENTIFIERS: LCCN 2021063067 (print) | LCCN 2021063068 (ebook) |
ISBN 9781108844482 (hardback) | ISBN 9781108948234 (paperback) |
ISBN 9781108951357 (epub)
SUBJECTS: LCSH: Foot-and-mouth disease–Mexico–History–20th century. |
BISAC: HISTORY / Latin America / General
CLASSIFICATION: LCC SF793. R38 2022(print) | LCC SF793(ebook) |
DDC 636.089/458–dc23/eng/20220222
LC record available at https://lccn.loc.gov/2021063067
LC ebook record available at https://lccn.loc.gov/2021063068

ISBN 978-1-108-84448-2 Hardback

Contents

Figures and Table

Figures

Table

Acknowledgments

First, I would like to thank everyone who helped me to conduct research, particularly Donna Glee Williams, who talked to me about her parents' experiences and suggested other sources; the Wellcome Trust, whose grant allowed me to conduct preliminary research; Melleta Bell and her colleagues at the Archive of the Big Bend, Alpine, Texas; Fabio Ciccarello at the Food and Agriculture Organization; Christopher Boyer, who generously shared his knowledge of Mexican archives and catalogs; Juan Manuel Cervantes Sánchez and Ana Román de Carlos at the Universidad Nacional Autónoma de México (UNAM); Yolande Yates, who kindly sent me the as-yet-unpublished memoirs of her father, agricultural economist Paul Lamartine Yates; the dedicated staff at the state archive of Guanajuato, the Truman Presidential Library, and the Archivo General de la Nación, Mexico City; and Ashley Black, Alex Aviña, Diego Hurtado, Jayson Porter, Julia del Palacio Langer, Myra Ann Houser, Aaron Moulton, and Elizabeth O'Brien, who helped me gather and make sense of far-flung documents.

Parts of this book have been reprinted with permission in revised form from "Burning the Archive, Building the State? Politics, Paper, and US Power in Postwar Mexico," *Journal of Contemporary History* 55:4 (2020): 764–792 and "A Tale of Four Laboratories: Animal Disease, Science, and Politics in Cold War Latin America," in *Itineraries of Expertise: Science, Technology and the Environment in Latin America's Long Cold War*, edited by Andra B. Chastain and Timothy Lorek (Pittsburgh: Pittsburgh University Press, 2020), 159–77.

While writing I benefited from the advice and encouragement of Bill Booth, Ernie Capello, Mark Carey, Andra Chastain, Ben Fallaw, María

Teresa Fernández Aceves, Vanessa Freije, Paul Gillingham, Alex Goodall, Gema Kloppe-Santamaria, Alan Knight, Christopher London, Tim Lorek, Nicola Miller, Nathaniel Morris, Andrew Paxman, Pablo Piccato, Garbriela Ramos, David Sim, and Jeffrey Taffet. Noemi Morales Sánchez made some handsome maps of some disparate places. Ben Smith and Paulo Drinot deserve a special thanks for reading the whole manuscript – colleagues who wear big professional hats and can corral a herd of insights. All the usual disclaimers apply. My biggest debt is to my family and especially Hema, who takes care of me while I am busy making other book-writing plans. The book is dedicated to the memory of Kayte, who loved animals.

Abbreviations

BAI	Bureau of Animal Industry
CMAEFA	Comisión México-Americana para la Erradicación de la Fiebre Aftosa
CNC	Confederación Nacional Campesina
DFS	Dirección Federal de Seguridad
FAO	Food and Agriculture Organization
MAP	Mexican Agricultural Program
OIE	Office International des Epizooties
PAHO	Pan American Health Organization
PANAFTOSA	Pan American Center for Foot-and-Mouth Disease
PASB	Pan American Sanitary Bureau
PAHO	Panamerican Health Organization
PRI	Partido Revolucionario Institucional
SSG	Subsecretaría de Ganadería
UN	United Nations
UNS	Unión Nacional Sinarquista
USDA	United States Department of Agriculture

Introduction

The disease went by many names and people told different stories about it. Scientists called it *aftosa*, or foot-and-mouth disease. The other anglophone term, hoof-and-mouth disease, was more precise: cloven-hoofed animals carrying the virus typically foamed at the mouth, developed painful blisters, and lost weight. Some aborted and a handful – mainly newborn animals – died. US and Mexican officials argued that the disease was a "dread plague" – a terrifying and grave threat to national well-being, akin to floods, storms, or earthquakes.[1] From 1947 to 1954 a bilateral commission waged a campaign across central Mexico against this dangerous enemy. Many Mexicans regarded the campaign as a farcical and cruel affair. Most animals seemed to recover quickly, and many farmers believed that the disease was simply a version of a mild, familiar illness which they called *mal de yerba* or *mal de boca* – grass or mouth sickness. Few had seen anything quite like the anti-aftosa campaign before: brigades of pith-helmeted veterinarians, cowhands, and soldiers who dressed in bizarre heavy rubber overalls, drove through the country in jeeps, personnel carriers, and souped-up former ambulances, traipsed over the sierra on horses or mules, or paddled along rivers in wooden canoes, imposing quarantine, exacting fines, and dousing farms with acrid chemicals. At the start of campaign, they corralled hundreds of thousands of cows, pigs, goats, and sheep and shot them dead. Compared to run-of-the mill *robavacas* – cattle rustlers – their motives were hard to understand. Unlike Santiago *matamoros*, Spain's legendary Moor-slayer,

[1] USDA press release draft, September 1950, HP, box 5, foot and mouth.

these men seemed menacing but cowardly, even slightly ridiculous – mere *matavacas*, or cowkillers.[2]

A letter sent to the campaign's headquarters in Morelia in September 1947 espoused one of the most popular theories about the campaign, mocked its leaders, and urged them to come clean:

> Once more we notice that you are continuing to slaughter our livestock and that you believe or rather are trying to make us believe that there is a disease. I wish to advise you that there is no such disease and that all you want to do is to slaughter all our livestock so you can bring in yours. Say it outright, and don't come to us with these fucking bullshit stories (*chingaderas*). If you want to bring your cattle in go ahead and do it but don't come to us with fucking stupid stories (*cabronadas*) about disease and don't fuck about killing our animals. We won't stand for any more of your idiocy. Listen Doctor, we Mexicans will not stand for it. We are tough fuckers (*chingones*). If some of our cattle get sick it is because the airplane drops powdered soda on the pastures, so in your mother's name we beg you to stop bothering us as we have our children and we feed them with that milk.[3]

This letter puzzled its recipient, Dr. Richard Omohundro, a US veterinarian working on the campaign. Was it from one person, or many? The letter oscillated between the first and third person, and claimed to represent a large group who referred to themselves, menacingly, as Omohundro's "friends." Why, deep down, were people so angry? Had they not received the cash indemnities the commission paid? Did they really believe the story of the poison-dumping planes, or were they exploiting the affair for other ends? Were they peasant farmers who, as some of Omohundro's colleagues believed, enjoyed a peculiar sentimental attachment to their livestock? The commission had already suffered its share of opposition and bloodshed. Did the letter augur more? Perhaps it was nothing to worry about. Major Vargas, a Mexican army officer attached to the commission, insisted the letter "didn't mean a thing" and was simply one of the anonymous threats local officials received "quite frequently" from Catholic "fanatics" opposed to Mexico's post-revolutionary regime. But were the judgment and motives of Mexican officials entirely to be trusted? Omohundro had his doubts. Despite playing it down, Major Vargas still took the letter and passed it to Mexico's "secret police." Omohundro carefully made his own copies, nodded along with his colleague's assurances, kept his true opinion to

---

[2] Gipson, *Cow Killers*, 6.
[3] Transcription of letter, contained in Omohundro, Morelia, to CMAEFA, Mexico City, September 9, 1947, CMAEFA, Operations, box 29, Oaxaca.

himself, and then composed a confidential report for his own government describing his confusion and unease.[4]

The sheer size, novelty, and complexity of the campaign against aftosa practically guaranteed an outbreak of competing narratives. Like some strange, hulking piece of machinery or a convoluted work of architecture, it afforded multiple vantage points, and looked very different depending on where you stood. Absorbing over half of US economic aid to Latin America between 1947 and 1951, and involving thousands of veterinarians and ranchers from both countries, battalions of Mexican troops, and scientists from Europe and the Americas, the campaign against aftosa was unprecedented in scale.[5] When it first began, US officials working on the campaign boasted that their budget exceeded that of the early Marshall Plan: "We were spending two million dollars a month and they were spending less."[6] For five years, the joint US–Mexico commission counted, mapped, quarantined, sacrificed and vaccinated millions of livestock across a swathe of central Mexico – from the tropical eastern coast of Veracruz across the densely populated central plateau, to Guerrero and Oaxaca in the west – and sought to encourage new practices of husbandry and mechanized farming. By 1952, the commission had inspected more livestock than any other sanitary campaign in history.[7] When the campaign finally came to an end, its success even surprised many of the officials who ran it. Understandably, both governments boasted of a feat "unequalled in the annals of animal-disease eradication."[8]

Public congratulations notwithstanding, the campaign was also a rather opaque operation. The popular theories and rumors that arose around it, like the one outlined above, were almost entirely wrong in their specifics. The campaign was not designed to destroy Mexican agriculture, crush the peasantry, drive US cattle southwards, steal meat to feed US soldiers in Korea, poison farmers and their lands, or annex a chunk of Mexican territory. However, taking these theories literally may not be best approach. If we read conspiracies and rumors analogically (as social historians of medicine suggest we should), they appear more insightful, pointing to some underlying political truths.[9] Sure enough, the aftosa campaign was not quite what it claimed to be. It was not simply the result

---

[4] Ibid.
[5] United States Agency of International Development, *US Overseas Loans and Grants Dataset* (Greenbook), https://data.usaid.gov/Administration-and-Oversight/U-S-Overseas-Loans-and-Grants-Greenbook-Data/7cnw-pw8v (accessed December 2019).
[6] Interview with Patrick F. Morris, February 12, 2007, FAOHP.
[7] USDA, *Campaign*, 291.   [8] Ibid., iii.   [9] Ramírez, *Enlightened*, 215.

of disinterested economic measurements and technical judgment – of "the science," as a contemporary British politician might put it.[10] Rather, it was shaped by a host of undeclared political and economic interests, among which US groups and institutions loomed very large. The campaign was not simply an effort to spread the benefits of modern science and illuminate the dark corners of rural ignorance like a candle in a peasant shack. US and Mexican officials acknowledged some of the campaign's practices and effects; others they carefully concealed. The bonfire with which Mexican officials incinerated their share of the commission archive in August 1952 was only the most dramatic way this was done.[11] The USDA's in-house historian wrote a long, detailed, and sometimes fascinating account, but the government declined to publish it.[12] In short, the campaign had plenty of its own hypocrisies – its own *cabronadas*, we might say. It kept secrets, but not precisely the ones that most of its critics were looking for.

In one way, this book is a response to the challenge implicit in the anonymous letter stuffed into a post box in Morelia in 1947 – to tell an accurate, coherent, and compelling story of why this campaign was waged, how it worked, and why it mattered, keeping idiocy and bullshit to a minimum. The story of the campaign necessarily fans out in many directions. As Joshua Specht has noted, histories of modern agriculture tend to be at once deeply local and thoroughly global.[13] It is a story of man-made institutions and attitudes, and their entanglement with ecological processes. Tying these parts together is a simple central argument: that Mexico's aftosa crisis was just that, a crisis. The epizootic posed a concatenation of political, economic, social, technical, and geopolitical problems whose solution was genuinely uncertain or, in historians' parlance, contingent. As tempting as it is to liken the crisis to an analytical cross-section, slicing through the carcass of Mexican and US society and exposing hidden relationships, this is not sufficient. Like other crises and disasters – epidemics, earthquakes, hurricanes – it uncovered preexisting power structures, and was shaped by them. But the conflicts and debates unleashed by this epizootic had a dynamic and momentum of their own.

---

[10] Butler, "Follow the Science."   [11] Rath, "Burning."

[12] USDA, *Campaign*. A copy of this manuscript is available at ABB. The main author was Darel McConkey of the USDA's Agricultural Research Service. Various correspondence, September 1992, ABB, N82–4A, box 1.

[13] Specht, *Red Meat*, 11.

Their effects were more than the sum of preexisting structures, traditions, and expectations. For this reason, they are worth reconstructing in detail.

Taking this story seriously as a crisis helps us answer some big historical questions – questions which Dr. Omohundro, in his own hurried way, was forced to ponder one morning in his hotel room in Morelia. One conundrum was Mexico's place in the world. In the 1940s, Mexican and US societies integrated as never before. Wartime cooperation was underpinned by a shared vision of capitalist modernization and industrialization that emerged among Mexican and US elites. Mexican farm laborers and raw materials flowed northward; US loans, investment, technical expertise, consumer culture, and political propaganda poured into Mexico. This study joins a growing body of work concerned with clarifying the parameters within which Mexicans – both citizens and government officials – were able to resist, reshape, or deflect the power and world-making ambitions of the United States, and trace how Mexico's international and domestic politics were intertwined.[14] Some studies argue that integration unleashed a vast wave of US influence steadily eroding Mexican sovereignty, or pushed Mexican diplomacy into a "feeble balancing act" along a tiny wire of political options.[15] And yet, even as the end of the Second World War robbed Mexico of its bargaining power as a wartime ally, the country retained room for maneuver, and access to diplomatic techniques honed in earlier confrontations with the United States. Mexico's dependence on US credit and markets, and hardening anticommunism in the United States surely created constraints. But integration could also offer new kinds of leverage and routes of international engagement.

Fundamentally, both countries were concerned with aftosa because it threatened their livestock industries and their trade. US experts estimated that while aftosa killed no more than 5 percent of infected cattle (and sometime far fewer pigs, goats, and sheep), it reduced the overall productivity of meat and dairy production by 25 percent.[16] Aftosa was at once a matter of security – a threat to already established prosperity and production – and a brake on the wheels of future development. This study thus

---

[14] On the international and domestic politics of health and medicine see Cueto, *Cold War*, and Soto Laveaga, *Jungle*. For studies focusing on diplomatic, military, and economic ties, see: Moreno, *Yankee*; Jones, *The War*; Alexander, *Sons*, 123–14; Pettinà, "Adapting"; Thornton, *Revolution in Development*; Zolov, *Last Good Neighbour*; Buchenau, "Ambivalent"; Keller, *Mexico's Cold War*; Lopes and Zuleta, *Mercados*.

[15] Buchenau, "Ambivalent," 459. See also, Niblo, *War*.

[16] Shahan, "La fiebre aftosa," 578.

intersects with recent works exploring the long, pre-war roots of development, the tensions within US Cold War-era development projects, and how different societies engaged with them.[17] To prevent the spread of aftosa northward, the US government tried mightily to impose its own solution to the epizootic – mass slaughter of infected and exposed livestock – but could not. The project which emerged represented a compromise between older US models of animal-disease control, new virological knowledge and technology, the Mexican state's approach to development and security, and the interests and attitudes of rural Mexicans. In turn, the campaign transformed both countries' understandings of the institutions they needed to build to achieve security and development, and had ramifications across the Atlantic and into South America. In short, the aftosa campaign in Mexico underscores the contested, heterogenous nature of twentieth-century development projects, their entanglement with notions of national security, and the ecological forces that shaped them. This is a story of the world's germs, animals, expertise, money, and geopolitical interests in Mexico. It is also about "Mexico in the world."[18]

Other questions concern the Mexican government's relations with its citizens. One of the great themes of Mexican historiography is the growing power of the central state and official party that emerged from the revolutionary upheaval of the 1910s, and governed the country under one name or other until 2000. Conventionally, the two decades or so after 1940 are seen as the heyday of what in 1946 became known as the Party of the Institutional Revolution (*Partido Revolucionario Institucional*, PRI). In some ways this book is one sustained attack on the idea that in these decades Mexico largely lacked political events as such, but followed the synchronic patterns imposed by the PRI's ingenious and perfectly equilibrated corporate system: a system whose foundations had already been laid by the social reforms and institution-building of 1930s, in which political actors circled the presidential center like the planets around the sun, or engaged in a fruitless game of political poker in which president and party always held aces up their sleeves.[19] Rather, it joins a body of

---

[17] A helpful overview of a large field is Macekura and Manela (eds.), *The Development Century*. For a path-breaking account connecting development history with animal disease, see McVety, *Rinderpest Campaigns*.

[18] Thornton, "Review," 16.

[19] The best-written, and surely the most influential version of this interpretation is Krauze, *La presidencia imperial*. It also frames various secondary studies of the aftosa campaign, for example Soto Correa, *El rifle*, 18–19. For broader (and critical) overviews of the historiography, see: Schmidt, "Making it Real"; Knight, "The Weight of the State in

work that has gradually disassembled the narrative of successful Cardenista corporatism, and sought to come up with a better account of state formation reflecting the historical evidence of central weakness, instability under the edifice of national calm, and the diachronic power of unanticipated events.[20] It also aims to bring the character of political mobilizations and the PRI's tactics of ruling into sharper focus. Historians who have written about the politics of aftosa have tended to reduce the story to a stark struggle between Mexico's campesinos and modernizing US and Mexican elites.[21] While this captures some political dynamics, it obscures others. Peasants certainly contested the campaign, but so did newspapermen, scientists, well-connected commercial ranchers, and factions within the Mexican state itself. Put simply, a less Manichean framing and a larger cast of characters is needed to understand the politics of this epizootic and its lasting effects.

It is also a story about the relationships between domesticated animals and the people who farm them or regulate their lives. The attractions of telling history with animals – and their various afflictions – are numerous. Domestic animals provide an excellent lens for tracing the transformative effects of human societies on the planet; if there is an Anthropocene, livestock are surely one of its key components. They also offer a helpful route for historians to move beyond dichotomous understandings of human culture and nature. Mexico's cows, for example, were not nature. Commission officials were sometimes quite clear about this, referring to cattle herds as "stuff" – blank, inert matter, awaiting human manipulation.[22] Cattle were deeply embedded in systems of commercial and subsistence farming: as commodities, units of food and energy, and stores of liquid capital; they could also pose as a kind of technology-devices for

---

Modern Mexico." Despite growing critique, this image of sweeping state and "near imperial" presidential power lingers. Alexander, *Sons*, 14.

[20] The most sophisticated case for interpreting the PRI in terms of a hegemonic pact of shared revolutionary discourse and party mediation is still Vaughan, *Cultural*. For qualified critiques of this model, see Gillingham and Smith (eds.), *Dictablanda*; Fallaw, *Religion*. For a similar critique of an "excessive and misleading image of presidential power," and the need to analyze national politics as "a process that developed episodically, rather than in a linear or progressive fashion," see Loaeza, "Dos hipótesis," 58, 53. The relative importance of consensus, repression, and surveillance in PRI rule – and the appropriate conceptual vocabulary and periodizations – all remain subject to some debate. See, for example Pensado and Ochoa, "Introduction," 3–18, 8, 14 n21. I return to these topics in the conclusion of Chapter 4.

[21] A deeply researched and very useful book in this vein is Soto Correa, *El rifle*.

[22] Miscellaneous phone logs 1947–1948, CMAEFA, Operations, box 29, Jalisco and Veracruz.

hauling a plow or cart, or vessels for improving breeds. In the 1940s they were used to produce a complex and state-of-the-art vaccine. Cattle could also act as symbolic tools, boosting the status and rugged, virile image of their owners. On the other hand, cows were not entirely man-made. They fled from, bit, or maimed their handlers. They carried unwanted viruses, bacteria, and insects. The commodity value of beef cattle derived, at least in part, from the work they did finding food and feeding themselves and rearing their young, while a fighting bull without the appropriate level of wildness was symbolically worthless.[23]

Scholars in many disciplines are increasingly interested in how capitalism, state formation, and the transformation of science and biomedicine remade human relations with animals in the modern world.[24] Still, we know very little about how these broad processes – which, for convenience, we can crudely term modernization – influenced how people thought about and interacted with animals in different places and different societies. In one way or another, the aftosa campaign exemplified some key modern trends in animal history: the globalization of trade and veterinary science, the growth of state regulation, and the intensification and mechanization of farming.[25] It also shows how these processes were mediated by the Mexican context – the postwar geopolitical conjuncture, divisions among scientists, the postrevolutionary state's distinctive political style, and the interests and attitudes of rural Mexicans – and how, in turn, events in Mexico reverberated beyond the nation's borders. Some historians approach the history of human–animal relations as a story of contrasting and clashing cultures and worldviews. This framework fits some times and places, but does not work so well in mid-twentieth-century Mexico.[26] The animals at the center of this story had long been

---

[23] For debates about applying sociological categories to animals, see Russell, "Can Organisms be Technology?"; Hribal, "Animals." On bullfighting in 1940s Mexico see Gillingham, "Maximino's Bulls."

[24] Ritvo, "Animal Turn"; Kean and Howell (eds.), *Routledge Companion to Animal–Human History*.

[25] Brown and Gilfoyle (eds.), *Healing the Herds*; Franklin, *Animals and Modern Cultures*; Mikhail, *The Animal*. For criticisms of the Eurocentric (or often simply Anglocentric) perspective of many attempts to theorize the relationship between processes of modernization and human–animal relations, see Bulliet, *Hunters*, 36–7. For a path-breaking Latin American collection covering the colonial and postcolonial eras, see Few and Tortorici (eds.), *Centering Animals*.

[26] For fascinating applications along these lines from different contexts see García Garagarza, "The Year the People Turned into Cattle"; Norton, "The Chicken and the Iegue"; Demuth, "The Walrus and the Bureaucrat."

conceived of primarily as livestock, or *ganado* – that is, as things to be used for human advantage. The conflicts and debates we will examine concern competing interpretations of how best to exploit animals as resources for human development; they largely stem from tensions between or inherent in different facets of modernization, and so often echo those triggered by similar campaigns around the world. For better or worse, the story of Mexico's aftosa epizootic is a variation on a theme of global efforts to modernize the countryside. When officials and observers talked about the aftosa crisis as a cultural conflict between rural traditions and urban forces of science and progress they offered a very partial account at best; they were participating in struggles over aftosa policy and not describing them.[27] As we will see, aftosa arrived in Mexico and spread as rapidly as it did, precisely because of earlier processes of capitalist development, market integration, and biotic homogenization.[28]

Twenty years ago "a lot of ink" had already "been spilled" examining this history.[29] More has been spilled since, to good effect. This book aims to build on this work, and avoid some of its pitfalls. Early surveys were hamstrung by a reliance on published sources, some crude, broad-brush assumptions about Mexican politics and society.[30] More recent studies have deepened our knowledge of key aspects of the campaign, tracing changes in the veterinary profession, or using oral histories, national archives, and the press to examine regional experiences.[31] Other articles have shed light on the experiences of US participants in the program and the campaign's effects on the US–Mexico border.[32] However, existing works offer diverging claims about policy aims and outcomes, the nature of US–Mexico relations, the depth and breadth of popular resistance, and

---

[27] For a critique of accounts of Latin America that emphasize cultural and ontological difference, see Tenorio Trillo, *Latin America*.

[28] On biotic homogenization, urbanization, and industrialization in another North American context, see Kheraj, "The Great Epizootic."

[29] Téllez Reyes-Retana, "Cuando," 6.

[30] Saucedo, *Historia*; Machado, *Aftosa*. Machado's early studies provide a useful narrative, but echo official sources in portraying rural opposition as sporadic and fundamentally irrational – a handful of outbursts from impulsive, gullible, and drunken mobs of peasant villagers, stirred up by a few malcontents and "petty demagogues." Machado, *Industry in Crisis*, 51–3.

[31] Key works on veterinary history include: Cervantes Sánchez, Román de Carlos, López Montelongo (eds.), *La medicina*; Mayer and Adler de Lomnitz, *La nueva clase*. The most detailed local studies: Castro Rosales, "La aftosa"; Figueroa Velázquez, *El tiro de gracia*; Soto Correa, *El rifle*; Guzmán Urióstegui, *Oxtotitlán*. For a useful overview of the campaign that generally emphasizes peasant resistance, see Ledbetter, "Fighting."

[32] Fox, "Aftosa"; Mendoza, "Battling Aftosa"; Alvarez, "The US–Mexico Border."

rest on fragmented primary research. Some studies take the campaign's stated aims at face value.[33] Others echo the popular theories mentioned above, portraying a deliberate campaign by a power-hungry Truman administration and callous Mexican elites to proletarianize campesinos – an elaborate excuse to "force the peasants to buy machinery and industrial inputs; to coerce them into the national market; and to make them buy industrial goods."[34] Some studies argue that the campaign was truly devastating, delivering a "coup de grace" to smallholders' and peasant farmers' livelihoods, a sign of the PRI's centralized and repressive system and the "feebleness of political opposition and public opinion."[35] Others emphasize how Mexicans successfully mobilized to defend their interests, thereby writing another chapter in Mexico's long history of campesino rebellion.[36] Few make comparisons to other cases of aftosa and animal-disease control, which officials did at the time, and which this highly transnational story would seem to demand. Other than the USDA's own in-house researchers some seventy years ago, no historian has consulted the single largest trove of related archival materials: around eighty boxes holding the main US records of the commission in Washington DC. The fact that these "rather complete" organizational and financial records exist is itself an indication of the campaign's unusual significance for US officials. While regular archival purges were "a good policy in most cases," in the late 1960s diplomatic relations with Mexico and the preparation of sanitary campaigns elsewhere still generated a "seemingly constant need to refer to old files."[37]

The records in Washington DC are not easy to navigate, and cannot be read on their own. US officials had various agendas of their own. Sometimes they had no idea what they were talking about. At times the sheer quantity of detail seduces us with verisimilitude: daily phone-logs which seem to replay events almost in real-time or which, perhaps,

---

[33] Machado, *Aftosa*; Dusenberry, "Foot and Mouth."

[34] González Martínez, "Political Brokers" 102, n2. Ana Figueroa Velázquez argues that the US and Mexican governments "designed" the slaughter campaign to target only "poor campesinos." Figueroa Velázquez, *El tiro de gracia*, 21, 136. José Carmen Soto Correa goes further still, arguing that the aftosa campaign was a pretext for the US military – the "Pentagon" – to "dismantle and destroy all national agriculture and livestock," first in Mexico, then Latin America – a "Marshall plan in reverse." Soto Correa, *El rifle*, 14, 27.

[35] Figueroa Velázquez, *El tiro de gracia*, 11. See also ibid., 32–5.

[36] Bartra, *Los herederos*; Soto Correa, *El rifle*.

[37] R. J. Anderson, associate director, US–Mexico commission for the prevention of foot-and-mouth disease, to Knierim, budget division, USDA, August 11, 1967, FMDRL, box 1, folder 1.

might make a half-decent screenplay. Of course, many incidents simply never made it into reports. US officials preferred to keep particularly sensitive or embarrassing topics off the radio logs and out of written reports. Once back in Mexico City, Dr. Omohundro typically summoned district supervisors to report in person, preferring to "have dope on things that cannot be said over radio."[38] Decades later, a US veteran of the campaign remembered facing a hostile crowd in Huajuapan, Oaxaca. Under orders not to carry guns, a Mexican colonel, "tough as nails but only five foot four," improvised:

> Well, the colonel filled a big syringe with strychnine, waved it in front of the crowd, and injected it into a nearby cow. The cow went into paralysis; the crowd dispersed ... We quickly inspected and killed the infected animals, paid compensation to the presidente municipal, and drove away with our big syringe taped to the hood of the jeep – in clear sight of anyone who might be watching. I never told that story around headquarters. They would have canned me had they known how we did business in the boonies.[39]

Despite these problems, the Washington DC archive offers a crucial view of the campaign's workings that escaped, or were deliberately kept from the public record, and are not necessarily apparent from local sources and perspectives. US officials were not always invited to the room where political negotiations with Mexican governors, generals, and local mediators took place, but commissions' records often indicate where and when deals happened and their likely outcomes. Read alongside memoirs and interviews, the plans, reports, and complaints lodged in other archives in Mexico (which thankfully escaped destruction), and the papers of related international organizations and actors, it allows us to illuminate the local, national, and international dimensions of this story.

As Priscilla Wald has argued, the stories we tell about outbreaks of disease can be formulaic and too neat.[40] Animal diseases emerge out of long and broad historical contexts; some are recognized as significant public problems; most others are not.[41] The Mexican campaign was nothing if not eventful; as the USDA's official but never-published history put it, "every sort of thing seemed to happen."[42] It is impossible to streamline all of these many happenings into one narrative. Outbreaks often have messy and contested endings, and are equivocal in the lessons

---

[38] Omohundro, Mexico City, to Barnes, Guadalajara, December 17, 1948, CMAEFA, operations, box 29, Jalisco.
[39] Ewing, *Ranch*, 199.   [40] Wald, *Contagious*.
[41] Woods, "Patterns of Animal Disease."   [42] USDA, *Campaign*, 168.

they teach, and this case was no different. With these problems in mind, Chapter 1 begins with a wide-angle lens, sketching the history of relations between domestic animals and state formation in Mexico from the colonial to the postrevolutionary era. Along the way, it discusses different accounts of how aftosa arrived in Mexico in 1946, and their political stakes. The lens then zooms in on the different aspects of the campaign in Mexico, seeking to balance regional variations with national trends. Chapter 2 explains how and why the campaign adopted the policies it did, focusing on the high politics of bilateral diplomacy, the main political and economic interests on both sides of the border, and the bureaucratic infrapolitics of the commission. Chapter 3 explores Mexican opposition to the aftosa campaign, drawing on hundreds of complaints, local studies, and an original database of over 450 incidents of civil disobedience, riots, and rebellions. Rather than portraying resistance as rooted in the Mexican peasantry or rural tradition, this chapter emphasizes the geographical breadth, cross-class character, and the self-consciously modern public discourse of many opponents, and the vigorous but localized focus of most action. Chapter 4 examines how the aftosa commission understood and countered opposition, using threats and targeted violence, carefully calibrated concessions, propaganda, mediation by regional bosses and powerbrokers, and information-gathering. It argues that this blend of tactics illustrates the Mexican state's conceptions of order and security, and supports the notion of the PRI regime as a "dictablanda" – authoritarian but institutionally weak, and reliant on a complicated blend of repressive and consensual mechanisms. The last two chapters zoom out again to explore the campaign's aftermath from different angles. Chapter 5 shows how the aftosa outbreak shaped the Mexican state's efforts to modernize and regulate livestock from the 1950s to the 1980s. By disrupting existing methods of production and consumption, creating new technical capacities, and offering an example of effective state action, the crisis prompted officials to contemplate more ambitious state intervention. At the same time the aftosa crisis offered painful lessons about the kind of political compromises and alliances – international and domestic – upon which government action rested. Along with the waning of Cardenismo, the Second World War, and the so-called Green Revolution, the aftosa campaign helps explain why Mexico's developmentalist state took the shape it did, and illuminates its strengths, weaknesses, and contradictions. Finally, Chapter 6 traces the global repercussions of the aftosa campaign, particularly its effects on new US efforts to govern animal disease across the Americas and Europe for economic and military purposes. By demonstrating the apparent threat aftosa posed to national security and improving vaccine technology, Mexico's aftosa campaign boosted the international ambitions of Mexican experts, inspired the creation of the new laboratories and international organizations in the Americas – from Rio de Janeiro to Long Island Sound – and reshaped the United States' scientific and military relations with its Cold War allies in Europe. As such, the story underlines the multilateral character of Latin America's Cold War, and the ecological contexts that shaped it.

I

Animals and Government in Mexico

Bill Leftwich grew up in Texas, joined the US Army in the Second World War, and then signed up for work on the aftosa campaign in 1949. For Leftwich, his work was a kind of journey through time. Mexico's cities, with their hotels, cars, asphalt, and amenities, were familiar enough, but the countryside was isolated and strange. "By going over a couple of mountain ranges from a paved road," he recalled, "you could go back a 100 years in time." John Hidalgo, one of Leftwich's colleagues, agreed but was less precise, describing a "strange land" stretching across the countryside that he simply called "Old Mexico."[1] Many other US and Mexican officials similarly noted "the backwardness of rural Mexico." As one visiting US congressman explained in a report, the customs and outlook of villagers in central Mexico were "ancient."[2] A US Army general advising the campaign warned colleagues not to be "deceived by emblems of civilization such as railroads, electric lights, and beautiful churches"; rural Mexicans themselves were rather childlike – "easily excitable and easily led" – with only a "thin veneer of civilization as we know it."[3] Of course, the countryside's backwardness could be blamed for many of the campaign's problems: "Irate *campesinos*, disease, snakes, gators, harmful insects, etc."[4] It also brought certain compensations.

[1] *Aftosa International*, 2, 16.
[2] Stoops, itinerary and reports on visit of congressional committee, July 11, 1947, CMAEFA, Reports, box 2, congressional committee.
[3] Corlett, confidential report on foot-and-mouth disease campaign, September 1947, CAP, box 7, foot and mouth.
[4] *Aftosa International*, 2.

Rural Mexico may have been a strange and sometimes dangerous place, but for many who worked on the campaign, leaping over these temporal chasms was exciting. Old Mexico was curious and picturesque, with its colonial architecture, quiet and dignified farmers, quaint customs, and "lovely young girls" who promenaded coquettishly around small-town plazas. Some became quite attached to Old Mexico, worried that their work on the commission was violating "customs" and trampling on farmers' traditional "way of life."[5] Another attraction was pay in US dollars that stretched far and provided ample access to hotels, swimming pools, tourist attractions, drink, and brothels.[6] In short, time travel made the Mexican countryside an excellent place (or an excellent time) for "adventures."[7]

Leftwich and his colleagues wrote in a well-established genre, echoing how travelers and novelists had portrayed Mexico for decades.[8] In some ways, such images were understandable. Mexico's cities really were different from their hinterlands: wealthier, more literate, and dense with modern industrial technology. However, rural Mexico was not a uniform landscape, nor an island cut adrift from historical change. People's lives and relations with domestic animals had been remade by conquest, war, commodity booms, depressions, and revolution. The aftosa campaign represented a huge effort to project state power into the countryside and intervene in the lives of livestock and their owners. But Mexico's government had never been indifferent to animals. To help us understand the kind of society the aftosa campaign confronted and what it really changed, this chapter sketches an outline of this earlier history. The story below focuses on domestic livestock, the main object of the aftosa campaign; where they shaped the fate of livestock or helped illustrate broader shifts in governance, other animals occasionally strayed into the story's path.

When Spanish conquistadors brought their domesticated animals to Mesoamerica, they released them into a propitious environment. Cows, pigs, sheep, goats, and horses lacked many natural predators. For centuries, oceans protected them from the worst animal plagues of the Old World. Indeed, livestock dominated the New World landscape further

---

[5] Eakin, *Borderland*, 36; Gipson, *Cow Killers*, 128; *Aftosa International*, 18.
[6] Pavia Guzmán, *Recuerdos*, 93–4.   [7] *Aftosa International*, 2.
[8] On Old Mexico as a "hunter's paradise" for "red blooded" US sportsmen, see Burnaman, *A Week*. For an overview showing how images of Latin American backwardness were often crosscut with anxious comparisons to the United States, see Leary, *Cultural History*.

and faster than the Spaniards. The speed at which New Spain's cattle herd grew and spread amazed observers.[9] How ecologically destructive this was is a topic of some debate. Melville argued that an onslaught of sheep-farming desiccated and degraded the Valle del Mezquital. Others suggest that Melville may have exaggerated the size and impact of sheep-farming, and argue that livestock roaming through a sparsely populated landscape normally found niches that allowed them to thrive without too heavy an impact on the surrounding ecology.[10]

Old-World livestock were also well suited to the demands of the new colonial society being made. Everywhere oxen and mules were the draft animals of choice – pulling plows and carts, toiling in the mines, and powering sugar presses. On the northern and tropical fringes of viceregal authority, where land was plentiful but disciplined workers were few or non-existent, cattle ranching was an efficient way for the Spanish to convert biomass into calories and animal bodies into commodities. Herds wandered freely, and a single vaquero could look after scores of animals. These cattle herds provided food, hides, and tallow to the mining towns of the center and north, the engines of the commercial economy. Where cultivable land and labor were more plentiful, livestock remained important, and many haciendas kept smaller herds alongside crops. Subsistence farmers also quickly saw the attractions of raising a few pigs, chickens, or cows to supplement their diets, trade locally, provide manure for fertilizer, and act as stores of (literally) mobile capital.[11] Trains of mules and donkeys stitched together the fabric of the colonial economy, creating meandering roads that competed against (and in marginal areas, defeated) the urban grids to which colonial authorities aspired.[12] By the eighteenth century, they had propelled muleteers to a position of some prestige and power within colonial society.[13] In the colder pockets of the Sierra Madre, pastoralists made a living herding goats and sheep between seasonal pastures and urban markets. By the eighteenth century, some of these "flying haciendas" had become "enormous enterprises," swooping up and down the valleys of the Mesa Central.[14]

[9] Crosby, *Ecological*, 281–2; Knight, *Mexico*, 24–5.
[10] Melville, *Plague of Sheep*; Sluyter, *Colonialism and Landscape*, 95–142.
[11] On the slow but steady spread of stock-raising in indigenous communities in Guerrero, and animals' role as "social security," see Dehouve, *Entre el caimán y el jaguar*, 134.
[12] Stanislawski, *The Anatomy*, 11, 67.   [13] Barragán-Álvarez, "Feet of Commerce."
[14] Smith, *Roots*, 88.

Given the ecological context and material incentives, much of this occurred without tight control or oversight from the Spanish Crown. Still, the authorities of New Spain concerned themselves with animals in various ways. Horses and mastiffs were regarded, rightly, as crucial military technologies; indigenous people were initially forbidden to own or ride horses – true "war machines" – on pain of death.[15] To represent the interests of large stock raisers, enforce property and grazing rights, and brand livestock, the Spanish imported and adapted a familiar institution from the Old World: a livestock guild, New Spain's Mesta.[16] The Spanish Crown craved information about the quantity and distribution of domestic animals, a key indicator of the prosperity and taxable surplus of different places. The first colonial surveys, the famous *relaciones geográficas*, counted livestock in different regions, and divided them into familiar Iberian categories: *ganado mayor* (cattle, horses) and *ganado menor* (pigs, poultry, goats, sheep). Some also noted how indigenous communities quickly adopted some of the new species alongside their own rabbits and "native chickens" – that is, turkeys.[17] Complaints about livestock trampling on crops became a mainstay of the viceroyalty's multilayered judicial system and a good indication of where the relations between haciendas and peasant villages were under strain.[18] When a rising "bovine tide" seemed to threaten stability, colonial authorities intervened and banned stock raising in some valleys, although "the sheer reiteration of such measures ... attested to their inadequacy."[19]

As crucial sources of food and energy, animals also had symbolic power of interest to colonial authorities. Tasked with upholding order and morality, priests condemned indigenous people when they engaged in what seemed to them idolatrous animal worship or diabolical attempts to take the form of wild animals.[20] One alarming by-product of the proliferation of domestic animals was, from the Catholic Church's point of view, the propensity of the young men who worked alongside them to use

---

[15] Saucedo, *Historia*, 21. On hounds and social control in the Spanish Caribbean and US south, see Parry and Yingling, "Slave Hounds."

[16] Dusenberry, *Mexican Mesta*.   [17] Alves, *Animals of Spain*, 100.

[18] Borah, *Justice by Insurance*, 48.   [19] Knight, *Mexico*, 25.

[20] Alves, *Animals of Spain*, 113–48. For a summary of the ontologies underpinning what the Spanish understood to be diabolical Indian shape-shifting, see Descola, *Beyond Nature and Culture*, 104–11.

female animals for heterosexual – or perhaps "heterospecial" – gratification.[21] Late-colonial reformers increasingly associated bullfighting with the unruly pleb, and some sought to restrict and discourage these events, without much success.[22] Around the same time in Mexico City, the "middling" and plebeian types who staged baptisms and marriages for their pet dogs at dance parties also aroused official suspicion. Inquisitors worried that these ceremonies – apparently hilarious for those who witnessed them – were sacrilegious or satirical, mocking viceregal ceremonies and church leaders.[23] New Spain's authorities and scientific elite prescribed popular practices but also had their own changing ideological uses for animals. In the face of European condescension, Creole naturalists defended the vigor and usefulness of New World nature, including its wild and domestic animals, and sought to gather more information about them. The *Gaceta de Literatura*, a key forum for eighteenth-century Creole scientists, published articles about the history and improvement of wool production, bee farming, alfalfa and acorns as livestock fodder, and smallpox inoculation using cattle.[24] Long before it became an emblem on Mexico's national flag, the council of Mexico City had already placed on the city crest an image of an eagle holding a serpent in its beak, appropriating a scene from the Aztec myth of the founding of Tenochtitlan.[25]

This symbolic continuity belied the upheavals brought by the wars of independence. Water flooded the silver mines, the commercial economy contracted, haciendas fragmented into smaller family ranches, and warfare pushed ranchers into formerly peripheral areas. Efforts by Spanish and Creole naturalists to catalogue and classify the viceroyalty's flora and fauna were likewise interrupted.[26] The instability and insolvency of the new Mexican state weakened governing authorities' administrative grip over people and livestock alike. Increasing raids on cattle and horses by indigenous people in the north dramatically illustrated the inability of the new government to control key resources and the indirect pull of new markets in the United States, to which the Comanche and other groups

---

[21] Tortorici, *Sins against Nature*, 137. For cases after independence, showing roughly the same social patterns, see Bazant, "Bestiality."

[22] Viqueira Albán, *Propriety*, 10–25.   [23] Proctor, "Puppies," 2, 15.

[24] Cervantes Sánchez, "Historiografía veterinaria," 3. The medicinal use of lizards was another topic of debate shaped by, but not reducible to, Creole–Spanish tensions. Achim, "Making Lizards into Drugs."

[25] Florescano, *La bandera*, 40.

[26] Tutino, *Heartland*, 173–88; Mociño, *Real expedición botánica*, volumes XII, XIII.

traded livestock and hides.[27] The hopes of a new prosperity for independent Mexico freed from its colonial shackles proved illusory, at least in the commercial economy. Even among these early hopes and plans, livestock did not inspire that much interest.[28] Mexico's Ministry of Development, Colonization, Industry and Commerce, founded in 1853, lacked funds to match its infrastructural ambitions; in any case, it initially prioritized transport, communications, information-gathering, and mapmaking.[29] When the government founded the country's first school of veterinary medicine in 1853, part of a wave of French-inspired schools created around the world round about the same time, its focus was squarely on the wellbeing of horses.[30] In this way, it built on older traditions of equine medicine (*albeytería*) – present in New Spain in one form or another since the late 1500s – and was an eloquent expression of the government's preoccupation with military matters.[31]

From around 1880, three interrelated processes began to transform livestock farming and Mexican authorities' role in it, eventually setting the scene for the drama of the aftosa campaign. First, markets and geography began to form three main regional patterns of livestock farming. The arid northern states had long been dominated by cattle ranching for hides and beef, but began to be reshaped by US markets and investment. After the Mexican government subdued the region's indigenous holdouts, northern ranchers began to export cattle on foot to meet mushrooming demand in the United States. The trade generated great profits but did not require huge changes in techniques. Ranchers in Chihuahua, Coahuila, and Sonora found niches in the emerging US meat-production system, first as sources of cheap seasonal grazing, and then as exporters of "feeder" cattle: young, light steers who ran with their mothers until their milk dried up, and were then sold to be fattened in the US Southwest before being shipped on to markets further east. The sprawling creature of transnational ranching was itself fed on US (and British) capital, and many US citizens raised money and bought up pasture lands in northern Mexico.[32]

---

[27] Delay, *War of a Thousand Deserts.*   [28] Saucedo, *Historia*, 26.

[29] Lurtz, "Developing."

[30] Mayer and Adler de Lomnitz, *La nueva clase*, 19–20; Uribe Mendoza, "La invención." For the case of Ottoman Egypt, see Mikhail, *The Animal*, 144–50.

[31] Little is known about colonial-era *albeytería*; surviving manuals focus on horses but also include other animals and prescribe some New World plants and apparently local remedies. Uribe Mendoza, "La invención."

[32] Lopes and Riguzzi, "Borders," 611–2, 618–9, 621–6.

In the late nineteenth century, Mexico's gulf coast slowly emerged as another region where beef cattle dominated livestock farming, particularly the states of Veracruz, San Luis Potosí, and, a little later, Tabasco. Here, however, the market for beef and hides was domestic, principally Mexico City. The famously rich and year-long pastureland of the Huasteca was a pivotal piece of this emerging system: a place where cattle from the surrounding area could be driven and fattened before being sent to slaughter in Mexico City, and a partial ecological buffer against the decline in beef supply caused by seasonal variations in pasture elsewhere.[33]

A third region, extending across the central tableland and down to the Pacific Ocean, was defined chiefly by the enormous variety of ways people used livestock for subsistence and regional markets, reflecting the region's rugged and varied topography. In the early twentieth century, economic change was slower here, but not invisible. Urban growth and the spread of railroad hubs boosted demand for mules and horses. In the *tierra caliente*, where the central tableland sloped off to the Pacific, growing domestic markets stimulated beef-cattle ranching much like in the Gulf, though on a somewhat smaller scale.[34] In general, however, larger populations and pressure on crop land constrained the development of beef-cattle ranching in this region, and made it receptive to more land and capital-intensive dairy, pig, and poultry farming.[35]

As these regional patterns emerged, Mexico also saw a growing interest among government officials and farmers alike in improving domestic animals through breeding and nutrition. When a cross-bred racehorse owned by Porfirio Díaz won the first race at the new Mexico City racecourse, it sparked a new public interest in these techniques.[36] The Porfirian regime then encouraged them more directly. It created a course in breeding at the National School of Agriculture and Veterinary Medicine, published accounts of the latest advances in Europe and the United States, and sponsored the publication of helpful literature – such as the *Manual del ganadero mexicano*, penned in Mexico City by Dr. C. Dillmann, and adapted and expanded by Miguel García, a veterinarian at the Ministry of Development.[37] In 1887, the government

---

[33] González-Montagut, "Factors"; Ford, Bacon, and Davis Incorporated, New York, "Report: Refrigeration and Cold Storage of Food for Mexico, D.F.," to Villaseñor, Banco de México, December 1944, CMAEFA, reports, box 1, "refrigeration and cold storage," 26–45.

[34] Léonard, *Una historia de vacas*, 66–73.

[35] Yates, *Mexico's Agricultural Dilemma*, 90–1.   [36] Saucedo, *Historia*, 26.

[37] Uribe Mendoza, "Invención"; Dillmann, *Manual del ganadero mexicano*.

sponsored the first national livestock show in Coyoacán; by 1909 sixteen such events had been held around the country.[38] The aim was to encourage farmers to cross their hardy, disease-resistant but scrawny "creole" animals with improved pedigree breeds from abroad, achieving a supposedly optimal blend of characteristics. It all chimed well with the generally Europhiliac and outward-looking bent of Porfirian modernizers.[39] As the opening speech at the 1894 livestock fair put it, "we are a young country, and we have to take advantage of the learning of others."[40] Porfirian officials hoped that these events would help Mexico transform all of its domestic species, forming "races with diverse aptitudes; for provisioning and feeding cities at a good price; to provide excellent primary materials for industry; good horses for the army; strong and hard-working beasts for work in the fields and transport; and models of shapeliness and speed to satisfy the desires and caprices of the sportsman."[41]

Inspired by these efforts or their own initiative, some farmers began to dabble in improvements of their own. By the late nineteenth century ranchers in Veracruz had also begun to experiment with new grasses for pasture, principally *guinea* and *pará*; around the same time, ranchers in the *tierra caliente* fattened livestock with ground maize and sesame seed cakes.[42]

Many early experiments were small scale and rather ad hoc, and some failed spectacularly. Some ambitious government researchers sought to create a cross between a pig and a sheep that would thrive in Mexican conditions, without success.[43] In the 1940s, residents around Lake Chapala still remembered a "silly" Porfirian-era landlord who wanted to breed dairy cattle but foolishly imported Black Angus beef cattle for the purpose.[44] The most dramatic attempt to modernize the production and marketing of meat was by the unfortunately named John DeKay, to whose corporation the Díaz regime awarded a concession to remake Mexico City's supply along the lines of the Chicago meatpackers. The threat to

---

[38] Saucedo, *Historia*, 13, 41.

[39] Creole stock were also said to have a "nervous temperament." In the colonial period, farmers differentiated between several different types of "native" or "corriente" cattle. González-Montagut, "Factors," 103.

[40] Saucedo, *Historia*, 46.

[41] Don José Segura, Head of National School of Agriculture and Veterinary Medicine, c. 1894, transcribed in ibid., 50.

[42] Lopes and Riguzzi, "Borders," 612 n25; González-Montagut, "Factors," 106; Léonard, *Una historia de vacas*, 69.

[43] Lurtz, "Developing," 450.   [44] Bedford, *A Visit to Don Otavio*, 153.

existing butchers and middlemen, and customers' suspicions of chilled meat combined to trigger a "sausage rebellion" that quickly condemned the project.[45] Setbacks aside, these initiatives heralded a lasting shift in how the government and many farmers thought about livestock and their role in national progress; animals were not just units of property to be multiplied, but objects of systematic investment, whose bodies and diets could be manipulated to adjust their size, yields, docility, and profitability.

The third major trend was a growing official awareness of animals as victims and vectors of disease. By the 1870s the veterinary school had broadened its scope beyond equine illnesses, and produced an elite group of influential and cosmopolitan veterinarians, thoroughly apprised of advances in germ theory and hygiene in Europe and the United States, and regular contributors to Mexico's medical periodicals. Veterinary researchers were few but, as in Europe, at the forefront of new microbiological knowledge. José de la Luz Gómez, a member of the first intake to graduate from the veterinary school and who later taught there, was a central figure. He successfully replicated Pasteur's anthrax vaccine, drafted sanitary protocols on imports and consumption of animal products modeled on European and US legislation, joined and corresponded with the American Veterinary Association, and taught Mexico's first course on microbiology in 1883, five years before a similar course was taught at the medical school.[46] By the early twentieth century the government had posted small corps of veterinary inspectors at ports of entry, and branches of the Ministry of Agriculture started to produce vaccines for anthrax and pig cholera. At first the ministry distributed vaccines for free but in 1910 it started to impose a small fee to encourage farmers to use vaccines sparingly and carefully.[47]

From 1910 to 1920, the Mexican Revolution interrupted these three trends in dramatic fashion. Warring revolutionary bands bought or stole livestock for their own provisions, or to sell for precious dollars. Sometimes armies killed animals to enact reprisals, or simply to prevent them falling into enemy hands. Herds of cattle declined precipitously, perhaps by around 50 percent, and the northern cattle industry was "practically liquidated."[48] Government-backed improvements or sanitary regulation in these circumstances was impossible. In 1911, the Ministry of Agriculture created twelve regional experiment stations, the country's first

---

[45] Pilcher, *Sausage Rebellion.*   [46] Uribe Mendoza, "Invención."
[47] Cervantes Sánchez, Román de Carlos, López Montelongo (eds.), *La medicina*, 111.
[48] Saucedo, *Historia*, 28.

US-style extension program aimed at diffusing new farming techniques. Most of them quickly ground to a halt and at least one, in Oaxaca, was taken over by surrounding villages.[49] Major rebellions continued into the 1920s, as did rebels' appetite for seizing livestock as a means or an objective of warfare. During the Cristero Wars, federal army generals stole livestock from the territories they commanded on an almost industrial scale, sending rail trucks filled with cattle to Mexico City.[50] In Jalisco, farmers and townspeople caught up in the conflict attributed similar motivations to the rebels and came up with a bitter twist on the Cristero slogan: "Long live Christ the King, bring me the best ox [Viva Cristo Rey, tráeme el mejor buey.]"[51]

Despite the destruction and upheaval, the revolution did not ultimately derail the formation of regional (and transnational) markets or the gradual growth in government intervention. In some ways, it served to stimulate these processes. In the 1920s, the postrevolutionary regime encouraged farmers to repopulate their herds – restricting exports until they had done so – and renewed the Porfirian effort to modernize livestock farming. The postrevolutionary Ministry of Agriculture created a department dedicated to breeding, began to sponsor livestock shows once more, and sent at least one veterinarian to tour US land-grant colleges to absorb the latest techniques in animal husbandry.[52] In 1930, a first national agricultural census provided officials with a clearer map of the genetic resources they aimed to upgrade. Census-takers divided Mexico's livestock into unimproved *corriente* animals and "fine" specimens that showed signs of improvement, using hazy criteria and their own variable judgment.[53] Government attention could be rather inconsistent; a group at the Ministry of Agriculture carried out research on one of President Calles's own pedigree bulls, but when they discovered its poor breeding "performance" and dubious pedigree, a humiliated Calles swiftly and politely canceled the project.[54] Still, an interest in livestock breeding extended far beyond the presidential chair and veterinary circles, and arguably became part of a wider revolutionary, nationalist, and modernizing sensibility. This is particularly clear among

---

[49] Cervantes Sánchez, Román de Carlos, López Montelongo (eds.), *La medicina*, 67–84.
[50] Various correspondence, 1929, AHSDN X/III/1-8 (Máximino Ávila Camacho), and AHSDN X/III/1-16 (López Morales).
[51] Rodríguez and Shadow, "Religión," 678.   [52] Saucedo, *Historia*, iii, 14.
[53] Ervin, "The 1930 Agrarian Census"; Secretaría de Economía, *Primer censo agrícola*. A first national livestock survey was attempted in 1902, but was perforated by huge gaps in data collection and "questionable procedures." Lopes and Riguzzi, "Borders," 607 n12.
[54] The story is from Enrique Beltrán, in Olea-Franco, "One Century," 496.

the revolution's sizeable tier of ranchero leaders, with their carefully crafted rustic, hands-on and individualist style. Maximino Ávila Camacho – admittedly an extreme and unusually violent example – boasted that the origins of his fortune lay in his entrepreneurial drive and his experiments with "breeding cattle" around 1900 – that is, when he was only nine years old.[55] On the other end of the revolutionary personality spectrum, we find the cerebral anthropologist Manuel Gamio who, when he was working on a dig at Teotihuacán, brought villagers imported goats and a "blooded bull and boar" so they could remedy the "unproductiveness of the valley's cattle" and wean themselves off pulque.[56] Conversely, other postrevolutionary reformers tried to discourage what they believed were wasteful and disruptive uses of domestic animals, but faced an uphill battle. Venustiano Carranza's 1916 ban on bullfighting was flouted almost immediately and reversed in 1920. Rural teachers discouraged cockfighting, but struggled to make an impression. Many revolutionary leaders were themselves aficionados of blood sports, or at least understood that they provided a useful way to burnish their popular credentials.[57] In Morelos, some "progressive" villagers successfully campaigned to do away with their local bullring – according to Lola Romanucci Ross, "the symbolic center of the machismo subculture"– but most of the surrounding villages kept theirs.[58]

By the 1930s, modernizing livestock production had become an important part of the postrevolutionary regime's most ambitious project: land reform. Officials aimed to break up large estates and ranches not just to redress old injustices, demobilize armed villagers, or destroy bases of conservative support. They also argued that this would ultimately create a more efficient use of resources. Initially, the postrevolutionary regime seemed rather unclear about how reform might apply to ejidos' domestic animals, and in the 1920s no agrarian laws touched on the subject directly.[59] By the 1930s, the census had revealed just how many ejidatarios and villagers owned small numbers of livestock, and a new agrarian code formally recognized common pasture lands as part of the ejido. As land reform peaked under President Cárdenas, the official interest in small-scale animal production became quite clear. For Dr. Pedro Saucedo, a veterinarian whom Cárdenas appointed to organize and lead

---

[55] Quintana, *Maximino Ávila Camacho*, 33.   [56] Gruening, *Mexico*, 521.

[57] Lear, *Workers*, 341; Fallaw, *Religion*, 76–7, 84–5; Lomnitz, *Exits*, 167, 174. Some ranchers found cattle-breeding a useful source of metaphors with which to justify their families' supposedly natural, hereditary dominance of local society. Ibid., 172.

[58] Romanucci Ross, *Conflict*, 152, 153, 154.   [59] Saucedo, *Historia*, 14.

a new livestock division in the Ministry of Agriculture, "extensive" ranching represented an "antieconomic, antisocial," "feudal," and "false" conception of stock raising, which had dominated the country before 1910, and formed a pillar of the old regime that needed to be dismantled.[60] Truly "modern stock raising," by contrast, was "intensive"– it did not require "great tracts of land," was closely integrated with agriculture, and was not "an obstacle for social justice for ejidatarios."[61]

In this, Saucedo echoed the views of the man who appointed him. Cárdenas directed the Ministry of Agriculture to give ejidatarios preferential access to its breeding stock and technical assistance. To this end, it established courses in animal husbandry for agronomists at Chapingo, sent agronomists to rural schools and ejidos, boosted the number of federal "breeding posts" from five in 1934 to twenty in 1939, and invited ejidatarios to use the ministry's animals to improve their cattle, goats, and sheep, or swap the eggs of their chickens for improved varieties.[62] In 1936, Cárdenas sent a team of agronomists on a fact-finding tour of indigenous communities in Guerrero, Oaxaca, Querétaro and Michoacán to find out how they raised animals and how their techniques could be improved.[63] One important influence on Cárdenas's thinking was apparently the US-born rancher Raymond Bell, who bought a hacienda in Durango in 1923 and sought to turn it into a model of efficient, integrated animal and crop production.[64] Cárdenas visited the ranch, befriended Bell, and sent teams of agronomists there to learn about new techniques in breeding, water and feed management before dispatching them to rural communities.[65] Officials argued that the rational exploitation of resources on a small scale, adapted to local conditions, would allow them to reconcile land reform with both the imperatives of production and another Cardenista objective: conserving the nation's wild flora and fauna.[66]

Big cattle ranchers were obviously alarmed by much of this. Many joined the provincial opposition to Cardenismo that began to corral the administration's radicalism, and eventually Cárdenas hashed out an uneasy compromise with them. In fact, some of the cattlemen's arguments

---

[60] Ibid., 61. [61] Ibid., 63.
[62] *Memorias de la Secretaría de Agricultura, 1938–1939*, 199–207.
[63] Various correspondence, 1936–1937, AGN, LC, 506.25/27.
[64] Reeves, *Hacienda de Atotonilco*. [65] Corrales, *Hacienda de Atotonilco*, 55.
[66] Boyer and Wakild, "Social Landscaping."

against expropriation were hard to dismiss and raised "disquiet" even "within the very ranks of agrarismo": cattle exports raised crucial revenue and foreign exchange, while large-scale ranching suited areas of thin pastures or populations, and allowed ranchers to accumulate the capital with which to make the kind of improvements the government urged.[67] In 1937, Cárdenas issued a decree allowing farmers to apply for a certificate of immunity from expropriation for twenty-five years for pasture lands on which they raised up to 500 beef-cattle, or 300 dairy cattle. Cárdenas argued that this was only a temporary pause on the path to intensification: twenty-five years would allow enough time for ranchers to plan and invest in their businesses, and permit the government to obtain more information about the true carrying capacity of Mexico's pastures; ranches were only supposed to receive protection if the authorities were convinced that all the agrarian needs of neighboring communities had been met; ranchers were even supposed to donate 2 percent of their calves (or 5 percent of their piglets, lambs, and goat kids) each year to ejidos, to allow them to gradually build up their own enterprises. For all these caveats, the move represented a clear concession to ranchers' power. Cárdenas's conditions were subject to the vagaries of subsequent administrations or, in the case of the annual donations of calves, were a dead-letter from the start. Still, northern ranchers regarded the decree and its conditions skeptically, the sign of an uneasy political truce at best. The goal of Cárdenas' Ministry of Agriculture remained to help the country slowly but surely "transition from extensive to intensive" animal farming.[68]

As the postrevolutionary regime encouraged improvements, and tried to democratize access to the necessary genetics and technology, it also re-established efforts to regulate animal diseases. Microbes posing a direct threat to human health were the main concern. In the 1920s, the Rockefeller Foundation and Mexican authorities waged a campaign against yellow fever and the mosquito, state governments organized sporadic campaigns to vaccinate dogs against rabies, and government veterinarians inspected dairy farms and tested cattle for tuberculosis.[69] Teachers sent out to spread the gospel of revolutionary reform were also expected to gather data about local health conditions, including the number of villagers who shared living quarters with their domestic livestock, taken as a key indicator of uncouth habits and unsanitary

[67] Saucedo, *Historia*, 37.
[68] Ibid.; *Memorias de la Secretaría de Agricultura, 1938–1939*, 210.
[69] McCrea, "Pest to Vector"; Sowell, *Medicine on the Periphery*, 35.

conditions.[70] Compared with education and public health, official support for veterinary education and services remained modest, but efforts against diseases that afflicted livestock still grew. By the 1930s, the Ministry of Agriculture was vaccinating livestock against half-a-dozen different diseases. These campaigns aimed to control local outbreaks, not to launch national-scale eradication. During the largest Cárdenas-era initiative, brigades administered 54,000 doses of anthrax vaccine across twenty-two states, around 2,500 per state and affecting less than 1 percent of the country's livestock.[71] Still, these services were clearly important to the farmers who increasingly wrote to the federal government to request them. In 1936, the Ministry of Agriculture received so many requests for veterinary services from ejidatarios that it exhausted the dedicated funds and requested more.[72]

By the early 1940s, as revolutionary radicalism faded, Mexico displayed quite similar regional patterns of livestock production as it had in the early twentieth century. After the revolution, northern ranchers gradually restocked, pursued, and re-established (admittedly intermittent) access to US markets, and finally enjoyed an export bonanza as US demand surged during the Second World War. In the gulf states, beef-cattle ranching slowly gathered pace again to meet growing demand in Mexico City, and spread south from Veracruz; by the 1940s the size of Veracruz's cattle herds and the political weight of its ranchers began to rival those in the north.[73] Mexican officials and experts also generally agreed that market integration, improvements to breeding and nutrition, and increased control of disease were all important ingredients in the recipe for national progress in livestock farming.

In theory, these different processes would all reinforce each other, but in practice they often clashed. Mexico's revolutionary context made some tensions particularly clear: the struggle between land reformers seeking small but efficient enterprises and large, profitable, and powerful estates.

[70] Various education ministry questionnaires, c. 1929, TA, box 40, Mexico.

[71] Author's calculation based on Secretaría de Economía, *Primer censo agrícola*, and figures in Cervantes Sánchez, Román de Carlos, López Montelongo (eds.), *La medicina*, 148.

[72] E. Méndez, Banco Nacional de Crédito Ejidal, to Cárdenas, December 31, 1936, AGN, LC, 705.1-1. Dozens of requests for veterinary services can be found in AGN, LC, 506.17/8-30.

[73] Lopes and Riguzzi, "Borders," 632; Ford, Bacon, and Davis Incorporated, New York, "Report: Refrigeration and Cold Storage of Food for Mexico, D.F.," to Villaseñor, Banco de México, December 1944, CMAEFA, reports, box 1, "refrigeration and cold storage," 26–57.

Another contradiction was shared by many other countries: the tension between the attempts to police microbes and the imperatives of global trade and investment. Mexican officials and experts had long been aware of this potential problem. They were well aware that imports could carry disease – like the Duroc pigs imported from Kansas in the 1890s that brought triquinosis and cisticercosis to Guanajuato – and created sanitary inspections to try to prevent it; from the 1910s, they could hardly miss the USDA's tighter regulation of cattle ticks at the US-Mexico border.[74]

The difficulty of reconciling genetic improvement and disease control is particularly clear in arguments over how aftosa arrived in Mexico. Since the mid-nineteenth century, governments, scientists, and farmers in Europe and the Americas had come to fear aftosa. By the 1920s, it was common for states and scientists in Europe and the Americas to group the disease alongside rinderpest as one of the two great devastating livestock plagues. Yet, there was little that was self-evident or natural about this. Aftosa was highly contagious, but its clinical symptoms, particularly among low-bred livestock, could be very mild- unlike the highly fatal rinderpest. It was only the interplay of several factors through the nineteenth century which allowed the idea that the disease was a serious – even existential – problem to gradually take hold: the developing art of statistics to measure and model harm to national wellbeing, economic interests of elite livestock breeders, and the growth of increasingly professional and ambitious veterinary experts. To an unusually obvious degree, aftosa was a plague "manufactured" by human interest groups and expertise.[75]

By the early twentieth century, two main policies emerged in Europe and the Americas to deal with the problem of aftosa: the so-called "stamping out" method using quarantine and slaughter to eradicate the virus; and the use of quarantine, serums, and vaccines to restrict and ameliorate it. Many factors interacted to produce these protocols in different states: changing perceptions of disease, the relative sophistication of laboratory research, the prestige of veterinarians, state capacity, national identity, the shifting nature of rural societies and the meat and dairy trade. However, once the contagious (rather than spontaneous) nature of the disease was recognized, geography and the scope of infection imposed a general pattern on policies. In much of continental Europe

---

[74] Saucedo, *Historia*, 34–5. On the effects of the BAI's vast, slow-moving anti-tick campaign on border policing after 1914, see Strom, *Making Catfish*, 111–16, 173, 199–203.
[75] Woods, *Manufactured Plague*, xiv. See also, Berdah, *Abattre ou vacciner*. On rinderpest, see McVety, *Rinderpest Campaigns*.

and South America, where aftosa was widespread or enzootic, and particularly where extensive trade or land borders threatened future reinfection, a mix of vaccination and serums proved to be compelling and cost-effective. By contrast, the UK – largely free of the disease, and relatively isolated geographically – became the leading exponent of "stamping out." Early US and Mexican protocols followed suit, and increasingly recognized the need for some form of international coordination to tackle this problem.[76] In 1926, Mexican veterinarians diagnosed an outbreak of aftosa in the coastal lowlands of Tabasco; officials believed that a shipment of bulls from Louisiana was the most likely cause. The USDA sent a handful of veterinarians to help Mexico's Ministry of Agriculture and, over six months, veterinary brigades quarantined the area, slaughtered a few thousand infected cattle, and eradicated the outbreak, greatly aided by the lack of major commercial arteries and marshy terrain hindering the movement of herds. As a result of the Tabasco outbreak, in 1928 both governments signed an international sanitary accord restricting imports of stock from infected areas of the world – that is much of South America, mainland Europe, and Asia – and agreed to assist each other in case of future outbreaks.[77]

This sanitary agreement was very difficult to enforce. Mexico's veterinary officials were sparse, and the accord itself was vague and full of loopholes. Mexico imported breeding cattle from France and Spain in the 1930s, through murky procedures that are not entirely clear.[78] Ranchers in the north – often with investments and properties on both sides of the US–Mexico border – moved breeding cattle to and fro across the international boundary with few obstacles. As one US rancher remarked decades later, the men involved in the trade for elite breeding stock – the cattle industry equivalent of high-end capital inputs – were powerful and well-connected; in postrevolutionary Mexico the breeding business was "full of colonels and generals."[79]

In 1945–6, the political weight of these groups was particularly clear in a dispute over two shipments from Brazil of several hundred *cebu* bulls. Aftosa had been widespread in Brazil since the late nineteenth century, but the cebus' hardiness, resistance to disease, and suitability for tropical

---

[76] Woods, ibid., xiv. On continental Europe, particularly the Netherlands, see also Swabe, *Animals, Disease and Human Society*. For the United States, see Olmstead and Rhode, *Arresting Contagion*, 115–37. On the spread of aftosa in Argentina and Brazil in the late nineteenth century, see Machado, *Aftosa*, 3–19.

[77] Sigsworth, "Mexican Epizootic," 24–6.   [78] Ibid., 39.   [79] Ewing, *Ranch*, 173.

ranching, ensured that they were much in demand. In the 1930s, Richard Kleberg, a powerful Texan rancher and owner of the vast King Ranch, bred a new cebu hybrid called the Santa Gertrudis; in 1941, Kleberg persuaded the USDA to recognize it as the first beef breed produced in the United States, using the "tremendous amount of pull" he enjoyed as a conservative Democratic congressman.[80] In Mexico, elite politicians and businessmen also sought out cebu genes. One of the recipients of a shipment of several hundred Brazilian cebu in the autumn of 1945 was none other than ex-president Cárdenas, who had recently stepped down as Minister of Defense and begun to cultivate an inscrutable and Sphinx-like public demeanor, but remained one of the most powerful figures in the country; future president Miguel Alemán received another.[81] The most visible driver of the next shipment of cebu bulls to Mexico in 1946 was Colonel Carlos Serrano, a senator from Veracruz, who had been involved in the cattle breeding business since the 1930s. Given Serrano's involvement, it is difficult not to conclude that incoming president Alemán also had some interest in the shipment. Serrano was well-known as Alemán's stooge, bagman, and pistolero; soon he would run Alemán's presidential spy agency, and help him muscle in on the drug trade, among other enterprises. (During the aftosa campaign, Alemán seized some northern ranches for his portfolio, and Serrano flew there in person to threaten their owners at gunpoint.)[82] Serrano was also probably working with one Colonel Dan Breen, a US-born Coahuila-based rancher and breeder, with whom he had gone into business in the 1930s, and who reportedly shared Serrano's habit of using a fake military rank.[83]

A far-flung triangle of diplomats favored or acquiesced in these shipments. Brazil had imported cebu cattle from India in the late nineteenth century and its breeders and diplomats had long sought to export their acclimatized "indu-cebu" cattle to the rest of the Americas. A group of Brazilian ranchers and congressmen, aided by the Mexican ambassador, had arranged Mexico's first import of cebu in the mid-1920s.[84] Mexico's Ministry of Foreign Relations welcomed the cebu trade to strengthen ties with South America and diminish economic and political dependence on the United States, an enduring objective of Mexican diplomacy. In this,

[80] Ibid., 72.   [81] Saucedo, *Historia*, 224; Castro Rosales, "La aftosa," 222.
[82] Williams and Williams Irwin, *Let the Tail*, 212–3.
[83] Ewing, *Ranch*, 172–3; Sigsworth, "Mexican Epizootic," 47.
[84] Wilcox, *Cattle in the Backlands*, 206, 190; various reports, Boyle, 1937, Rio de Janeiro, NA, MAF, 35/857; various correspondence, 1923–4, AHGE, 4/043.56(81-4)/1IN 1923.

they had the support of Mexican President Manuel Ávila Camacho, who wanted to avoid insulting Brazil's President Vargas, and whom US officials suspected also had a personal stake in the transaction.[85] The US ambassador George Messersmith decided that whatever sanitary risks the shipment presented, it was not worth antagonizing the major Latin American interests at stake, and he made a series of public statements which suggested that the US would acquiesce to more shipments from Brazil provided appropriate checks and inspections were made.[86] After all, those favoring the imports argued that cebus were not just a private business matter, but a crucial source of the genetic capital demanded by national development. Unusually, Cárdenas was willing to be publicly associated with the trade. In 1945, he attended the opening of a small quarantine station at Sacrificios Island off the Veracruz coast, built to inspect the first shipment and facilitate more. The press reported that he made a toast to the "happy continuation of the importations."[87]

While the 1945 shipment of bulls arrived unimpeded, the second in 1946 generated more conflict with sanitary authorities on both sides of the border. The more relaxed Messersmith had been replaced at the end of 1945, and the US government now began to take a harder line, under pressure from the USDA and, Mexican and Brazilian breeders suspected, from US breeders like Kleberg, who wanted to control the market in cebu stock. The US government warned that if the shipment went ahead it would close the US–Mexico border to livestock. According to his exculpatory memoir published the following year, Marte Gómez, then Mexico's Minister of Agriculture, tried stop the second shipment and never authorized the bulls to land at the station on Sacrificios Island, but was overruled by higher authorities – presumably President Ávila Camacho. In the summer of 1946, both governments came up with a compromise to resolve the dispute. A team of four veterinary experts from both countries was assembled and sent to inspect the bulls on Sacrificios

---

[85] "Summary of Developments in the Mexican outbreak of Foot-and-Mouth Disease," January 28, 1947, TP, Official File, 395; Nash Carter, *One Man*, 157–8.

[86] Sigsworth, "Mexican Epizootic," 40–1. In general, Messersmith argued the United States' long-term interests would be best served by continuing to foster Mexico's industrial and technological development after the war, given that "the industrialization of Mexico will go forward whether we help it or not." Messersmith, Mexico City, to Hull, State Department, March 9, 1944, Messersmith Papers, University of Delaware Library, box 14, F106, https://udspace.udel.edu/bitstream/handle/19716/7552/msso109_1587–00.pdf (last accessed December 1, 2020).

[87] Ibid., 42.

Island, and to conduct follow-up inspections on bulls from the first Brazilian shipment scattered throughout eighteen different ranches in Veracruz, San Luis Potosí, Nuevo León, Michoacán, Tamaulipas, and Yucatán. After this group reported no signs of aftosa, the bulls finally arrived on the Mexican mainland in October 1946, and their first port of call was Colonel Serrano's nearby ranch.[88]

A few weeks later, a Mexican veterinarian reported cattle with aftosa-like symptoms very close to Serrano's ranch. By December, only a few weeks after Alemán had become president, Mexican researchers confirmed that the virus was probably aftosa. A polemic ensued in the Mexican press over the origins of the virus. For some, the answer was obvious: the shipment of Brazilian cebus, whose inspectors had clearly erred or, perhaps, been led astray. Others argued that the virus could easily have been the result of earlier unregulated shipments, a holdover or mutation from the 1926 outbreak. The Brazilian embassy made statements to the press alleging that aftosa must have been present in the region in some form for decades.[89] Eventually the Mexican government settled on the Brazilian shipment as the most likely cause, but never clarified exactly who had been involved in it. Rather than spend time sifting through the uncertainty of past bull imports, it argued, the priority was to deal with the task of eradication at hand. US officials agreed, and in early 1947 the US Secretary of Agriculture Clinton Anderson struck a conciliatory tone. Anderson admitted that the US government ought to take a share of blame for the outbreak, since some of its citizens were also involved in the cebu business, and should also play its part in planning a response.[90]

The traditional focus of histories of livestock has been economic production and markets. As historians increasingly emphasize, animals can also tell us a lot about broader changes in governance and notions of development. Long before the 1940s, Mexican authorities were interested in animals – as sources of wealth, energy, symbolic power, and disease – and harnessed them to projects to govern and develop resources. In this way, human-animal relations were part of debates over the meaning of

---

[88] Wilcox, *Cattle in the Backlands*, 191; Sigsworth, "Mexican Epizootic," 44–8; Saucedo, *Historia*, 228.

[89] Mexico's veterinary historians now argue that aftosa most likely arrived from a 1946 shipment of Spanish fighting bulls, cattle smuggled into the country from Venezuela, or a mutation of a vesicular disease already present in Mexico. Cervantes Sánchez and Román de Carlos, "Las consecuencias," 18.

[90] Saucedo, *Historia*, 230–2.

modernization; animals could, at times, become touchstones of national progress. Animals were not necessarily models for governing people (or vice versa) although, in some areas – microbiology – animals helped produce knowledge that was given much wider application. Most important for us, looking at state formation from the perspective of animals highlights political and ideological tensions within projects of control and modernization: between moral regulation and legitimation; production and social reform; genetic management, global integration, and disease control. Tracing conflicts over breeding stock also reveals some political dynamics that resist neat categorization; the interests involved crossed national borders, traversed Mexico's factional and ideological divides, blurred boundaries between state and society, and revealed fault lines within states themselves. In other words, this historical background introduces us to some of the precursors, institutions, and interest groups and expectations that would shape the aftosa crisis. It also provides a foretaste of the messy political dynamics of the aftosa campaign, which would shortly become "the biggest thing going in Mexico."[91]

---

[91] *Aftosa International*, 2.

2

Sharing Sovereignty in a Technical Commission

Frank Mulhern did not expect to spend his time in Mexico spying on colleagues. Twenty-five years old and "just out of vet school," Mulhern was one of the first veterinarians to join the US–Mexico Commission for the Eradication of Foot and Mouth Disease (*Comisión México-Americana para la Eradicación de la Fiebre Aftosa*, CMAEFA). In May 1947, the commission sent him to scout local conditions in a northern stretch of the State of Oaxaca that traversed the tropical basin of the Papaloapan River, a section of the Sierra Norte, and the windswept Isthmus of Tehuantepec. In his first reports topographical and cultural obstacles loomed large: rope-bridges "like Tarzan swings in the movies," impassable and unmapped forest, "roads that twisted and turned like a snake," disease, mosquito nets "as hot as if they were solid cloth," Indian dialects which his Mexican colleagues could not understand and "resemble Chinese." Still, after meeting local cattle owners and "preaching to them for days," he found them cooperative, and the surroundings were "a botanist's dream ... beautiful sights that in the future will bring back fond memories."[1] Four months later, Mulhern's mood had curdled, soured by endless delays and threats which prevented him inspecting or slaughtering infected animals. On October 3, Mulhern sat in the campaign's headquarters in Oaxaca City, and eavesdropped on a phone call. He heard Dr. Gama, his Mexican colleague, agree not to slaughter any animals in the district, breaking CMAEFA protocols. Mulhern then searched the CMAEFA's office, found some telegrams from Nazario Ortiz Garza,

---

[1] Ewing, *Ranch*, 197; Mulhern, Tuxtepec, to Shahan, Mexico City, July 20, 1947, CMAEFA, operations, box 29, field reports, Oaxaca.

Mexico's Minister of Agriculture, confirming the orders. He made copies and reported his find to US officials in Mexico City: "It is beginning to look as if we're doing this on our own and that the people in Mexico City don't want us to do it."[2] US officials confronted the Mexican government with these telegrams and in a few days slaughter restarted, but six weeks later the Mexican government officially suspended slaughter and announced plans for an alternative policy, vaccination.

The CMAEFA was an exercise in animal disease eradication of unprecedented scale, "the largest undertaking ... of this sort that has ever transpired," and officials like Mulhern worked closely with Mexican officials to implement it. US and Mexican co-directors ran the campaign, created parallel US and Mexican administrative "sections," and adopted the general principle that each US official or employee – district directors, veterinary inspectors, paymasters, appraisers, engineers, cowhands – should work in tandem with a Mexican counterpart. The resulting, rather unwieldy organization employed around 3,000 US citizens and 5,000 Mexicans at its height.[3] Without a surviving archive, it is not so easy to access the Mexican section's perspectives, but other government archives and memoirs offer telling glimpses. One Mexican veterinarian stationed in Veracruz recalled a revealing incident: a US veterinarian argued that, since the campaign was funded, equipped, and run by the United States anyway, the district's jeep effectively belonged to him, and refused to let his Mexican colleagues drive it; one day, one Mexican colleague lost patience and threw a fistful of mud into the driver's face, muttering "this is certainly my land."[4] If the CMAEFA was a jeep, its journey consisted of three main stages: from March to November 1947, the engine of policy was quarantine and slaughter, and it was steered overwhelming by US interests and policy preferences; by November, the wheels of the campaign were clogged by the mud of Mexican public opposition and official obstruction, and it then entered a 12-month period of maintenance and refurbishment; finally, with the engine of vaccination fully installed, US and Mexican officials found the sociopolitical terrain easier, and directed this peculiar bilateral vehicle to a successful completion.

One way of seeing this campaign is as a reflection of the growing cooperation of capital and modernizing elites on both sides of the

---

[2] Mulhern, Oaxaca City, to Noyes, Mexico City, October 4, 1947, CMAEFA, operations, box 29, field reports, Oaxaca.
[3] Supplement to statement of General Johnson, November 1948, FMDRL, box 1, folder 18.
[4] Torres y Elzaurdia, *Botas de hule,* 222.

US–Mexico border, eager to sanitize, integrate, and develop the country-side.[5] The campaign certainly received support from the transnational cattle complex that connected northern Mexico to the US Southwest. The campaign's objectives, the kind of secondary benefits it aimed to spread – roads, mechanization, credit, new meat-packing plants – and its general indifference to agrarian and distributive conflicts, all chimed with an emerging "interstate consensus on modernization" that prioritized generic technical and market-oriented solutions to rural problems.[6] Local studies of the outbreak have unearthed vital insights into popular attitudes and resistance, but tend to portray the commission itself as an institutional monolith.[7] However, this perspective reveals little about the conflicts that emerged between (and within) both governments over how best to confront the epizootic, why these conflicts mattered to people at the time, and how they were resolved, masked and, later, forgotten. To answer these questions, this chapter combines a sense of shared economic interests and modernizing expertise with close attention to a kind of cross-border, or "stereophonic" bureaucratic politics.[8] The campaign was indeed a conflict between modernizing states and the country-side; but it was also a drawn out and murky struggle between and within those states.

The Bureau of Animal Industry (BAI) – a powerful and autonomous branch of the USDA – and Mexico's Ministry of Agriculture were primarily responsible for organizing the commission. However, many different groups and institutions sought to influence the project. Short-lived, and with a specific aim, the CMAEFA was not an international entity which enjoyed significant autonomy from the states that created it, but

---

[5] For accounts emphasizing these trends, see Niblo, *War*; Fein, "Everyday Forms." On the shift away from more peasant-focused agricultural research in 1947–8 specifically, see Harwood, "Peasant-Friendly."

[6] Fein, "Everyday Forms," 436.

[7] Soto Correa, *El rifle*; Figueroa Velázquez, *El tiro de gracia*. Two works that use state department files to illuminate international and intragovernmental tensions, without exploring their full breadth and dynamics: Torres Ramírez, *México en la segunda guerra mundial*; Ledbetter, "Popular Protest."

[8] Tenorio Trillo, "Stereophonic Scientific Modernisms." Scholars of international relations might prefer to speak of either bilateral relations or (in cases of weak executive control) transgovernmental relations between government agencies in different states. Given that the degree of central control over the commission varied over time, I prefer the more open-ended terms. For an examination of the proliferation of US agencies involved in US–Mexico relations, see Wiarda, "Beyond the Pale." For studies of transgovernmental dynamics in drug policy and water management respectively, see: Pérez Ricart, "U.S. Pressure"; Alvarez, *Border Land*.

these states were hardly unified.[9] In the United States, the livestock industry, Congress, state governments, and an emerging national security state all took an interest in and, in different ways, shaped the campaign. In Mexico, a weak central government, and the immediate costs imposed by the disease and eradication, ensured more acute divisions between federal, military, and subnational authorities and serious limits on the power of the Ministry of Agriculture to formulate and impose policy. However, for the United States, such divisions did not make Mexico "submissive, docile ... and easy to manage."[10] As weak as it was, over time Mexico's government developed a coherent if unspoken strategy to help minimize the costs of US-backed slaughter, and shift policy towards its favored solution, vaccination. The strategy had two key components: the kind of obstructionism and delay witnessed by Mulhern in Oaxaca; and a search for international ties to balance the influence of the USDA and its allies in the US Congress.

In 1946, the outbreak and galloping spread of aftosa shocked the US and Mexican governments, but it is not surprising that it generated a bilateral commission. The 1926 outbreak of aftosa in Tabasco provided a precedent of sorts, but not much guidance; small and hastily organized, the earlier campaign generated no enabling legislation or clear organizational blueprint and in negotiations, neither Mexican nor US officials mentioned it often.[11] More important were the various bilateral commissions that emerged in the 1940s to organize wartime cooperation on security, trade, US loans, and migration, in whose footsteps the CMAEFA followed. Mexico initially suggested that the aftosa campaign be organized through the Joint US–Mexico Commission on Agriculture, founded in 1944 to support postwar planning, but US officials insisted that the scale of the problem demanded a stand-alone commission.[12] In any case, several veterans of wartime agencies were recruited to the CMAEFA: Don Stoops, agricultural attaché at the US embassy, whose fluency in Spanish allowed him to follow Mexican officials' informal discussions during and after meetings, "a rather important assignment"; Pancho Scanlan, US expatriate, procurement officer and all-purpose political fixer, who had worked for Mexican railways in the 1930s before

---

[9] Barnett and Finnemore, "Politics, Power, and Pathologies."

[10] Soto Correa, *El rifle*, 52.

[11] Comments by Fladness, Minutes of Advisory Committee, May 27, 1947, afternoon session, CMAEFA, reports, box 1, advisory committee.

[12] Stoops, confidential report covering January 18–June 22, 1947, CMAEFA, reports, box 1.

running wartime rail shipments of strategic materials for the US government. The campaign's tents, jeeps, steam shovels, people carriers, and insecticides, all sourced from postwar US Army surplus, made the connection to the wartime mobilization of resources still more obvious.[13]

In theory, the authority both governments delegated to the CMAEFA was merely technical. Both states were committed to eradication, initially via slaughter, and it was the commission's job to find the most efficient way to carry it out. In public, US and Mexican officials tended to frame aftosa as a technical problem, to be addressed through the application of scientific and administrative expertise. In Mexico, for example, the government ensured that all announcements about commission policy were made by the CMAEFA's Mexican co-director, Oscar Flores, to lend them the appearance of neutral appraisals of economic and epidemiological conditions.[14] Maintaining this distinction between the technical and political was far from simple. Any method of control or eradication would necessarily rest on a series of assumptions – who ought to shoulder the program's costs, who should enjoy its benefits, the character of Mexican society and how it ought to develop in the future – and navigate a welter of competing interests.

The BAI had long advocated stamping out aftosa with slaughter. This adoption of UK protocols in the late nineteenth century was not based on the prestige of British scientists or their knowledge of the virus and its stubborn array of types – which was relatively underdeveloped. Rather, the BAI believed that it fitted a context of geographic isolation and freedom from enzootic infection similar to that of the United Kingdom. By the 1940s, the slaughter method was thoroughly institutionalized in the agency, and considered a "time-tested, proven procedure."[15] It had been implemented successfully during outbreaks in the 1910s and 1920s, and veterans of these campaigns crafted BAI policies and defended the advantages of slaughter in pamphlets for farmers and the general public. Many at the BAI doubted that recent aftosa vaccines – such as had been developed in Germany by Dr. Otto Waldmann after 1938 – were as

---

[13] B. Simms, BAI to Secretary, June 18, 1949, CAP, box 7, foot-and-mouth; Scanlan, Mexico City, to Simms, BAI, May 27, 1948, CMAEFA, reports, box 2, procurement and property; L. Greene, Personnel, Mexico City, to DeVaughan, Personnel, BAI, May 12, 1948, CMAEFA, reports, box 2, "personnel: general."

[14] Confidential report, 30 November 1947, CMAEFA, reports, box 1, weekly reports.

[15] Ewing, *Ranch*, 200. Soto Correa mistakenly claims that slaughter was rarely used in the United States before the 1940s. Soto Correa, *El rifle*, 51.

reliable or as cost-effective as slaughter as a means of eradication.[16] Past experience reinforced skepticism. The BAI blamed several earlier outbreaks of aftosa on livestock owners smuggling unreliable vaccines into the country and unwittingly spreading the virus.[17] Conversely, campaigns in California and Texas increased US officials' faith in the efficacy of quarantine in Mexico. Their research suggested that earlier worries about the role of migratory and carrion-eating birds as disease vectors had been exaggerated. In 1924, the BAI had hunted down and killed 22,000 wild deer during an outbreak in California, but believed that more isolated populations of such animals in Mexico would make such measures unnecessary.[18] John R. Mohler, who headed the California and Texas campaigns and wrote their official histories, retired in 1943, but several of his former colleagues were sent down to Mexico: Maurice Shahan, a mild-mannered veterinarian, renowned virologist, and veteran of the California campaign who headed the US section of the CMAEFA from its founding to mid-1948; Leroy "Sparkplug" Noyes, a famously hard-bitten and forceful administrator from the BAI office in Texas, known among US officials for his willingness to "knock a few heads together," who effectively ran the everyday administration of the US section for five years.[19]

Besides pointing to long-established protocols and earlier successes, the BAI supported its prescribed policy in other ways. As in the UK, the BAI also sometimes presented the choice to slaughter as a test of national character: it showed that the United Kingdom and the United States were the kind of determined, virile, and efficient nations that could wage an outright war against disease, and handle the bitter medicine of slaughter, unlike lax Latin or oriental nations (or, for that matter, the feckless Irish).[20] In a June 1947 speech to drum up support for the campaign, the BAI's Dr. Fred Shigley made the parallel with British policy and rhetoric explicit. Shigley quoted a prayer by the Bishop of Salisbury for release from the "evil" of the disease during a recent outbreak, argued

---

[16] Various USDA pamphlets and reports, 1910s–30s, FMDRL, box 1, folder 2.

[17] Ibid. For an overview, see Olmstead and Rhode, *Arresting*, 115–37.

[18] Minutes of Advisory Committee, May 27, 1947, afternoon session, CMAEFA, reports, box 1, Advisory committee.

[19] Smith, Aguascalientes, to Anderson, Mexico City, 4 pm, June 15, 1948, CMAEFA, field reports, Aguascalientes, radio log; "From Foot to Mouth," Aftosa newsletter, October 2, 1947, CMAEFA, general subject files, box 1. On the influence of "veterans" of the 1924 and 1929 California outbreaks in Mexico, see Ewing, *Ranch*, 199.

[20] For Britain, see Woods, "Why Slaughter?"

that experiments with vaccines were only safe where the disease had already been allowed to become endemic, and congratulated Mexico on adopting the "same policy" as the United Kingdom and the United States since their experiences provided "proof that man can be master of the infection if he has sufficient determination."[21] Behind closed doors in Washington DC, the BAI lobbied Congress discreetly, creating backchannels to avoid accusations of open politicking; rather than visiting senators to drum up support, they asked members of their industry advisory committee – made up chiefly of Southwestern US cattlemen – to act as go-betweens, lobbying senators or inviting them to visit the USDA offices to be briefed on the matter.[22]

Key US interest groups were receptive to lobbying. As Alan Olmstead and Paul Rhode have shown, although the BAI's sanitary campaigns often provoked initial criticism from farmers, over time their success boosted support and even generated further calls for government regulation of livestock production and markets.[23] Republicans, who controlled both houses of Congress for the first time since 1931, worried about the size and expense of the Mexican campaign. Occasionally Republican politicians and newsmen associated it with New Deal era agricultural regulation that they wanted to roll back. BAI officials in Texas complained that "vultures" in the press lazily likened the commission to 1930s public works projects. Henry Luce's publications in particular dwelled on the campaign's supposed wastefulness, but such criticisms were vague and opportunistic in the main. Republicans generally accepted the principle that some kind of eradication campaign was necessary, and focused on scrutinizing budgets while agreeing to fund the commission. After the former actor and broadcaster Robert Montgomery accused the campaign of being a "welfare state pork barrel" in April 1952, a bipartisan Senate committee summoned and chastised him.[24] The BAI also benefitted from

---

[21] F. M. Shigly, "Eradicating FMD in Mexico," Assistant to co-director of CMAEFA, June 10, 1947, to Union Church, CMAEFA, General subject files, box 1, "Dr Shigly."

[22] Minutes of Advisory Committee, May 27, 1947, afternoon session, CMAEFA, reports, box 1, Advisory committee.

[23] Olmstead and Rhode, *Arresting Contagion*, 8.

[24] Dr. Sneider, Albuquerque, to Dr. Wardlow, Monterrey, June 13, 1947, CMAEFA, operations, box 29, field reports, Nuevo León; various press clippings, 1948, FMDRL, box 1, folder 8; John Bell, "Robert Montgomery Turns Tables at Quiz," *Washington Post*, April 10, 1952. On disputes about New Deal and wartime price supports, and the "Farm Problem," see McDonald, *Food Power*, 74–104.

early, backstage support for the campaign from the chief of staff of the US Army, General Dwight Eisenhower.[25]

For the beef-cattle industry, eradicating aftosa in Mexico by slaughter had a specific appeal. Its noisiest advocates were the Texan ranchers gathered around Richard Kleberg, who argued it was the only sure-fire way to defend the livestock economy, boost food production, provide American families with nutritious meat and milk, and thus wage the Cold War. In January 1947, Richard Kleberg briefly visited Mexico City to lobby for a slaughter policy, fueling conspiracy theories about hidden economic purposes.[26] Most theories focused on US ranchers' supposed plans to expand into Mexican markets. In private, USDA officials identified other more powerful motives, which had less to do with access to the Mexican market and more with US protectionism. Slaughter was certainly compatible with Kleberg and his supporters' desire to protect their breeding business from competing with Brazilian cebu shipments. However, US Secretary of Agriculture Clinton Anderson believed that the real reason why Kleberg's supporters and the beef industry as a whole were so wedded to slaughter and hostile to US research on vaccination was their desire to protect themselves from competition with cheap, high-quality beef from Argentina, whose status as an aftosa-infected country had barred imports to the United States since the late nineteenth century.[27] (Logically enough, when BAI officials sought to bolster US support for vaccination a few years later, they included fewer beef ranchers and more dairy farmers on their advisory committee.[28]) In 1947, however, critics of US beef interests were unable to dictate BAI policy, and few were willing to broach US protectionism in public. In a cabinet meeting in February 1947, Secretary Anderson complained that the bill authorizing the USDA to cooperate with Mexico in a slaughter campaign was "too strong" and "not a good bill," but was "the only thing that will satisfy the cattle people."[29] Whatever Anderson's misgivings, the BAI remained a steadfast supporter of slaughter, and did not

[25] Simms, "Deficiency appropriations report," July 21, 1947, CMAEFA, reports, box 1, "Congressional hearings of June 1947"; Shahan and Stoops, BAI, to Anderson, June 24, 1947, CAP, box 7, foot and mouth.

[26] Ledbetter, "Popular Protest," 396–7; R. Kleberg, to Truman, January 18, 1947, TP, box 1137, file 395, "foot and mouth disease."

[27] I discuss those interests supportive of virus and vaccine research in detail in Chapter 6.

[28] Miscellaneous correspondence, 1949, FMDRL, box 2, folder 2.

[29] Cabinet meeting minutes, February 7, 1947, TP, digitized cabinet meeting collection.

share Anderson's optimism that an effective aftosa vaccine was close at hand.[30]

Apparent unity on the US side contrasted with open divisions in Mexico. By December 1946, the Ministry of Agriculture had already dispatched teams of veterinarians and soldiers to set up quarantine lines and slaughter any infected herds connected with the outbreak in central Veracruz; in January Alemán allocated some 100 million pesos to fund a national campaign.[31] However, the disease quickly spread into neighboring Puebla and the outskirts of the Federal District, and lax or nonexistent quarantine ensured that further spread north was only a matter of time. In Querétaro, the state government accused officials manning quarantine lines of being drunk or literally asleep on the job, but still allowed cattle to enter the state to feed the city and or fight in the state's main bullring.[32] The same month, federal officials drew up two main policies for consideration. One was to pursue eradication by slaughter with US support. The main advantages of this course were that it had worked previously and, it was assumed, the USDA would fund most or all of the program while ceding some administrative control to Mexico. Mexican officials recognized that any US-style slaughter campaign would need to be adjusted to national conditions: disruption to milk supply to the cities was a particular concern, and officials hoped that US support would include some 20,000–40,000 replacement dairy cattle, and credit and technical support for modernizing centers of dairy production. The second option was a long-term program of quarantine and vaccination, likely to be pursued without US assistance of any kind, and very likely in the face of US opposition, supported by collaboration with scientists from Europe and South America.[33]

In early 1947, Mexico's political establishment split over the question. In the cabinet, the Minister of Foreign Relations, Jaime Torres Bodet, opposed slaughter, and urged Mexico to rely on quarantine and slowly develop a vaccination program modeled on European and South American initiatives. This was a longer and more uncertain path but, he argued, it would avoid dependence on the United States and the enormous difficulty of implementing slaughter in poor, isolated, traditionally

---

[30] Simms, BAI, to advisory committee, September 15, 1947, CMAEFA, reports, box 1, advisory committee.

[31] Saucedo, *Historia*, 221.   [32] Figueroa Velázquez, *El tiro de gracia*, 121.

[33] Ortiz Garza, Agricultura, to Alemán, December 16, 1946, AGN, MAV, 4255-2-33.

independent peasant villages reliant on animals for draft power. Lurking off the stage of formal politics was ex-President Cárdenas, an ardent defender of Mexico's economic and territorial sovereignty, who had nationalized foreign oil companies in 1938 and limited US military ties during the Second World War; Cárdenas was characteristically silent but widely known to oppose slaughter. Nazario Ortiz Garza, Mexico's Minister of Agriculture, was one of the few Cardenistas left in the cabinet; he and officials at his ministry were privately uneasy about a US-backed slaughter campaign prosecuted with the "sanitary rifle" and preferred vaccination – or the "Argentine method" as they called it.[34] Most of Mexico's small group of 300 professional veterinarians would join the commission, attracted by the rare offer of steady employment and up to four times what they would usually earn, but many remained critical of slaughter. At the Veterinary School of the Universidad Nacional Autónoma de México (UNAM), Mexico's most prestigious researchers in the field openly advocated vaccination.[35] High-ranking military officers, including the head of the General Staff, General Francisco Grajales, and members of the military's medical corps, also pushed for the government to reject US-backed slaughter. Such attitudes worried the US State Department. US officials believed Mexican generals "didn't know beans about *aftosa*," but understood that the military – as the sole, reliable "police power" in Mexico – would be indispensable in any campaign. The US State Department was further alarmed when the Mexican government invited veterinary scientists from Brazil and Argentina to Mexico to advise on vaccination policy.[36]

The US government exerted enormous political and economic pressure on Mexico to quieten these divisions and adopt slaughter. US congressmen and ranchers warned Mexico that, unless adequate eradication measures were taken, the United States would have little choice but to completely seal the border, not just to livestock, but all movement of

---

[34] Torres Bodet, *La victoria*, 36–7; Report on 1946 cabinet, NA, FO 371/51590, 84; confidential report, September 30, 1947, CMAEFA, reports, box 1, weekly reports; Torres y Elzaurdia, *Botas de hule*, 38; Figueroa Velázquez, *El tiro de gracia*, 69.

[35] Interviews in special issue of *Imágen Veterinaria* 1:4 (2001); various clippings, 1947, CMAEFA, operations, box 5, information reports.

[36] Stoops, minutes of advisory committee meeting, May 27, 1947, morning session, CMAEFA, reports, box 2, advisory committee; Soto Correa, *El rifle*, 63; copy of Thurston, US embassy, to State Department, February 16, 1947, CMAEFA, reports, box 1, weekly reports.

goods and people.[37] In practice, this measure would have been extremely difficult to enact, but the physical border was far from Mexico's only point of weakness. Much like the rest of Latin America, the end of the Second World War eroded Mexico's bargaining power with the United States. To maintain the national drive for industrialization, Mexican officials were anxious to stem the flood of US imports and the resulting drain on dollar reserves, renegotiate wartime trade agreements, maintain some control over trans-border migration and, most important, secure access to US credit and investment.[38] US officials also pushed Mexico to clamp down on press coverage of dissenting government views. After newspapers reported General Grajales's criticisms of slaughter in February 1947, Don Stoops had some conferences with the Ministry of Agriculture and told them that "if this kind of publicity were going on we might as well call the whole thing off right away; if you don't have the cooperation of all your government behind it there is no use spending a bunch of money to try to get rid of the disease, because you can't do it."[39]

Moreover, slaughter enjoyed support among Mexico's powerful beef-cattle interests in Sonora, Coahuila, and Chihuahua.[40] The disease had yet to reach these northern states, and US border restrictions paralyzed livestock exports and cross-border grazing. Indeed, in many ways northern ranches were transnational enterprises, reliant on US markets and credit, and were often part owned by US citizens. (Carlos Ronstadt, a rancher from New Mexico who advised the USDA on the campaign, portrayed north Mexican cattle enterprises as thoroughly dependent on US investment, and so powerful locally as to be practically indistinguishable from state governments; in Sonora, for example, the cattlemen's associations and state government were "the same people."[41]) Northern

[37] Clinton Thompson to Truman, February 11, 1947, TP, box 1137, file 395, "foot and mouth"; confidential report, May 18, 1948, CMAEFA, reports, box 1; Torres Bodet, *Victoria sin alas*, 32.

[38] Confidential report from Thurston, Mexico City, to Truman, December 1, 1947, TP, Presidential Secretary's Files, box 161, foot and mouth. On the erosion of Mexico's foreign currency reserves since 1945, and negotiations around oil, labor, and US credit, see Alexander, *Sons*, 123–48.

[39] Stoops, minutes of advisory committee meeting, May 27, 1947, CMAEFA, reports, box 2, advisory committee, 22.

[40] Figueroa Velázquez, *El tiro de gracia*, 53.

[41] Ronstadt, minutes of advisory committee meeting, May 27, 1947, CMAEFA, reports, box 2, advisory committee, 48.

ranchers had long been aware of the obstacles unwanted microbes, ticks, and increasing USDA regulation posed to their operations. In the 1930s, they had formed a cross-border livestock sanitary association which met annually, the venue alternating between cities in Mexico and the US Southwest.[42]

At first, US pressure was effective. On February 21, the Mexican government announced it would wage a joint eradication campaign with the United States using quarantine and slaughter, and in March the CMAEFA came into being. President Alemán's appointment of Oscar Flores to co-direct the commission reassured US officials of the Mexican government's commitment to a vigorous program of stamping out. Flores was an up-and-coming *político* from Chihuahua, closely tied to the state's cattle interests and landowning elite, and a political enemy of Ortiz Garza.[43] Both governments promised to make roughly equal contributions to the campaign, and to split indemnities – by far the largest anticipated expense – down the middle: the US section would pay compensation for cattle (*ganado mayor*), and Mexico would compensate owners of the less valuable, but more numerous pigs, goats, and sheep (*ganado menor*).[44] The USDA created funding arrangements designed to induce steady Mexican compliance. The US Congress initially appropriated 9 million dollars to fund the first few months of cooperation; on July 30, 1947, it passed an "emergency appropriation" allowing the Secretary of Agriculture to transfer as much funding to the campaign from other sources as necessary. This "blank check" given to Clinton Anderson raised Republican hackles in the US Congress, but supporters argued that it enhanced the USDA's negotiating leverage, reflected the uncertain duration and scope of the campaign, and avoided the pitfalls of fixed annual sums which "would imply to Mexican officials ... a commitment to spend a certain sum of money during the year regardless of the course of the disease or the eradication campaign."[45]

---

[42] The group met in Albuquerque in 1941, and in Mexico City in 1942. Various correspondence, 1942, AHEG, III/368(72).

[43] Corlett, confidential report on foot and mouth disease campaign, September 1947, CAP, box 7, foot and mouth. In 1945, Flores had been secretary of the livestock association in Chihuahua, under its president Rodrigo Quevedo, and had protested against the shipments of Brazilian cebu bulls. Saucedo, *Historia*, 225.

[44] Stoops, report covering January 18–June 22, 1947, CMAEFA, reports, box 1.

[45] *Excélsior*, July 22, 1947; "Appropriation History," c. 1951, FMDRL, box 2, folder 32, 9–10.

While the commission largely followed US protocols on aftosa control, the BAI agreed to some important adjustments for Mexican conditions. Along with individual cash indemnities for livestock, the commission also offered mules as direct replacements for draft oxen, and subsidized credit for tractors for those who wanted them.[46] Just as important were the arrangements for "salvage" operations, whereby the USDA paid indemnities for exposed cattle which Mexican officials then transported and sold to Mexico City's slaughter house, on the formal (but loosely enforced and unaudited) understanding that proceeds would be reinvested in the aftosa campaign.[47] US veterinarians considered salvage less than ideal from a sanitary perspective, but it allowed for the campaign to empty regions of susceptible cattle before the arrival of US heavy equipment necessary for digging slaughter pits. Mexican authorities also argued it was an essential means of addressing shortages in the Mexico City meat supply, whose reliance on fresh rather than chilled and frozen meat made it particularly vulnerable. Salvage also functioned as a discreet subsidy to the Mexican state- a compromise solution after the US government rejected a Mexican request for a loan to fund 50 percent of the campaign costs. It generated around 6 million pesos, roughly equal to Mexico's official contribution to the campaign before November 1947.[48] On this hastily conceived basis, in April and May the commission began to order equipment and vehicles from the United States, recruited veterinarians, paymasters and appraisers, and created a basic administrative structure for the campaign, with US and Mexican personnel working, wherever practicable, in parallel. The arrangement helped counter the impression that the campaign was an US imposition. It also allowed for both sections of the commission to keep an eye on their counterparts and share responsibility for all levels of implementation – an implicit recognition that negotiations over the campaign were far from over.

[46] Minutes of advisory committee meeting, May 27, 1947, morning session, CMAEFA, reports, box 2, advisory committee; confidential report, July 6, 1947, CMAEFA, reports, box 1.

[47] Richards, BAI, to Anderson, Agriculture, 17 March 1947, CAP, box 7, foot and mouth.

[48] Unsigned report, c. July 1947, CEFMD, reports, box 1, "Congressional Committee"; "Examination of Fiscal and Administrative Procedure and Controls, Mexico–United States Foot and Mouth Disease Project," Mexico City, c. 1949, BP, box 5, foot and mouth disease; various correspondence, February 1947, CAP, box 7, foot and mouth; author's calculation, based on figures in Sigsworth, "Mexican Epizootic," 120, 216, 405 n349.

From April to November 1947, the CMAEFA's quarantine and slaughter operations intervened dramatically in everyday life. Quarantine lines surrounded the area of known infection – a swathe of central Mexico covering much of Veracruz, Puebla, Morelos, Mexico State, Oaxaca, Guerrero, Guanajuato, Michoacán, Jalisco, San Luis Potosí, Querétaro, Hidalgo, and Aguascalientes – and funneled all traffic through checkpoints and clouds of disinfectant solution; smaller checkpoints were established along strategic arteries within this area. Checks disrupted commerce, inconvenienced travelers, and scandalized some onlookers by forcing "respectable young women" to expose their legs and remove stockings while walking across vats of disinfectant.[49] Religious pilgrimages and countless local festivals were temporarily banned.[50] The commission created three centers to gather, strip, and spray northbound *braceros* and their effects with disinfectant; by May 1948, the main work of the commission's office in Aguascalientes was "processing" 800 braceros in this manner each day.[51] The commission strained to "get ahead" of the virus, finding those northernmost outbreaks that were recent and virulent, before working back southwards into areas of old infection. In theory, the CMAEFA was equally concerned with the spread of aftosa south to Guatemala, but privately officials recognized that it prioritized the northern boundary of the infection.[52]

It is easy to see why critics and supporters of slaughter likened it to a military campaign. After veterinarians discovered infection in a village, the village typically waited for a follow-up inspection at which a handful of veterinarians gauged the scope and virulence of the outbreak, determined which animals had been exposed to the virus, and fixed a time and place for owners to assemble their livestock. The commission then sent a team of engineers, steam shovels, and bulldozers to dig burial pits; longer was needed if they had to arrange for local people to dig pits by hand. When the day for slaughter arrived, at dawn several dozen commission officials and soldiers arrived in a convoy of jeeps and people carriers or, in remote areas, via mule trains and on horseback, and waited for owners to assemble at the agreed location. US and Mexican appraisers then slowly inspected the assembled livestock, agreed prices, and issued receipts to the

[49] *La Prensa*, September 4, 1947.   [50] Figueroa Velázquez, *El tiro de gracia*, 185–6.

[51] Smith to Noyes, May 25, 1948, CMAEFA, operations, 29, Aguascalientes radio log. On organized labor's opposition to the spraying of braceros in Tampico, see report, May 28, 1948, CMAEFA, reports, box 1, confidential weekly reports.

[52] Shahan, minutes of advisory committee meeting, May 27, 1947, afternoon session, CMAEFA, reports, box 2, advisory committee, 6.

FIGURE 2.1. Photograph of a farmer leading a cow into a slaughter pit in Aguascalientes, summer 1947. ABB, N82-4A. Archives of the Big Bend, Brian Wildenthal Memorial Library, Sul Ross State University, Alpine, Texas.

owners. Around early afternoon, commission employees then slowly drove the cattle, pigs, and goats to the pit one-by-one, and commission-designated "killers" (usually soldiers in civilian clothes) shot and dumped each animal into the pit below. Early in the campaign, officials sometimes allowed locals to hack meat from a handful of carcasses left above ground, on the condition that they cook and eat the meat that evening and burn the remaining carcasses, but US veterinarians soon discouraged the practice. After the killings, owners then formed a queue and a pair of US and Mexican paymasters exchanged the appraisal paperwork for cash compensation, while a platoon of soldiers stood guard. If the commission's estimate of livestock numbers had been fairly accurate and the operation had gone smoothly, by the evening work drew to a halt. Commission "slashers" cut the hides of animals and dumped buckets of lime over them, before diggers closed the pit. Any given operation took at least a day and, for larger towns, sometimes as long as a week (Figure 2.1).[53]

[53] Description taken from, USDA, *Campaign*, 33–51.

Following slaughter, a smaller disinfection brigade arrived. Charles Bernhardt, head of the US section's public relations, likened one brigade's work in an isolated part of Querétaro to a kind of counter-insurgency campaign against a hidden enemy:

Disinfection lacks the tragic drama of slaughter and burial. But it has the same sort of vital significance that the work of mop-up squads has in war – the painstaking, difficult work of small, lonely groups of fighters who seek out and dispose of the enemy wherever he may lurk ... Failure to disinfect one isolated, crag-hidden corral might allow foot-and-mouth virus to live, to spread, to re-infect the new herds that will eventually replace the slain animals.[54]

The USDA found the first months of this joint "sanitary warfare," from May to July 1947, relatively encouraging.[55] By then the disease had spread to nine states, but the campaign seemed to be taking effect and halting its spread. The US Congress only approved the major funding bill in July 1947 after a visiting congressional committee declared itself satisfied. The committee visited the CMAEFA's headquarters in Mexico City, toured slaughter operations in Guanajuato, enjoyed "some very delightful entertainment in the form of native dancing and a moonlight cruise to an island in the center of Lake Patzcuaro," and painted a fairly rosy picture of the campaign. Congressmen believed that it faced huge obstacles, but these were largely technical and topographical; they observed certain anomalies and incorrect procedures – outdoor butchering of carcasses, under-manned quarantine lines – but argued these could be rectified with better training and organization; the geographical isolation of many communities would be countered by better transport and planning; delays caused by rocky ground would soon be avoided with the arrival of heavy digging equipment from the United States. US ambassador Walter Thurston likewise urged approval of funding to shore up Mexican cooperation and US "prestige."[56] At the rate of current progress, the BAI predicted that the campaign would continue, slow during the rainy season, culminate with a "big drive" for slaughter in the dry months of January–June 1948, and be completed within a year.[57]

---

[54] Ibid., 56.   [55] Ibid., 36.

[56] Stoops, itinerary and reports on visit of congressional committee, July 11, 1947, CMAEFA, Reports, box 2, congressional committee; Thurston, Mexico City, to State Department, June 26, 1947, FMDRL, box 1, folder 21.

[57] Draft BAI statement on latest information on the campaign to eradicate foot and mouth disease, CMAEFA, reports, box 2, "For congressional hearings of June 1947."

The adoption of US prescriptions on aftosa also seemed to be paying other diplomatic dividends to Mexico. In March 1947, President Truman made an historic visit to Mexico City, laying a wreath at the memorial to the victims of the US–Mexico War.[58] The following month, Mexico received a 50-millon dollar loan from the US government for infrastructure and another loan of the same amount to stabilize the peso; in May, Mexican diplomats worried that US Ambassador Thurston might be replaced by a hard-line attorney from Texas, and were relieved when these rumors abated.[59] In July 1947, Mexico unilaterally imposed tariffs to protect industry, contravening Mexico's 1942 commercial treaty with the United States; it did so again in November. Following an "exhaustive consideration of all angles of the problem and with overall US–Mexico relations in mind," US officials decided not to impose diplomatic reprisals.[60]

However, many problems quickly surfaced. Everywhere, people simply hid animals or engaged in other kinds of passive resistance. Official cooperation was also halting. "High-ranking army officers" and the occasional state governor were, according to field reports, the members of Mexican officialdom most likely to refuse to have their baggage searched and disinfected at checkpoints.[61] More seriously, a group of military officers opposed to slaughter wrote letters to Cárdenas seeking his views, hand-delivered by trusted allies, while a few military commanders openly questioned the wisdom of slaughter.[62] State authorities were expected to cover 50 percent of the cost of maintaining quarantine lines and disinfection stations, but cooperation was also lacking in places.[63] In Querétaro, the state government refused to order the local police force to assist in the slaughter campaign.[64] In Veracruz, US officials noted that state authorities "don't want anybody there." The state governor (and future president), Adolfo Ruiz Cortines, had promised that no slaughter would occur in the state for at least 18 months, and when US section officials tried to travel to the port of Veracruz he called Mexico City and simply "canceled the tickets," delaying their arrival for over a month;

---

[58] Soto Correa, *El rifle*, 57–9.
[59] Pettinà, "Adapting"; Various correspondence, May 1947, AHGE, III/510(73-0) "48"/2-S.
[60] Charles "Chip" Bohlen, State Department, quoted in Pettinà, "Adapting," 11.
[61] Confidential report, August 30, 1948, CMAEFA, reports, box 1.
[62] Soto Correa, *El rifle*, 207.
[63] Various correspondence, AHEG, 3.40 (78), fiebre aftosa, 1947; confidential weekly report, August 8, 1947, CMAEFA, reports, box 1.
[64] Figueroa Velázquez, *El tiro de gracia*, 147.

later Ruiz Cortines promised to help the campaign only if the CMAEFA supply his own ranches around the port of Veracruz with disinfectant, but the US section refused.[65] Elsewhere, veterinarians grafted on the campaign budget, and colluded with livestock owners to pad the slaughter record with fictitious animals. In Michoacán, ex-Governor General Félix Ireta was handsomely paid for driving his pigs into a grave later shown to be empty, an affair the press dubbed "the dance of the pigs."[66] Groups crisscrossed the countryside buying up cattle on the cheap from panicked farmers and driving it to slaughter elsewhere for a steep profit; *La Prensa* accused Querétaro's state governor and federal deputies of running such a scheme; in Jalisco and Guerrero, commission field reports indicated that state and military officials protected or helped to organize similar ruses.[67] Profiteering drained the CMAEFA budget and generated discontent, but some veterinarians shrugged: the "silver lining" was that profiteers at least helped to depopulate swathes of the surrounding countryside, provided the animals were slaughtered.[68] More damaging to the campaign were bribes paid to soldiers, officers, and veterinarians to prise open quarantine lines or stymie slaughter operations. At night in Jalisco's central valley around Guadalajara, ranchers moved "tremendous" herds of cattle, offering between 500 and 2,000 pesos to soldiers as bribes.[69]

In Guanajuato, many of these problems converged in the person of General Miguel Z. Martínez, the commission's military liaison for the state, and a hardliner with a reputation for ruthless repression and corruption. Through the summer of 1947, the southern municipalities of Guanajuato saw some of the most intensive slaughter operations as the commission raced to depopulate the area before the rainy season. Martínez supervised most operations in person, shouted threats at uncooperative villagers, bombarded Mexico City with requests for more

[65] Mendenhall, Veracruz, to Dr. Rice, Mexico City, July 1, 1947, CMAEFA, operations, box 30, Veracruz; confidential reports, Shahan, Mexico City to Simms, BAI, February 24 and March 5, 1948, CMAEFA, operations, box 29, Veracruz.

[66] Machado, *Industry*, 71.

[67] Figueroa Velázquez, *El tiro de gracia*, 169. From thirty-three incidents of illegal cattle movements, culled from a database of CMAEFA field reports and a chronology based on Mexican veterinarians' recollections, officials identified seven as profiteering operations. In Jalisco, reports implicated the state government, in Guerrero the state veterinarian. In Veracruz, a group of twenty to thirty men on horseback roamed the south of the state buying up cattle.

[68] Hackenberg, Querétaro, to Noyes, Mexico City, October 14, 1947, CMAEFA, operations, Querétaro radio logs.

[69] Lewis, *Children*, 198, 199.

funding to speed up operations, and suggested that President Alemán fund aftosa eradication through a forced tax on wealthier citizens collected, presumably, by officials like himself.[70] Martínez and his officers feuded incessantly with veterinarians for "control of indemnity funds" in Guanajuato, and oversaw several dubious operations. In one notorious case in Salvatierra, the Mexican section claimed that Martínez's forces slaughtered some 80,000 oxen and 10,000 domestic cattle, a figure US officials regarded as absurd on its face.[71] At Valle de Santiago, Martínez refused to inspect hundreds of head of cattle hidden in a nearby volcanic crater, and threatened to kill the attending US livestock appraiser who had located the animals. Mexican officials in Guanajuato did not admit to graft, but privately conceded that the commission had to "work against the military opinion as they consider themselves more apt than the technical personnel"; the actions of Martínez and his officers were intended to "signify... that all work or organization undertaken by the commission should rest only with them; they consider it obligatory to send complaints everyday."[72] Shahan also trod lightly around General Martínez. Rather than investigate the main dispute in Valle de Santiago – the origins and fate of the mysterious cattle in the crater – Shahan explained to superiors that the dispute was likely a personal and intercultural misunderstanding; Martínez was known for "bullying tactics" but "some American citizens of Mexican parentage" – like the appraiser, Enrique Aguirre – "have a feeling of superiority which they conceal with difficulty"; in any case, "little can be done by us to absolutely preclude such incidents."[73]

As the campaign wore on, evidence gathered not simply of central weakness, but of a coordinated Mexican strategy to blunt the slaughter policy, or at least, to minimize its political and financial costs to the Mexican federal government. Even General Alejo González, the officer Alemán hand-picked to act as military liaison to the CMAEFA,

[70] Various field reports on Guanajuato, June–September 1947, CMAEFA, operations, Guanajuato; various correspondence, General Miguel Z. Martínez, Guanajuato, to Alemán, April 2, 1947, AGN, MAV, 4255-2-33.

[71] Wardlow, Guanajuato, to Shahan, Mexico City, May 7, 1947, CMAEFA, operations, Guanajuato; copy of Alfonso Suárez Serrano, Report on Restocking, March 17, 1948, and Hopkins, US embassy, to Shahan, May 8, 1948, in CMAEFA, reports, box 2, "operations: restocking."

[72] Rafael Levy Pérez, Mexican section, Salvatierra, to Shahan, October 30, 1947, CMAEFA, operations, box 29, Guanajuato.

[73] Shahan, Mexico City, to Simms, BAI, November 4, 1947, CMAEFA, operations, box 29, Guanajuato.

sometimes mediated disputes in a way that the US section found, at very best, distasteful and unhelpful. At a village in Querétaro, González handed out meat from a slaughtered cow to locals. When confronted by US officials, the General "got quite excited and remarked that ... he personally would be responsible for the giving of the meat and payment for the same," started handing out 100-peso bills to a gathering crowd, and made "several speeches to the people, causing much turmoil and excitement." During the speeches, the US officials "heard the General mention something about the 'damn gringos,'" and the "crowd responded with shouts of 'Viva el General!'"[74]

More important, the supply of federal resources was sporadic. Time and again through August, the Mexican section's budget dried up, forcing the US section to either cease operations altogether or cover costs temporarily from its own elastic budget.[75] The US section also struggled to obtain troops and transport. Whichever bureaucratic route the US section pursued – Flores and the Mexican section; General Alejo González; the provincial zone commanders; the Ministry of Defense – US officials encountered countless efforts to "bluff us out of those soldiers."[76] Off-the-record, military officers attached to the commission blamed their inability to provide troops and other support on a lack of federal money channeled through the Mexican section. Given the nature of the original bilateral agreements – hastily drawn-up, vague – such ongoing bargaining over finances is not surprising. While Secretary Anderson had anticipated that Mexico would spend a similar amount on the campaign as the USDA, or even somewhat more, Mexico's government considered slaughter viable only insofar as ample US funding could compensate for the enormous anticipated political costs.[77] Moreover, original discussions regarding military expenses had been left deliberately ambiguous. While the responsibility of the Mexican government, Mexican diplomats had understood that the US government might reward cooperation with military loans, and US diplomats had encouraged this impression.[78]

[74] Hackenberg, Querétaro, to Noyes, October 1947, CMAEFA, operations, box 29, Querétaro.

[75] Various confidential reports, August 1947, CMAEFA, reports, box 1; and AHEG, 3.40 (78), fiebre aftosa, 1947, vol. II.

[76] Omohundro, Mexico City, to Mackery, Guadalajara, November 26, 1948, CMAEFA, operations, box 29, Jalisco, phone log.

[77] Anderson, handwritten memo, c. March 1947, CAP, box 7, foot and mouth; Garza Ortiz, Agricultura, to Alemán, December 16, 1946, AGN, MAV, 4255-2-33.

[78] Confidential report, January 6, 1948, CMAEFA, reports, box 1.

The Mexican section of the commission often dragged its feet on costly slaughter operations, particularly in politically restive areas. One recurrent source of friction was the initial diagnosis of disease outbreaks, since it crystallized very different understandings of risk. The early clinical symptoms of aftosa among cattle were very hard to distinguish from relatively harmless cases of vesicular stomatitis. US veterinarians were instructed to assume the worst in all new outbreaks, and proceed to slaughter; Mexican veterinarians were more circumspect, preferring to recommend quarantine measures and wait until clinical tests (which took at least four to five days) confirmed the presence of aftosa. An exchange between Noyes and the field office in Tampico captures a typical dispute:

Dr. Dicke: They found a sick herd of about 20. Dr. [illegible] and Dr. Castillo are checking on it. They didn't come in yet.

Noyes: We can't play around with that. Don't look back at it at all. We can't afford to mess around. Just bury it.

Dr. Dicke: I don't know if I can do that, it might take a little pressure.

Noyes: Then use some pressure ... The best thing on Foot-and-Mouth is to take and kill and don't look back.[79]

In another dispute at San Vicente, San Luis Potosí, Noyes was equally clear: "In the future be sure that nothing is diagnosed as stomatitis in that area, but that it is diagnosed as foot and mouth, and buried immediately."[80] A shared concept of "contact animals" – that is, those animals which showed no symptoms but had likely had some contact with the virus – was even harder to establish. Even in a smoothly-functioning commission, it would have been difficult to reconstruct the kind of reliable "herd histories" veterinarians needed: open-range or common grazing was common; fences were few; livestock censuses were wholly unreliable, and the routes along which livestock traveled were unmapped and seasonal, with many rivers barring movement one month but allowing it the next.[81] In any case, many Mexican officials within and outside the commission considered the US section's sweeping classifications of contact animals "absurd and damaging to the economy."[82]

[79] Dicke, Tampico, to Noyes, 5 pm, December 31, 1947, CMAEFA, operations, box 29, Tampico, phone logs.

[80] Noyes, CMAEFA, to Connolly, SLP, December 31, 1947, CMAEFA, operations, box 29, SLP.

[81] Omohundro, Ixtlán, to Noyes, Mexico City, August 21, 1948, CMAEFA, operations, box 29, Nayarit.

[82] Unsigned memorandum on meeting with General Alejo González, in Valle de Santiago, Guanajuato, November 6, 1947, AHEG, 3.40 (78), fiebre aftosa, 1947, vol. VI. Based on

Disagreements over prices were particularly fraught for small numbers of prized dairy herds and fighting bulls. In early meetings, Shahan and Flores had tried and failed to agree on a formula for valuing these animals, and the commission often failed to agree a price and was forced to quarantine premises indefinitely, and move on elsewhere. These disputes, combined with the Mexican section's aims to minimize slaughter, and the US section's dependence on Mexican officials, interpreters and local guides for information, ensured the scope for arguments and delays was enormous.

Early on, US and Mexican officials also tended to assess the pliability of local communities quite differently. On average, Mexican appraisers held out for higher indemnity prices than their US counterparts.[83] In Querétaro, the US district co-director described disagreements about the urgency and political viability of slaughter:

The Mexican supervisor and myself are not in agreement as to what action should be taken in case the owners of the cattle will not accept the price offered. I request that the animals should be killed, if necessary with the use of troops. He thinks that the people should be persuaded. Due to the fact that his method takes too much time (in one case, a week for 200 cattle), I feel that we should no longer follow his system, but have been unable to get him to adopt mine.[84]

Like Mulhern sitting in his office in Oaxaca City, many US officials began to question Alemán's wholesale commitment to the slaughter strategy. When Mexican veterinarians negotiated with the owner of a dairy herd in the State of Mexico during a tour of Alemán to the area, cut US officials out of the administrative loop, and then refused to provide evidence of the costs and burial of the animals, the US section suspected that Alemán had personally undercut in the campaign. US officials also began to find the degree of newspaper criticism of slaughter operations suspicious, coming as it did both from more independent outlets like *La Prensa*, but also from those close to the Alemán administration.[85] All this was perceptive; on August 4, Alemán had secretly told the US ambassador that although "he had nothing against slaughter" he felt a vaccine trial would be desirable,

---

other memoranda in this archive, the author was probably Luis Palacios, an official of the state government.

[83] Various confidential reports, September 1947, CMAEFA, reports, box 1.

[84] Dr Hackenberg, quoted in USDA, *Campaign*, 59.

[85] Various correspondence, July 1947, CMAEFA, operations, box 1, "Mexico, Toluca." In January, *Excélsior* had even reported that the governor of the State of Mexico had refused Alemán's telephoned order to sacrifice cattle unless he put it in writing. Soto Correa, *El rifle*, 64.

and that slaughter was "not the solution to Mexico's problem."[86] Soon after, Alemán made the ostensibly generous offer to hand the slaughter campaign over to a hand-picked, personal representative of President Truman, but USDA officials and State Department advisors quickly decided that this was a backhanded offer which it would be "unwise" to accept. Such an appointment, they believed, would only heighten the political exposure of the Truman administration, entrench de facto Mexican non-cooperation, and strengthen Mexican officials' hand in shifting financial costs to the United States.[87] An apparent concession, the offer served only to demonstrate Alemán's seeming loyalty while reminding US officials of the limits of their power and the need for Mexican cooperation. Still, Truman's response was not altogether discouraging. He asked his brother to introduce CMAEFA officials in Mexico City to George Bergdoerfer, a family friend from Ohio; Bergdoerfer offered to share a vaccination method he had been taught by a Swiss veterinarian after the First World War who had since died, but was politely rebuffed by the commission. Alemán and his cabinet well understood that Truman was irritated by Kleberg's efforts to dictate policy and was not a particularly dogmatic opponent of vaccination. [88]

Throughout 1947, the Alemán administration also secretly kept the options for vaccination open. The Ministry of Foreign Relations sought out information on vaccination programs abroad, as did officials at the Ministry of Public Health.[89] In April 1947, the USDA demanded that Alemán disband continuing experiments with vaccination being conducted by Mexican veterinarians and dairymen in the Valley of Toluca.[90] After more threats to cut off all support for aftosa eradication and close the border, the Mexican government complied, but continued to quietly gather information and canvass support for an alternative

[86] Thurston, Mexico City to State Department, August 4, 1947, CAP, box 7, foot and mouth.

[87] Presidential assistant to Truman, August 14, 1947, TP, Presidential Secretary Files, box 161, foot and mouth.

[88] Truman to Clinton Anderson, August 25, 1947, TP, Presidential Secretary's Files, box 161, foot and mouth; Memo to Alemán, September 8, 1947, AGN, MAV, 4255-2-35 B; Rex Smith to Alemán, c. August 1947, AGN, MAV, 4255-2-38.

[89] Torres Bodet, *Victoria sin alas*, 32; report on visit to Denmark, Miguel Bustamante, dir. Instituto de Salubridad y Enfermedades, August 27, 1947, SSA, box 10, file 9, "generalidades, aftosa."

[90] USDA press release, April 29, 1947, TP, box 395, foot and mouth.

strategy. Behind the scenes, in June 1947, Alemán asked Senator Isidro Fabela, the powerful ex-governor of the State of Mexico and a major backstage supporter of vaccination, to organize a meeting between the veterinarians who worked on the Toluca project and the Minister of Agriculture, Ortiz Garza. Soon afterwards, the same veterinarians traveled to Europe ostensibly on a purely private quest to gather information on the latest vaccination techniques. When US congressmen visited, Ortiz Garza quietly quizzed them on their openness to a change to vaccination and one of the Ministry of Agriculture's own researchers, Dr. Antonio Ladrón de Guevara, handed a congressman a letter outlining his objections to slaughter.[91] A military veterinarian, Lieutenent Colonel Teófanes López Arista, also traveled to Buenos Aires and met with Argentine vaccine manufactures at a livestock show. When US officials questioned his presence there, their Mexican counterparts replied that he was simply a private citizen who had won a travel contest from a Mexican airline.[92] According to Arizona rancher Ben Williams, Flores himself – Alemán's hand-picked director of the campaign – hoped that slaughter would be stopped and quietly built political support for this change among US and Mexican stockmen.[93] In July 1947, someone in the upper reaches of Mexico's Ministry of Agriculture privately reminded Alemán of the long-term advantages that vaccination might offer; carefully managed, the campaign represented an opportunity to permanently enhance Mexico's scientific capacity and prestige; it could even be used to create a laboratory that would meet both Mexico's needs and serve as an "international centre to combat foot-and-mouth disease," supported and funded by countries across the hemisphere or perhaps the entire world.[94] Far from showing "indifference" to alternatives to slaughter,

[91] Fabela, Mexico City to Alemán, July 16, 1947, AGN, MAV, 4255-2-35 B; Fernández and Quesada, *El problema*; Stoops, itinerary and reports on visit of congressional committee, July 11, 1947, CMAEFA, reports, box 2, congressional committee. For Ladrón de Guevara's earlier work in the Ministry of Agriculture, see Harald Johnson, Rockefeller Foundation, to Hanson, Montgomery, Alabama, July 19, 1944, RAC, group 1.1, series 323 Mexico, box 15, "Instituto Pecuario, Téllez Girón."

[92] *Novedades*, June 30, 1947; Gottfried and Ortega, CMAEFA, to Secretaría de la Defensa Nacional, Mexico City, July 1, 1947, CMAEFA, administrative correspondence, box 5, clippings. At some point in the campaign, the Mexican Ministry of National Defense set up its own laboratory to research animal diseases, headed by Dr. Manuel Sarvide. Mayer and Adler de Lomnitz, *La nueva clase*, 69.

[93] Williams and Williams Irwin, *Let the Tail Go*, 210–11.

[94] Unsigned memo, Agriculture, to Alemán, July 31, 1947, AGN, MAV, 4255-2-35 A.

the Alemán administration was acutely aware of them, and carefully explored them while ducking overt confrontation with the USDA.[95]

For their part, through late summer and early autumn the US section debated how to shore up the slaughter program. Occasionally US and Mexican officials pondered whether the campaign should include an integrated program of rural credit, education, and public works to help affected communities.[96] However, the idea never got far, and the BAI in particular was eager to define compensation narrowly; anything beyond individual cash indemnities for livestock risked shifting the campaign away from its supposedly technical remit and into the domain of political and social problems, which were Mexico's responsibility. General Charles Corlett, a retired US Army officer sent by Truman to advise the campaign, was more modest. He suggested Shahan be provided with an "entertainment fund" with which to woo state and municipal officials, since the War and State Departments did this "in similar situations," and such activities are "quite important in Mexico."[97] Some ranchers on the BAI's advisory committee went further, urging the commission to find new ways to pay Mexican officials for cooperation. Rather than pursue "an apparent effort to institute American governmental bureaucratic methods in a country that does not understand them," the BAI should understand that "we are dealing with a foreign people and that methods understood by them and applicable to their country should be instituted."[98] BAI officials rejected this invitation to "off color" transactions. Money was their main source of leverage in Mexico, and could hardly be surrendered without guaranteed increases in US administrative control and effectiveness of quarantine; such a relaxation of "American bureaucratic methods" would also leave the agency vulnerable to Republican critics in Congress, some of whom had already begun

[95] Figueroa Velázquez, *El tiro de gracia*, 11. For a similar argument that Alemán only adopted vaccination "reluctantly" and that application was characterized by official "laziness and carelessness" see Soto Corea, *El rifle*, 236, 239.

[96] USDA, *Campaign*, 44.

[97] Corlett report, September 1947, CAP, box 7, foot and mouth.

[98] Reports of Subcommittee, July 19, 1947, in Brock, Mexico City, to Albert Mitchel, Chairman of Advisory committee of the US section of the Commission on Foot and Mouth Disease in Mexico, Albuquerque, CMAEFA, reports, box 2, advisory committee. Rancher Carlos Ronstadt had rehearsed similar arguments about engrained corruption in an earlier committee meeting in May. Minutes of Advisory Committee, May 27, 1947, afternoon session, CMAEFA, reports, box 1, advisory committee.

to criticize Mexican graft in general and the salvage arrangements in particular.[99]

Rather, the US section pushed to build informal support, formalize agreements, or engaged in selective non-cooperation of their own. General Corlett endeavored to meet with Cárdenas but, despite overtures from Cárdenas's rancher friend Raymond Bell, was rebuffed.[100] US officials tried to avoid disputes about operational procedures by pushing their Mexican counterparts to sign day-to-day working agreements in writing, normally without success. Near the northern limits of the infection, US field officials deemed slaughter strategically vital and decided to cover any disputed costs for small animal indemnities and military protection to get operations moving. In other places, they responded to Mexican obstruction or a lack of federal funds by suspending operations altogether. Operations in the State of Mexico – the center of vaccine experiments supported by state politicians and local dairymen – were particularly fitful. After Alemán's visit in June, the US section refused to work in the state until the Mexican section and state officials allowed US participation in all operations, as per bilateral agreements. The state government then funded their own stop-gap slaughter campaign, before the US section agreed to begin work again in late July. However, in August the district was again at an impasse: Mexican veterinarians made "objections" to how the US section approached cattle owners; Mexican funds for small animal indemnities were lacking; US officials refused to send infected cattle to salvage; and the state governor accused the US section of going "on strike" again and endangering the state with further infection. US district co-director Dr. Louis Smith fumed that "lack of Mexican money is disrupting this program in this state as much as anything I know of, although they accuse me of doing so by stopping the kill. I believe this accusing me of disrupting the program is just something for them to hide behind." Amid growing signs of stalemate, in October Noyes again threatened to "take our entire force out of Mexico and go some place else" unless Dr Rubio Lozano of the Mexican section signed an agreement on dairy appraisal procedures.

---

[99] Shahan, CMAEFA to Simms, BAI, March 5, 1948, CMAEFA, operations, box 29, Veracruz; Simms, BAI, to Anderson, September 15, 1947, CMAEFA, reports, advisory committee.

[100] Corlett, Mexico City, to Anderson, Agriculture, August 20, 1947, CAP, box 7, foot and mouth.

Rubio Lozano was happy to continue discussions and reach a general oral agreement but, Noyes sighed, "I can't get him to write it."[101]

In this context, some officials within the BAI began to make contingency plans for a possible shift to vaccination. As early as July, the Southwestern cattlemen on the campaign's advisory committee urged the BAI to pursue more scientific research on the virus, if only as a concession to Mexican public opinion and to better defend the rationale of slaughter. In August, the BAI co-sponsored a conference in Mexico City to inform the public on the latest knowledge in the field, trusting that scientists known to be generally skeptical of vaccination – principally the UK's Ian Galloway – would be given top billing. As a piece of propaganda, the conference betrayed its origins as a diplomatic fudge. Flores and Shahan simultaneously amplified and dampened expectations: twenty years of scientific research projects in Europe and South America "have little to show for their labor to date"; a major US-funded international research drive on aftosa would emerge at some point in the future, but such a drive could not help Mexico since "barring a miracle" even preliminary results would take a year to arrive.[102]

Still, the USDA also began to gather more information on vaccination techniques from European laboratories but, in an echo of Mexican strategies, insisted that this program be kept secret and exempt from congressional discussion, lest it weaken Mexico's resolve to continue the slaughter policy.[103]

In the wake of the single largest incident of violent resistance – the lynching of a Mexican veterinarian, an army officer, and six soldiers in the village of Senguio, Michoacán – the US section pushed for a new slaughtering arrangement which started in October. This agreement essentially guaranteed more US funds for the campaign in exchange for Mexico ceding some administration control, putting into practice the blunt and confidential advice given by General Corlett: "In my opinion our people can tactfully dominate and lead the Mexican side, if we control all the money."[104] Rather than covering all small animal indemnities, Mexico would now pay a fixed monthly sum of 3 million

---

[101] Omar, Toluca to Shahan, Mexico City, June 10, 1947; Smith, Toluca, to Shahan, August 1947; Noyes, Mexico City, to Smith, Toluca, October 31, 1947, all in CMAEFA, operations, box 29, Mexico.

[102] Reports, August 1947, CMAEFA, reports, box 1; press release, August 1, 1947, CMAEFA, General Subject Files, box 1, press releases.

[103] Confidential reports, January–February 1948, CMAEFA, reports, box 2.

[104] Corlett report, September 1947, CAP, box 7, foot and mouth.

pesos a month into a joint commission account. The mule replacement program and the controversial salvage operation, previously run by Mexico, would now be administered jointly and subject to US audit. Mexico's contribution was half of what US officials had originally wanted, but Shahan argued that the main objective was simply to agree some kind of fixed figure, avoid wrangling over implementation, and ensure the Mexican government "act much more in earnest in prosecuting the campaign." The US section also obtained a vague commitment to greater military cooperation, and President Alemán issued a presidential decree formally granting the commission authority to slaughter animals without owners' consent – a measure requested by the US section since the start of the campaign.[105] The deal also probably included an informal agreement that Mexico crack down on the most egregious cases of graft: General Félix Ireta – who was also known as a political ally of Cárdenas – was arrested shortly afterwards.[106]

The new agreement was short-lived: it did not elicit more popular cooperation, and more violent opposition and threats appeared in several states; it failed to eliminate operational tensions and settle all financial disputes, as the US section refused to re-start campaign operations until past program expenses were settled, and Mexico stalled; the campaign still had no agreement on how to deal with dairy herds, or a workable definition of contact animals.[107] Despite the hardships of the slaughter campaign, the virus continued to penetrate porous quarantine lines, traveling along major rail, automobile, and livestock routes west into the central valley around Guadalajara, south into Tabasco, and (most alarming for the USDA) north across the Tuxpan river in Veracruz (see Figure 2.2). On November 25, 1947, Flores announced that the Mexican section had suspended slaughter operations indefinitely and, due to the strain slaughter was placing on Mexico's national economy, would search for alternative eradication methods.[108]

Cárdenas and his allies provided a major political impetus behind the change, but to some degree were pushing on a political door that was already ajar. Alemán met with Cárdenas in mid-November. According to Cárdenas, the president was still weighing the merits of vaccination and

---

[105] Shahan, CMAEFA, to Simms, BAI, August 23, 1947, CAP, box 7, foot and mouth.
[106] Confidential reports, October 1947, CMAEFA, reports, box 1.
[107] Sigsworth, "Mexican Epizootic," 137; Various reports, Guadalajara to CMAEFA, October–November 1947, CMAEFA, operations, boxes 29–30, Jalisco.
[108] Stoops, confidential report, December 13, 1947, CMAEFA, reports, box 1.

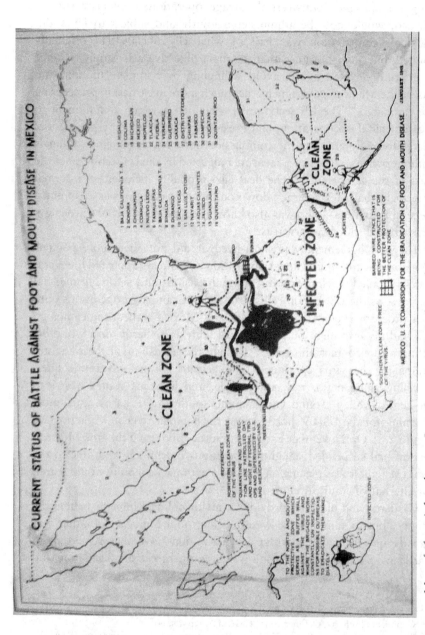

FIGURE 2.2. Map of aftosa-infected zones, January 1948. ABB. Archives of the Big Bend, Brian Wildenthal Memorial Library, Sul Ross State University, Alpine, Texas

worried about US reprisals if he moved away from slaughter. Arguing that any new system of vaccination could not begin for a year at the earliest, Alemán invited Cárdenas to take charge of the Mexican campaign in the meantime and handle remaining slaughter operations. Understandably, Cárdenas declined this poisoned political chalice, and urged Alemán to push the United States harder in negotiations and end slaughter as soon as possible.[109] Manuel Mora, an agrarian leader from Senguio who acted as a go-between for Cárdenas and his allies in the army, told a somewhat different story. When Cárdenas heard that "forty-two generals" had met in Querétaro and were plotting a coup for Christmas Day, he phoned Alemán and three hours later the president suspended slaughter.[110] The story is hard to verify but, in any case, Alemán's skepticism towards slaughter long predated November. As a result, the change of policy did not take the BAI or the commission hierarchy by surprise and the US government immediately agreed to the proposal. Throughout September and October, the commission hierarchy had repeatedly argued over policy: Shahan and the BAI argued that slaughter was perfectly feasible and sound policy, provided the Mexican government gave it full support; Flores and the Mexican section insisted that slaughter policy simply could not work.[111]

Out in the field, the change was met with more surprise and some consternation. In a call to Mexico City from Guanajuato, Dr. Schaulis reported that the news had sown confusion and sapped already low morale, and demanded to know "what's going on?"[112] Some US officials were angry at the abandonment of a policy they had strained to implement, and blamed Mexican obstructionism. Louis Smith, US district co-director in Aguascalientes, wondered that, if the Mexicans were so keen on vaccination, "maybe they all better handle and finance their own program," and later refused to accompany vaccination crews in the field.[113] Some Mexican officials and communities also felt betrayed. The people of Tarandacuao, Guanajuato rued their decision not to oppose slaughter; while recalcitrant neighboring towns had kept their animals, they were "left in the most painful humiliation, and all because we were

[109] Cárdenas, *Apuntes*, 580–1.   [110] Soto Correa, *El rifle*, 219.

[111] Various correspondence, October 1947, CAP, box 7, foot and mouth.

[112] USDA, *Campaign*, 55.

[113] Smith, Aguascalientes, to Shahan, Mexico City, November 29, 1947, and Smith, Aguascalientes, to Omohundro, Mexico City, August 4, 1948, CMAEFA, operations, box 29, Aguascalientes.

respectful and obedient."[114] To soften the blow, the governor of Guanajuato spent months urging the CMAEFA to classify towns in the south of the state devastated by slaughter as infection-free, so they could at least be placed outside of quarantine, but to no avail.[115] Dr. Robenstein, weary and ill after months killing cattle across northwest Jalisco, thanked Shahan for allowing him to break his contract and return to the United States, and was relieved to avoid a new round of negotiations: "I don't begrudge you people the responsibility of working out a program which will be acceptable to the Mexican Section ..."[116]

Such reactions were symptomatic of the next, uncertain, phase in CMAEFA history as, over the next 12 months, the US and Mexican governments endeavored to shift to a new means of eradication. Pending further agreement, the US section evacuated its personnel from the areas of active infection in Michoacán, Jalisco, and Guanajuato and concentrated them in a "buffer" zone just south of the quarantine lines, and sent small inspection teams to keep track of the limits of infection – the operational equivalent of a holding pattern until a landing strip of viable policy could be located. As in the previous phase, the CMAEFA's bureaucratic structure and organizational minutiae were both the object of negotiations over power and resources, and the means through which they took place.

With slaughter suspended, Flores argued that Mexico could not contribute more than 500,000 pesos a month to any new program – a figure the US section considered wholly unreasonable – and opened the next phase of negotiations with a "constant flow of criticism" about current arrangements.[117] One notable new demand was that all commission employees be subject to Mexico's federal labor law – since 1931 a crucial Mexican resource in bilateral disputes over US investment, notably in oil. In January 1948, a union of joint commission employees first broached the issue, demanding protection from "the caprice of the commission, which throws us into unemployment without cause and without

---

[114] Presidente municipal, Tarandacuao, Guanajuato, January 19, 1950, to Nazario Ortiz Garza, Agricultura, Mexico City, AHEG, 3.40 (78), fiebre aftosa, 1950, vol. I.

[115] Governor Castorena, to presidente municipal, Romita, Guanajuato, May 11, 1948, AHEG, 3.40 (78), fiebre aftosa, 1948, vol. III.

[116] Robenstein, Loveland, Colorado, to Shahan, Mexico City, December 22, 1947, CMAEFA, reports, box 2, "personnel: general."

[117] Lord, CMAEFA, to Mynatt, BAI, February 12, 1948, CMAEFA, reports, box 2, "legal counsel."

explanations."[118] The Mexican section also took up the cause, which US officials found difficult to understand. In the 1920s and 1930s, bilateral commissions on water and boundary disputes had not been subject to Mexico's labor law. Besides, the US section lawyers argued, most commission staff would be categorized as state employees, rather than workers, with restricted rights to organize and strike.[119] US officials suspected that the Mexican section wielded the dispute as a hook to reel in some administrative control of the eradication operation. Flores also suggested that Mexican labor courts might also be used as a venue to settle past disputes over campaign expenses, which only hardened the US section's hostility to the idea.[120] When the US section's legal advisor Durrell Lord pressed the Mexican section's lawyer on the issue, Licenciado Tovar was evasive, remarking that he personally sympathized with the US position, but his legal opinion differed from his personal view, which also differed from the legal advice he was prepared to put in writing. Following this convoluted discussion Lord was "less able than ever to explain to Dr. Noyes exactly what Tovar's opinion is concerning the applicability of the labor laws to this commission" and he "told Tovar so."[121]

Oddly, Mexico's apparent support for a gigantic quarantine fence bisecting the country also strengthened their hand in negotiations. In late 1947, Flores began to advocate the construction of two massive fences enclosing the infected zone, running from Tuxpan to Colima and across the Isthmus of Tehuantepec, thereby effectively dividing the country into an infected and disease-free zone for the foreseeable future. In private meetings, he insisted that such a plan was feasible, and even suggested that military planes could patrol its length machine-gunning stray cattle from the air.[122] Crucially, Flores argued that such an arrangement would allow for the re-opening of the US–Mexico border to the cattle trade, and the proposal enjoyed the support of northern cattle ranchers.[123]

---

[118] Translated copy of R. Cereza, and E. Fernández, "Invitation to all the Workers of the Mexico–United States Commission to Eradicate Foot and Mouth Disease," February 1948, attached to confidential report, February 14, 1948, in CMAEFA, reports, box 1.

[119] Lord to Noyes, June 23, 1948, CMAEFA, reports, box 2, "legal counsel."

[120] Lord, CMAEFA, to F. Mynatt, BAI, August 7, 1948, CMAEFA, reports, box 2, "legal counsel."

[121] Lord, CMAEFA, to F. Mynatt, BAI, July 3, 1948, CMAEFA, reports, box 2, "legal counsel."

[122] Corlett report, September 1947, CAP, box 7, foot and mouth.

[123] Confidential reports, December 6 and 20, 1947, CMAEFA, reports, box 1.

Like Alemán's earlier offer to concede administrative control to Truman's personal representative, some US officials (and Texas livestock interests) saw in this offer not a sign of Mexican cooperation but hard-nosed negotiation or even Latin American solidarity. Since the late 1930s, Argentina had sought to prise open access to the US meat market by proposing a system of subnational sanitary zones. While Argentina argued that a zonal system offered a more rational and realistic basis for trade, the United States insisted that the principle of national sovereignty and effective disease control demanded that agreements must made at the national level.[124] In this context, it is hard to imagine that the Mexican zoning proposal could ever have been acceptable to the USDA or the US Congress. Quite apart from the practical and political difficulties of erecting such a barrier, it would have forced the USDA to concede the possibility of subnational zones for disease control and undermined the US government's stance towards Argentina. However unrealistic, Mexico's argument did serve to demonstrate apparent cooperation, subtly highlight divisions and points of weakness among US interests, and served as a reminder of Mexico's capacity for autonomous action. It also encouraged the US government to agree to an alternative solution for northern ranchers during the crisis: new meat-canning facilities in the northern states, supported by US technical assistance and access to US tin-plate, whose output the Economic Cooperation Administration purchased at a generous price for postwar relief programs in Europe.[125]

For their part, the US section demanded that Mexico continue to contribute around 3 million pesos a month to the campaign (the sum agreed in October), settle unpaid indemnities and military expenses, and remove remaining administrative obstacles. Bypassing the military entirely was not realistic, but US officials hoped that jurisdictional tweaks could induce commanders to provide more troops. To avoid lengthy discussion with overlapping zone commands or with the Secretary of Defense in Mexico City, each of the nine district offices of the commission

---

[124] For worries about Mexico reviving the Argentine proposal for subnational zones for FMD, see unsigned report, c. July 1947, CEFMD, reports, box 1, "Congressional Committee." For the background of the dispute, see USDA report on "Protective measures against foot and mouth disease in the relation to the Argentine meat supply," April 1947, TP, box 395, foot and mouth.

[125] For negotiations over the costs of the canning project, see Mitchel, Bull Ranch, Albuquerque, to Anderson, USDA, August 5, 1947, CMAEFA, reports, box 2, advisory committee. For the final arrangements, see USDA, *Campaign*, 366–8.

was assigned a military officer "in charge of all military problems and necessities" connected to the campaign.[126] The US section reported a brief improvement in cooperation, but military zone commanders did not readily cede control and soon found another means of delay. Before they would agree to release troops, provincial commanders demanded they receive an advance, detailed description of where each detachment would be stationed and the tasks assigned each day, a level of detail the commission argued was impossible to provide.[127] Meanwhile bureaucratic skirmishes over military expenses continued. (In one of many petty but revealing examples, Flores argued that the costs of soldiers guarding US-only equipment and personnel should be borne by the US section, and that earlier agreements to the contrary were oral and thus unenforceable; in response US officials brandished the minutes of an earlier meeting indicating Mexican responsibility; Flores retorted that the minutes were also void since they had not been co-signed by both sections.)[128]

At the same time, the US section also recruited a new corps of livestock inspectors to compensate for the difficulties in recruiting veterinarians, and gradually diminish its reliance on Mexican personnel. In October 1947, Mexico had already ceded to US demands to bolster inspection teams; despite the suspension of slaughter, the US section pushed ahead with recruitment and by early 1948, dozens of these men began to arrive in Mexico. Recruited principally among cowhands from the Southwestern United States, the BAI hoped to create a hardy force of several hundred bilingual "cowpunchers," skilled at handling cattle, surviving off the land, and communicating with Mexicans; at least as important, such men were to act as the US section's eyes and ears in rural Mexico.[129] In a depressed labor market, flooded with returning veterans and stricken by recent droughts, such positions "came at a very opportune time," although the BAI relied on political networks of Democrat politicians and livestock associations to select suitable men.[130] The BAI hoped that these men would possess the social and linguistic skills to work effectively, but also envisaged an additional source of informal pressure on Mexican officials during field operations. BAI recruiters in El Paso hesitated to recruit cowpunchers who were "strictly of Mexican

---

[126] Confidential report, May 1948, CMAEFA, reports, box 1.   [127] Ibid.
[128] Various correspondence, March to July 1948, CMAEFA, reports, box 2, legal counsel.
[129] Aftosa newsletter, September 11, 1947, CMAEFA, general subject files, box 1.
[130] Quezada, *Border Boss*, 93.

descent and background," even if US citizens, either because they feared divided loyalties, subscribed to Shahan's theory about the haughty attitude of US citizens with Mexican backgrounds, or because such men had no powerful Anglo patrons to back them.[131] Livestock inspectors were not supposed to carry arms, but many did, with the US section's tacit approval.[132] Unsurprisingly, when the US section began to dispatch these men into the countryside in late 1947, the Mexican section baulked. Flores complained that such men operated with little Mexican oversight or control, were endangering themselves and the commission, and broke the spirit of the bilateral agreement by sometimes working without Mexican counterparts. The US section responded curtly that, if Mexico wished to keep up the parallel structure, all it needed to do was recruit its own share of livestock inspectors.[133]

In the summer of 1948, a dramatic plane crash suddenly exposed and ratcheted up underlying tensions over the scope of the US authority. On July 2, 1948, the pilot of a commission plane strayed into a treacherous mountain gully covered in cloud, and crashed into the summit of Mexico's highest peak, Citlaltépetl (also known as the Pico de Orizaba) on the border of the states of Puebla and Veracruz. The crash killed all the men on board – eight Mexican and eight US commission employees – and left a metal briefcase containing 250,000 pesos in the wreckage. Rain, mist, mudslides, and bitter cold hindered the commission's rescue and recovery operation, as did the heavy-handed style of the new US co-director, General Harry Johnson, and the political inexperience of Flores. Truman appointed Johnson only weeks before the crash, and in many ways the choice made sense. A retired cavalry officer and Texas oil executive, Johnson was a renowned administrator, and had served as allied military governor of Rome, during which the US military authorities had dispensed the aftosa vaccine; his ties to Texas oilmen and moderate Republicans like Nelson Rockefeller made him a logical choice to head off congressional criticism of the new phase of vaccination.[134] However, Johnson's actions in the aftermath of the crash betrayed a lack of diplomatic experience and fueled a short-lived scandal. First Johnson

---

[131] Winkler, El Paso, to J. Anderson, BAI, personnel, October 26, 1948, CMAEFA, reports, box 2, "file 24."

[132] *Aftosa International*, 48.

[133] Confidential reports, January–February 1948, CMAEFA, reports, box 1.

[134] "General Johnson Leaves Aftosa," April 1951, n.p., ABB, Dr. Albert Heflin papers, N82–3B, aftosa scrapbook; G. Kirksey, Houston, to Nelson Rockefeller, February 16, 1950, RAC, group 4, series III 4 L, box 80, "foot and mouth disease."

authorized a squad of armed US paratroopers, members of the US Air Force mountain rescue forces, to land on the volcano to support the pistol-carrying livestock inspectors Johnson had already sent to recover the bodies and money, ignoring the relevant treaties (which only authorized such actions within fifty miles of the border), breaking a long-standing political taboo against the presence of uniformed and armed US military personnel on Mexican territory, and angering the US embassy and State Department. Johnson then asked the Mexican section to order officials on the mountain to confiscate the cameras and photographs of the half-dozen Mexican journalists who had reached the crash site. Flores sent the order via telegram but, after a tense stand-off on the mountain-side, commission officials and soldiers eventually bowed to protests and allowed journalists to retain their films and equipment.[135] Over the following two weeks, newspapers from across the political spectrum excoriated the commission for trampling the freedom of the press and allowing US soldiers to penetrate Mexican territory and throw their weight around. Several hundred left-wing students marched in Mexico City, condemned rising US imperialism and the Mexican army's useless, melt-prone "chocolate generals," and stoned the US embassy.[136]

Four months later, Johnson looked back over his short time in Mexico and identified the crash as a nadir of "disaffection" within the commission. Since that point, Johnson insisted, the countries had been "cooperating as two free peoples should." While Johnson's account of "perfect harmony" in the CMAEFA was over-the-top, it was not entirely misleading.[137] By end of 1948 and through 1949 several related factors combined to decrease conflict within the commission, and enhance its capacity to present itself as a coherent bilateral and technical institution.

Just before the Citlaltépetl scandal erupted, the commission had begun to lay the main organizational pillars of the vaccination campaign. Mexico agreed to pay the costs of trial vaccines acquired from Argentina and the Netherlands, and a new monthly contribution of 750,000 pesos to the campaign, while the US would cover remaining campaign expenses. US officials considered Mexico's contribution too low, but it was 50 percent more than originally offered in January and

---

[135] For a detailed account of the crash, see Rath, "Burning."
[136] Various reports, July 1947, AGN, DGIPS, 2-1/261/80.
[137] Copy statement by Johnson to Senate Committee of Appropriations, November 16, 1948, FMDRL, box 1, folder 18.

"the most favourable that could be reached."[138] Having tested the imported vaccines in early 1948, the CMAEFA decided it needed to produce a vaccine locally to avoid problems of transporting the fragile vaccine long distances and to adapt to local strains of the virus. With a funding agreement in place, the commission began to organize a complicated system to produce the vaccine across several sites in the Valley of Mexico. Commission scientists purchased tens of thousands of disease-free cattle from Mexico's north, infected most of them with aftosa, "harvested" infective material from cattle by hand (principally from their tongues), mixed it with chemicals in centrifuges to attenuate the virus, and tested the innocuity of the vaccine on another group of cattle kept in secure stables. To help fund the laboratory, scientists also slaughtered these test cattle in controlled conditions and sent some of the meat and hides to the Mexico City market.[139]

Crucially vaccination received much firmer political support in Mexico. Vaccination had always enjoyed more support from Mexican officialdom, not least Mexico's professional veterinarians. The Alemán administration gave it clear backing, and even lent its name to the new "Alemán-Garza plan." When the commission unveiled a sparkling new animal disease research complex at Palo Alto (Figure 2.3), in the hills near Toluca, officials and diplomats gave speeches beneath a huge image of the president's face superimposed over a map of Mexico.[140] Alemán's federal spies also sought to clamp down more on public criticism of the campaign, privately urging newspapers to report unrest over vaccination "in such a way that they do not contribute to more agitation."[141] By the end of 1948, Alemán had also weathered the political storms triggered by the July devaluation of the peso, and emerged better able to push federal policy; he had come to terms with key military trouble-makers, boosted urban subsidies and food supplies, decapitated independent unions, and soon reintroduced restrictions on internal party primaries. Along with the move to vaccination, Alemán could also point to concessions won in negotiations over US loans and bracero labor.[142] Various other arrangements indicated new political compromises in Mexico. As head of the commission to develop the Tepalcatepec River basin, Cárdenas enjoyed

[138] Lord, CMAEFA, to Mynatt, April 5, 1948, CMAEFA, reports, box 2, "legal counsel."
[139] USDA, *Campaign*, 100.   [140] "Orgullo de México," *Mañana*, September 10, 1949.
[141] Memo, February 2, 1949, DFS to Gobernación, AGN, DFS, versión pública: Robert Proctor.
[142] Rath, *Myths*, 94–100; Gillingham, "We Don't Have Arms"; Alexander, *Sons*, 132, 137.

FIGURE 2.3. Photograph of staff housing and animal disease laboratories at Palo Alto, near Toluca, State of Mexico, c. 1949. ABB, N82-3A, Heflin papers. Archives of the Big Bend, Brian Wildenthal Memorial Library, Sul Ross State University, Alpine, Texas

enormous sway over the lowland *tierra caliente* of Michoacán. It was from or through these territories that much of the cattle to restock municipalities in Jalisco, Guanajuato, and eastern Michoacán came; Cárdenas reportedly helped organize these purchases, and some of the dairy cattle came directly from the Cárdenas family's own herds.[143] In June 1948, Cárdenas posed for campaign publicity shots, and was pictured smiling, standing alongside Alemán in a shallow vat of disinfectant.[144] At some point in 1948-9, Senator Carlos Serrano also "loaned" the very best of the Brazilian bulls the government had seized at the start of the outbreak to Cárdenas, and he trucked them to the *tierra caliente*,

[143] Davidson, review of national economic and political situation, Mexican Eagle Company, to Leigh Jones, Shell Directors, November 16, 1947, NA, FO371/60943; translated copy of Alfonso Serrano Suárez, Report on Restocking, March 17, 1948, CMAEFA, reports, box 2, "operations: restocking"; *La Prensa*, November 9, 1948.
[144] "Foot and Mouth Disease in Mexico" scrapbook, ABB, N82-3C, Gillespie papers, 9.

ignoring the protests of a group of US livestock breeders based in Tamaulipas who claimed to be their owners.[145]

Administering the vaccine still posed massive logistical and political obstacles. It only provided protection for 3–4 months. For the campaign to successfully "starve out" the virus, the commission organized three or four waves of vaccination and repeated inspections around the rim of the infected area before moving the quarantine line forward. To keep the vaccine cool and prevent spoilage, the CMAEFA retooled a fleet of refrigeration trucks, sent out mule trains laden with ice-packs and vacuum flasks, or hired planes to drop fresh ice to teams isolated in the hills. Field teams packed hundreds of extra syringes, since the vaccine was thick and "heavy" and "when they push hard, they break the barrels."[146] US inspectors had plenty of experience roping cattle and using portable cattle chutes to control large numbers of animals, and enjoyed swapping tips with Mexican cowboys. Most had never wrestled with pigs before, and had to learn from locals. Although incidents of unrest declined after 1948 and official Mexican support grew, many Mexicans continued to greet the CMAEFA with suspicion, non-compliance, and even violent protest.

Still, by the end of 1948, the commission was churning out such huge quantities of vaccine that it far surpassed the BAI's early expectations, and it gradually resolved, bypassed, or simply ignored older bilateral disputes. The confrontation over Mexican labor law resolved itself into a familiar pattern: the US section accepted the principle of Mexican jurisdiction, but made no efforts to enforce the law and the Mexican government did not push the matter. The US section still complained about the halting provision of troops, but eventually Johnson decided it was unnecessary to keep dwelling on military failings since overall Mexican cooperation was "good" and "nothing could be gained by asking the Mexican government to put more pressure."[147] In any case, with a larger group of livestock inspectors and greater support from ranchers themselves – gathered in lay inspection teams – the commission became less reliant on the vagaries of

---

[145] In 1950, Cárdenas confirmed that he held the bulls at a ranch in Apatzingán, Michoacán. According to their lawyer, the alleged owners included Ernest McCollum, William Daniel Cornelius, and George H. Echols. Fernando Coronado, Mexico City, to Alemán, June 23, 1950, AGN, MAV, 321(8)/2439.

[146] Report from Cerro Azul, Veracruz, February 25, 1948, CMAEFA, operations, box 30, Veracruz; Schaulis, SLP, to Omohundro, CMAEFA, April 23, 1948, CMAEFA, operations, box 29, SLP.

[147] Johnson, Mexico City, to Simms, BAI, September 30, 1949, FMDRL, box 1, folder 5.

military support. The campaign's fraught early years produced a contradictory and "chaotic mass of instructions and supplementary instructions." The US section briefly considered converting this paper into a coherent field manual, but eventually decided it was not worth the trouble.[148] In early 1948, the US section agreed to build a section of barbed-wire fence to reinforce the quarantine line running over 100 miles inland from Tampico – a particularly vulnerable point near the Huasteca's rich grazing lands and highways stretching to the border (see Figure 2.2). Soon the progress of the vaccination campaign made the question of a larger fence moot.[149] The border reopened for livestock in September 1952, closed again after another outbreak of aftosa in Veracruz, and then finally reopened again in 1954. The United States recognized Mexico as an aftosa-free nation, which allowed it to maintain its opposition to subnational aftosa-free zones, even as Mexico reassured it that it would only authorize livestock exports from the eight northern states which had been spared the epizootic and vaccination.[150]

These compromises allowed the commission to adapt and maintain its bilateral organization. When the slaughter program was suspended, critics in the US press subjected the commission's peculiar structure to stinging criticism. The *Farm Journal* denounced it as "one of the most cumbersome pieces of administrative machinery ever devised. Even Eisenhower with his Allied Joint Chiefs of Staff probably never had anything more unwieldy."[151] With the consensus around vaccination, these bureaucratic arrangements worked fairly well. Again, the commission paired US and Mexican scientists and engineers at every stage of vaccine production. The bulk of each vaccination team consisted of temporary Mexican employees, but they were directed by Mexican veterinarians and US inspectors. Some became good friends. Towards the end of the campaign, as it moved towards surveillance, lonely pairs of US and Mexican livestock inspectors crisscrossed the countryside conducting routine inspections, befriending villagers, dodging bandits, gathering information on suspicious animal maladies, and startling passing tourists. On their trek across the *tierra caliente*, Mary and Fred Del Villar met one Texan inspector who insulted his coworker, was "hopelessly prejudiced

---

[148] L. Munsil, Report on Administrative Inspection of District 4, September 1949, CMAEFA, administrative correspondence, box 5, "Military-Mexican Govt."
[149] Confidential reports, March 6, 1948, CMAEFA, reports, box 1.
[150] The final 1953 outbreak is discussed in more detail in Chapter 6.
[151] Clipping from *Farm Journal*, March 1948, CAP, box 7, foot and mouth.

against everything Mexican," and was "lucky not to have been found face down on the trail with a bullet in his back." All the "many" others they met "worked and lived with the Mexicans like brothers."[152]

The commission's leadership also developed a better (and largely unspoken, and unwritten) understanding of the constraints under which they worked. Chastened by the crash on Citlaltépetl, Johnson and the US section cooperated more closely with the State Department. Ambassador Walter Thurston helped defuse the scandal by hastily arranging for an exchange of diplomatic notes which made it unnecessary for Mexico to request, and the United States to issue, an official apology. Thereafter the State Department combed major public statements on the aftosa campaign for slights that could "offend Mexican nationalism."[153] In 1950, at the first sign of possible protests against a visit by US Secretary of Agriculture Brannan, Johnson canceled the trip; in 1951, Noyes replaced Johnson as co-director of the commission, with the US ambassador in a prominent advisory role.[154] In light of the crash, the US and Mexican sections also agreed to reduce US involvement in public events and propaganda. From now on, Johnson wrote to Flores, the US section would seek to contribute to propaganda events "quietly and unostentatiously."[155] For his part, Flores purged commission radio logs showing his controversial orders to censor the press; the US section were well aware of this, but did not pursue the matter.[156]

Similarly, the US section bowed to Mexican insistence that any remaining resort to slaughter be shrouded in secrecy. Despite the shift towards vaccination, the CMAEFA still agreed to slaughter any new, isolated outbreaks of infection, particularly those near the quarantine lines. Slaughter operations occurred somewhere in central Mexico "almost daily" until mid-April 1949.[157] Having shot 952,596 animals by November 1947, the CMAEFA shot a further 48,869 by September

[152] Del Villar and del Villar, *Where the Strange Roads*, 101.
[153] Iller, Assistant Secretary of State for Inter-American Affairs, to Elsey, Administrative Assistant to the President, September 21, 1950, HP, box 5, foot and mouth.
[154] Rubottom, State Department, to US Embassy, February 27 and April 30, 1951, IAMSD, 1950–4, reel 27, 219, 226; various correspondence, Johnson, CMAEFA to Brannan, Agriculture, July 1950, BP, box 5, foot and mouth.
[155] Johnson, Mexico City, to Flores, CMAEFA, August 6, 1948, CMAEFA, reports, box 2, file 34.
[156] Mitchell, "Diary of Search and Rescue," Engineering Division, CMAEFA to Noyes, Mexico City, July 9, 1948, CMAEFA, reports, box 2, file 34.
[157] "The Foot and Mouth Disease Research and Control Program," confidential summary for research committee, c. 1950, FMDRL, box 2, folder 32, 4.

1952.[158] The Mexican section argued that these operations should receive no publicity, and insisted that the word slaughter – *matanza* – be removed from all official correspondence, or replaced with a series of euphemisms.[159] US officials were initially uneasy; sporadic slaughter was still an important part of the campaign, secrecy risked further exposure and embarrassment, and officials were loath to exaggerate the flaws of the commission's initial policy. Besides, "although the matter might appear insignificant on first thought, experience to date shows that without clear cut instructions to the field there is often too much controversy and misunderstanding among the field forces as to what is meant."[160] The US section eventually relented, concluding that such secrecy offered necessary political protection for Mexican officials, and was an informal condition of continued cooperation. Commission and BAI officials purged mentions of slaughter from official correspondence, and replaced it with a new code word: *Operation Zero*.[161]

Looking back on the aftosa campaign in the 1960s, Mexico's former foreign minister Torres Bodet offered an acute if vague summary. The aftosa epizootic constituted "one of the most difficult diplomatic tasks of the Mexican government," but one which it ultimately engaged with some skill and success. Torres singled out Minister of Agriculture Ortiz Garza for praise, who did battle with the US agencies much like Tolstoy's General Kutusov: he refused open confrontation, and maintained a smiling, calm countenance at all times; he waited and waited, "sometimes not knowing quite what he was waiting for"; and when the conditions were right, he fought and "lost the least that he was obliged to lose – or won the most he could effectively win."[162] Torres never specified the tactics Garza deployed. His account was rather self-congratulatory, eliding the weakness and corruptibility of the Mexican state, and all the many ways that the Alemán administration was distinctly unresponsive to rural grievances. But it captured the essence of Mexico's strategy: to obey but selectively comply with bilateral agreements, use struggles of implementation to minimize the costs of the Mexican state, discreetly cultivate support for vaccination, and wait.

---

[158] Author's calculation, based on: USDA, *Campaign*, 116; summary sheet of "General History of Foot and Mouth Disease in Mexico," c. 1965, FMDRL, box 1, folder 19.

[159] Confidential report, January 24, 1948, CMAEFA, reports, box 1.   [160] Ibid.

[161] Report from Veracruz, December 12, 1947, CMAEFA, operations, box 30, Veracruz, radio log; various reports, May 1948, CMAEFA, operations, box 29, Aguascalientes.

[162] Torres Bodet, *Victoria sin alas*, 34, 38.

Historians usually portray the 1940s and 1950s as a period of relative harmony and consensus in US–Mexico relations. After all, the old revolutionary-era conflicts over oil, debt, and damages were settled, Mexico joined the allies and, from 1948, embraced anticommunism. Some historians argue that this elite consensus was premised on waves of US capital and diplomatic pressure eroding Mexican sovereignty. Alemán, to put it mildly, is not a nationalist icon. The story of the struggles over aftosa forces us to reconsider this image, the character of international conflicts, and where we look for them. A broadly shared vision of capitalist modernization still left room for disagreements over practice, whether over the governance of capital, trade, and migration, or cows, pigs, and germs. Besides, regardless of Alemán's own pro-business, anti-communist and "pro-*Yanqui*" inclinations, he had to work in a Mexican political context that he could not control.[163] The political levers in the cockpit of the imperial presidency were unreliable and sometimes jarred. However, while the US government was hugely powerful, it was also distracted, divided, and prioritized stability south of the border. Overlooked in many studies of the aftosa affair, neither Truman nor his Secretary of Agriculture were hell-bent on discharging the sanitary rifle and, over time, this provided useful leverage for Mexico. Moreover, two long-standing tactics, honed during periods of much more obvious confrontation with the United States, proved useful to Alemán: the cultivation of international ties to deflect US power, and what John Dwyer has called the "diplomatic weapons of the weak" – obfuscation, foot-dragging, and non-cooperation. The former tactics were mainly deployed at the level of high cabinet politics and diplomacy; the latter belonged to the murky "middle politics" of provincial implementation.[164] Indeed, it may be that in the 1940s US–Mexico relations was entering a veritable heyday of transgovernmental bureaucratic infrapolitics, as overt diplomatic and ideological clashes faded, and US and Mexican agencies integrated as never before.

This story also offers some clues as to why these kinds of conflict may have been overlooked or underestimated. Over time, US and Mexican officials also honed informal political skills, and learned to shield themselves from criticism. After all, bureaucratic battles and secretive diplomatic maneuvers could hardly be acknowledged publicly, lest they undermine the image of orderly bilateral relations and detached technical

[163] Soto Correa, *El rifle*, 27.
[164] Dwyer, "Diplomatic Weapons"; Ervin, "The 1930 Agrarian Census," 541.

authority that the commission cultivated. If government officials have to cultivate the "effect" of the state, this commission had to similarly cultivate the effect of sharing sovereignty.[165] Gradually new administrative routines and lexicons, propaganda techniques, and informal pacts – underpinned by high-level policy changes – helped to mask internal fissures and bolster the commission's image as a coherent, technical institution which channeled state sovereignty rather than undermined it. In private, US officials were well aware of the Mexican government's Kutusov-like strategy, but understood that "the true reasons for the subordination of the slaughter policy are such that their publication would do grave and irreparable damage to the commission and relations between Mexico and the United States."[166] Finally, officials framed the CMAEFA's own history in a way that deflected from internal politicking. Invariably officials blamed problems on obstacles residing outside the commission, belonging to the realm of the economy and society. One segment of society in particular was singled out: Mexico's peasant villagers, its *campesinos*.

[165] Mitchell, "The Limits of the State," 86.
[166] Stoops, confidential report, December 13, 1947, CMAEFA, reports, box 1.

3

Spiking the Sanitary Rifle

Argument and Opposition

Before they killed him, the inhabitants of Senguio warned Dr. Augusto Juárez Medina (Figure 3.1) not to slaughter their animals. At the end of August 1947, they met with him on outskirts of the municipality and, depending on the story, either begged him to spare a few of their calves, shouted threats at him, or fired bullets over his head.[1] Alarmed by these warnings, Dr. Juárez eventually discounted them. After all, he had worked as a government veterinarian for months across the state of Michoacán, and believed he understood the people who lived there well. CMAEFA officials in eastern Michoacán had already heard threats and rumors of violence. In July, someone took fifteen pot-shots at a commission vehicle in the neighboring municipality of Aporo, smashing the windscreen but leaving the traveling livestock appraisers unharmed. In August, veterinarian Dr. Thomas Berry and his brigade visited nearby El Oro:

An army captain and 10 soldiers went ahead of us. When they arrived at the village the Indians were armed with sticks and clubs. The officers finally persuaded them to lay them down and meet with us. When we arrived there were about 700 there, all mad. The church bell was ringing and smoke signals could be seen on the mountainside, which I was told meant trouble in the village. We talked to them for about 2 hours and made some progress towards examining their cattle at a later date.[2]

On the morning of September 1, 1947 Juárez departed for the village of Senguio and probably expected a similar outcome. He took standard

[1] USDA, *Campaign*, 81; interview with Simón Mora, in Pérez Escutia, *Senguio*, 288.
[2] Various reports, July 1947, CMAEFA, operation, box 29, field reports, Michoacán; Berry report, August 1947, transcribed in USDA, *Campaign*, 60–1.

FIGURE 3.1. Photograph of Dr. Augusto Juárez Medina (third from left), Dr. Albert Heflin (fourth from left), and military escort at Hacienda Tarimoro, near Senguio, Michoacán, August 1947. ABB, N82–3A, Heflin papers. Archives of the Big Bend, Brian Wildenthal Memorial Library, Sul Ross State University, Alpine, Texas.

precautions, bringing two jeeps, an army captain, and six soldiers armed with rifles and a machine gun. On the way to Senguio, the manager of the Hacienda Carindapaz warned the party to turn back, but Juárez pressed on. "I am going to convince them," he reportedly said. "I have convinced more stubborn people than these." Shortly before 11 am, Juárez and the military escort arrived on the outskirts of Senguio, heard cheers welcoming the army, and drove towards the main plaza. Near the plaza the jeeps confronted a crowd of between 500 and 2,000 men and women wielding knives, sticks, and stones. They hurled insults, and surrounded the jeeps.[3] Juárez climbed out of his vehicle and appealed for calm, but a man – probably local agrarista leader Manuel Mora – struck him from behind with a rock or pistol and knocked him unconscious. The crowd then disarmed the soldiers before they could raise their rifles, beat and stabbed the group to death, and ordered horses to trample the bodies. An army major, who happened to be in the town on other business, cowered in a house near the central plaza. A few hours later he crept away and quietly called the military post at Zitácuaro to raise the alarm.[4]

[3] *Novedades*, September 5, 1947.
[4] Ibid.; *La Prensa*, September 4, 1947; Pérez Escutia, *Senguio*, 288.

It is easy to understand why the massacre at Senguio grabbed the country's attention, and shaped interpretations of resistance to the aftosa campaign at the time and since. Leaving eight dead, it was the single most violent attack suffered by the campaign. The violence had a spectacular, transgressive quality typical of community lynchings in Mexico, and the press did not skirt around details. After the massacre, a woman kneeled over the army captain's corpse and gouged out his eyes with a knitting needle. In case the symbolism was not obvious, the press reported that the woman muttered an explanation to the corpse: "So you cannot see who killed you."[5] News of the massacre spread quickly and far. It elicited horror and condemnations from the press, political parties, and unions. The CMAEFA paused operations, and sought to streamline its finances and boost military support. The timing was also ominous. The massacre coincided with President Alemán's annual speech to Congress, and officials feared it formed part of a cresting wave of opposition.

The massacre also invited a particular understanding of the underlying character of resistance to the CMAEFA. Abutting the rugged Sierra de Chincua, the municipality of Senguio was a backwater, dominated by peasant farmers – who were typically referred to as campesinos by officials, lawyers, and journalists as well as by themselves. The village itself had a population of around 800 people, but the massacre drew in hundreds of people from the surrounding area, a patchwork of small ejidal plots and farms spread over "green valleys and mountains."[6] These farms produced no conspicuous agricultural surplus, although many farmers gathered wood from the nearby hillsides, and sold it at markets.[7] Most only had a few head of livestock, whose meat, fat, eggs, milk, and draft power they used themselves, selling whatever remained locally. A short distance over the sierra, the mines at El Oro had once provided employment and a market for produce, but by the 1930s they were in terminal decline, leading to a pronounced economic introversion noted by contemporary observers.[8] Reinforcing the sense of marginality, Cristero rebels had cut the village's telephone line in 1929, and Senguio would be without one for four decades.[9] Historians have long recognized that the aftosa campaign – and particularly the *rifle sanitario*, or sanitary

---

[5] *La Prensa*, September 4, 1947. For a systematic analysis of lynching in the 1930s–1950s, see Kloppe-Santamaría, *Vortex*.
[6] Pérez Escutia, *Senguio*, 245.   [7] Ibid., 230–1.   [8] Ibid., 257–8.   [9] Ibid., 267–8.

rifle – encountered opposition, and gave humble campesinos a leading role in the drama.[10]

This story has been told with differing emphases. One common explanation was that campesinos had a sentimental attachment to their animals, with whom they had lived and worked "for generations, in a family-like intimacy."[11] This idea – that a peasant's animals are "are almost as dear to him as members of his family" – seems to have emerged first among some officials in the Mexican section and newspaper reports from the Bajío. It was quickly echoed by US officials, congressmen, and ranchers, repeated in almost every memoir and novel written about the campaign, and later filtered into the historiography.[12] Such imagery fitted neatly into the Alemán administration's discourse on modernization, which identified peasant culture as the main cause of rural backwardness, and prescribed science, technology, and markets as solutions.[13] Other accounts have identified more precise, material, and political sources of campesino grievances: the integral role of livestock in peasant agriculture, as sources of draft power, food, fertilizer, and one of the few available forms of mobile capital. The apparent contradiction between subsistence agriculture and the cash and credit offered by the CMAEFA seemed to support the idea that peasants were particularly opposed to the campaign.[14] Indeed, some have portrayed the opposition as a would-be campesino rebellion against the inequities of the sanitary rifle and *alemanismo*'s general abandonment of peasant communities – a surge of campesino consciousness and "class unity" which brought the country to the brink of a "peasant war." In this narrative, opposition formed one link in

---

[10] Several studies recognize that some ranchers and dairymen in central Mexico argued against the sanitary rifle. However, analysis of their political actions is scant, beyond the publication of open letters in the press, and the main focus has been on campesino protest. Machado, *Aftosa*, 51–3; Soto Correa, *El rifle*, 62–7.

[11] Gipson, *Cow Killers*, 4.

[12] USDA, *Campaign*, 26; Stoops, itinerary and reports on visit of congressional committee, July 11, 1947, CMAEFA, Reports, box 2, congressional committee. Mexico's official report reviewing the campaign picked up on the idea, noting how peasant farmers gathered at the slaughter pits as if at a family funeral. *La fiebre aftosa en México* (Mexico, 1951), 55. Jaime Torres Bodet expressed regret that the US government consulted with veterinary experts rather than unnamed "anthropologists" who could have informed them about the "sentimental attitude of our humble campesinos, for whom cows and oxen in the backyard corral were almost like family members." Torres Bodet, *Victoria sin alas*, 34, 33–4. Jean Meyer suggested that the "animal worship (*zoolatría*)" characteristic of Mexico's campesinos was one factor underpinning resistance to the campaign. Meyer, *El sinarquismo*, 232. See also, Soto Correa, *El rifle*, 23.

[13] Warman, *El campo*, 192–3.   [14] Ledbetter, "Popular Protest," 402.

Mexico's chain of popular agrarian mobilization, the work of the "heirs of Zapata."[15]

In other words, historians have tended to shoehorn the conflict over aftosa into a dichotomous narrative underpinning much Mexican historiography: the clash between urban agents of capitalist modernization and marginal communities of campesinos. However, these existing interpretations rest on uneven and fragmentary research. Jean Meyer's pathbreaking (and much-cited) article on the topic is symptomatic. Meyer took campesino protest far more seriously than previous accounts, but misdated the Senguio massacre by three months, conflated and mischaracterized several other key episodes, and painted an image of an indifferent press bearing little resemblance to historical reality.[16] More recent local and regional studies have excavated fascinating layers of local experience, but their view of the broader political landscape is sometimes hazy.[17] International comparisons are almost wholly lacking, implying that we can understand this episode largely in terms of the particular character of Mexican society and its campesinos. Synthesizing archival research and local studies, this chapter places the Senguio massacre in those larger contexts to emphasize the geographical breadth, cross-class character, and the discursive and tactical variety of opposition. Campesinos certainly had good reasons to oppose the campaign, but the most important of these they shared with a range of groups living in central Mexico. Campesino is a somewhat ambiguous term of course, sometimes used narrowly to mean peasant or subsistence farmers, and sometimes referring to a broader range of rustic people who live off the land. Even at its most expansive, it is not adequate to describe the opposition that confronted the CMAEFA.

Writing the history of resistance to the CMAEFA raises methodological problems very familiar to social historians. Much of the documentary evidence was created by authorities tasked with eliminating opposition, rather than opponents themselves. However, the voices and arguments of opponents, though faint and shaped by their intended audiences and available cultural idioms, are by no means silent. Opponents wrote letters and petitions to the government, spoke to

---

[15] Soto Correa, *El rifle*, 105, 218; Bartra, *Los herederos*, 73–4.

[16] Meyer, *El sinarquismo*, 231–55. For another argument that the press responded to the aftosa crisis with "opaque silence," see Figueroa Velázquez, *El tiro de gracia*, 35.

[17] Soto Correa, for example, confuses street protests over the crash rescue on Citlaltépetl (discussed in Chapter 1) with protests against crop-duster planes supposedly spreading the virus. Soto Correa, *El rifle*, 106.

journalists who provided ample and sometimes critical coverage, penned and sang popular ballads, made bitter jokes, and decades later a few spoke to pioneering local historians about their experiences. Official reports also provide glimpses of rumors circulating at the time, and the kind of relatively unguarded expressions of popular attitudes officials confronted in Teotitlán del Camino, Oaxaca, where the townspeople smashed the commission jeep's windscreen, slashed its tires, and daubed "to hell with aftosa" on one side.[18] The discussion below first charts the main ebb and flow of opposition over time. It then sketches a synchronic picture of the kinds of criticisms made of the campaign, both in principle and in practice, and the different types of resistance it confronted – ranging from non-compliance to violent rebellion – illustrating throughout the wide range of social groups involved, and the combination of older traditions of protest with new tactics and arguments.

When officials worried that Senguio was simply the most obvious and violent note in a gathering crescendo of opposition, they were broadly right. A rough count of significant episodes of non-cooperation and civil unrest, culled from CMAEFA and other Mexican sources, confirms this impression.[19] Through the summer of 1947, opposition mounted as CMAEFA slaughter operations began in multiple states; it peaked in the autumn as the US section sought to bolster and intensify the slaughter operations, fell sharply with the announced switch to vaccination in November 1947, and then slowly tapered off until the end of the program (see Figure 3.2). Likewise, before November 1947 unrest and opposition roughly correlated with the scale of slaughter conducted (see Figure 3.3). After the adoption of vaccination, a disproportionate share of opposition arose in areas still experiencing slaughter of aftosa outbreaks, particularly southern Veracruz and Jalisco. The sources contain only fragmentary information on delays to the campaign caused by opposition. Still, the available evidence suggests that the CMAEFA tended to overcome delays

---

[18] Various reports, Mulhern, Tehuacán, to Shahan, September 1947, CMAEFA, operations, box 29, Oaxaca.

[19] Data are necessarily approximate. Reports are often vague, and difficult to quantify. Some dates are inferred from the contextual information. Fairly consistent series of US reports exist from June 1947 to the end of 1948, when Mexican institutions became more prominent in administering the campaign. US field officials were initially concentrated in states undergoing intensive slaughter (Guanajuato, Michoacán, Aguascalientes, Querétaro, México, Jalisco). The change of program in December 1947 shifted US personnel away from the main areas of infection, to undertake inspections along the northern quarantine line. Mexican archives and memoirs are less detailed but provide more even chronological coverage.

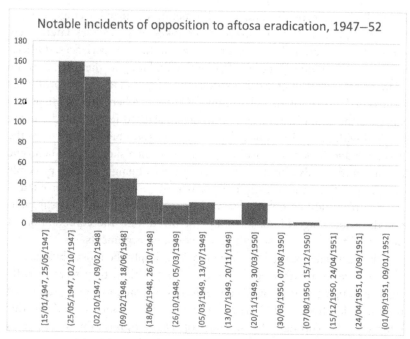

FIGURE 3.2. Notable incidents of opposition to aftosa eradication, 1947–52. *Source*: Field reports and phone logs, CMAEFA, operations, boxes 29–30; *Campaign in Mexico Against Foot and Mouth Disease, 1947–1952* (Unpublished 1954 report by Agricultural Research Service, USDA, available at Sul Ross University, Archive of the Big Bend, Aftosa Papers); confidential weekly reports, CMAEFA, reports, boxes 1–2; various correspondence AGN, MAV, series 5255–2; José Domingo Torres y Elzaurdia, *Botas de hule. Anecdotario de la campaña contra la fiebre aftosa en México* (Mexico City: Centro Nacional de Investigaciones Agrarias, 1956).

more quickly from December 1947 onwards.[20] In this way, the Mexican case, for all its peculiarities confirms a general principle of anti-aftosa campaigns everywhere: vaccination elicited less popular resistance than slaughter, and in this sense was an easier policy to implement (Table 3.1).

Opposition to slaughter doubtless had emotional, cultural, and religious dimensions, though they are difficult to gauge. Many people found slaughter operations shocking and sad things to behold. They were rushed, chaotic, and appeared wholly disproportionate or unnecessary to many; they took place on a scale, and at times and in places – fields on

---

[20] Data on delays exist for 63 out 292 incidents between January and November 1947. Based on these data, each incident delayed CMAEFA operations by 16 days on average. After December 1947, only 32 of 173 incidents contain data on delays, and indicate an average delay of around 6.5 days per incident. Author's calculation, based on data gathered for Figures 3.1 and 3.2.

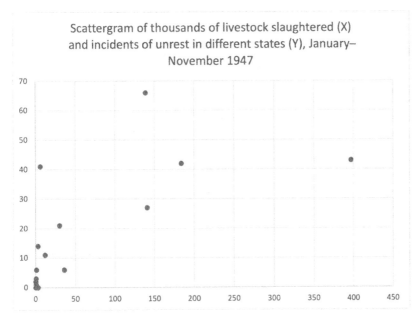

FIGURE 3.3. Scattergram of thousands of livestock slaughtered (X) and incidents of unrest in different states (Y), January–November 1947. *Source*: Field reports and phone logs, CMAEFA, operations, boxes 29–30; *Campaign in Mexico Against Foot and Mouth Disease, 1947–1952* (Unpublished 1954 report by Agricultural Research Service, USDA, available at Sul Ross University, Archive of the Big Bend, Aftosa Papers); confidential weekly reports, CMAEFA, reports, boxes 1–2; various correspondence AGN, MAV, series 5255-2; José Domingo Torres y Elzaurdia, *Botas de hule. Anecdotario de la campaña contra la fiebre aftosa en México* (Mexico City: Centro Nacional de Investigaciones Agrarias, 1956).

the outskirts of towns – which had no real precedent. If sanitary campaigns rely, in part, on translating their work into existing cultural idioms, it hard to see how the sanitary rifle could have been made familiar and edifying. Press reports and corridos depicted slaughter operations as macabre and thoroughly miserable episodes. *El Universal* reported on a "sordid and monotonous spectacle" in Guanajuato: "Dozens of animals fall and soak the dry ground with their blood. The church is visible far away and the heat is terrific ... There are cases when they don't die and turn and drag themselves painfully."[21] Just as they did decades later, many peasant farmers worked alongside their oxen for many years, came to know their particular quirks and personalities, gave them names and,

---

[21] *El Universal*, July 24, 1947, transcribed in USDA, *Campaign*, 36–7.

TABLE 3.1. *Head of livestock slaughtered and notable incidents of opposition in different states, January–November 1947*

Federal state	Head of livestock slaughtered (in thousands)	Notable incidents of opposition
Guanajuato	397	43
Michoacán	184	42
Querétaro	141	27
Jalisco	139	66
Hidalgo	36	6
Mexico	30	21
Veracruz	12	11
Guerrero	6	41
Oaxaca	3	14
San Luis Potosí	3	0
Puebla	1	6
Aguascalientes	0.5	1
Zacatecas	0.4	3
DF	0.1	2
Tlaxcala	0.02	0
Morelos	0.01	2

Source: Field reports and phone logs, CMAEFA, operations, boxes 29–30; *Campaign in Mexico Against Foot and Mouth Disease, 1947–1952* (Unpublished 1954 report by Agricultural Research Service, USDA, available at Sul Ross University, Archive of the Big Bend, Aftosa Papers); confidential weekly reports, CMAEFA, reports, boxes 1–2; various correspondence AGN, MAV, series 5255–2; José Domingo Torres y Elzaurdia, *Botas de hule. Anecdotario de la campaña contra la fiebre aftosa en México* (Mexico City: Centro Nacional de Investigaciones Agrarias, 1956).

in some cases, grew fond of them.[22] US veterans remembered campesinos' "faithful reverence for their animals" evident in their "sad teary, eyes."[23] *Excélsior* reported "teary-eyed" campesinos who preferred to shoot their own animals "since they were sure they could aim better than soldiers, who often missed and made the animals suffer more."[24] Adding to the sense of transgression and waste, poorly dug slaughter pits sometimes cracked open to emit "nauseous odors" in the weeks after slaughter, or flooded and were washed away in the rainy season.[25]

US officials recognized the incongruous, somber paradox of the sanitary rifle. In Guanajuato, Dr. Shaulis from Kansas spoke to the press: "Believe me ... I deeply regret this, but it must be done. This spectacle is

[22] On naming, see various testimonies in Soto Correa, *El rifle*, 108–9. For a later ethnographic description of such bonds in Oaxaca, see González, *Zapotec Science*, 135–6.
[23] *Aftosa International*, 17.   [24] Quoted in Soto Correa, *El rifle*, 78.
[25] USDA, *Campaign*, 169.

painful to me, who has studied to cure animals and not to exterminate them. I realize how all these people must feel. My one desire is to put an end to this as soon as possible so they can raise better animals."[26]

In villages around Arcelia, Guerrero, rural doctors attached to a Rockefeller Foundation program noted a distinct change in attitude after the aftosa brigade left: "The hostility of the Mexican farmer, staring hopelessly at the carcasses of his cattle lying in lime pits, is directed towards everything North American and medical"; families began to keep their children out of school, and refuse treatments for *pal de pinto*.[27] For its part, Mexico's Ministry of Public Health wanted as little to do with the aftosa commission as possible, fearing that any association in the public mind with the sanitary rifle would reverse growing acceptance of their efforts to vaccinate against smallpox and treat other diseases.[28] In 1949, one of the most useful things that priests in Puebla did, according to CMAEFA reports, was assuage fears of the aftosa vaccine by organizing mass blessings of peasant families' pigs and cows prior to the arrival of veterinary brigades. In this way, priests vouched for the vaccine, providing a kind of institutional insurance policy, and underlined the idea that animals had souls of some kind, and were not inert commodities or machines.[29]

The main problem for interpretations of opposition based on kin-like sentiment or religious belief is that there is not very much direct evidence. A family-like attachment to animals is almost always something imputed to others. Some stories – of women gathering at a slaughter pit dressed in black and weeping as at a funeral – became embedded in commission lore, and were repeated over and over by people who never witnessed them.[30] In his "semi-fictional" novel about the campaign in Michoacán, Ramón Rubín depicted some peasant farmers whose defense of their animals' God-given right to life was entirely cynical, simply a means to bargain for higher indemnity prices.[31] Rubín suggested that other campesinos may have mourned the deaths of their animals rather like those of family members, but rarely expressed such sentiments in public. These included the character of "Don Miguelito," who walked past a slaughter pit in which his four cows and two goats had been buried:

---

[26] *El Universal*, July 24, 1947, transcribed in USDA, *Campaign*, 36–7.
[27] Ruth Mulvey, "Cattle killing turns peon against doctor," *Washington Post*, January 4, 1948.
[28] Agostoni, *Médicos*, 200. In Michoacán smallpox vaccinators also complained the cash-flush CMAEFA outbade them in the market for local guides. Ibid.
[29] USAD, *Campaign*, 255.   [30] Porter, *Doctor*, 44.   [31] Rubín, *Ese rifle*, 26.

At the side of the road, in the dip between two hills, is the pit where they buried the cattle, recently coated in powdered lime which isolated the dangers of contagion and made the place feel rather like a great sepulchre ... And it is a kind of tomb, before which one might take off one's sombrero, cross oneself, or erect a cross. But Don Miguelito only showed himself, with the pretext of scratching his head, a little pained, and did not turn towards it or say anything.[32]

In the few petitions and witness statements where opponents of the CMAEFA do indeed compare their livestock to family members, it is clearly intended to underline animals' centrality to household production and labor.[33] Admittedly, another kind of research – local, ethnohistorical – might provide more direct evidence on these lines. But it is clear that most public and political criticism of aftosa eradication – in the press, in correspondence with the state, during public meetings – was not made on the discursive terrain of kinship or the religious significance of livestock. Still, officials and politicians imputing sentimental motives to peasants had very good reasons to seize on this particular aspect of the aftosa drama, and ignore all the other unsentimental and frequently scathing criticisms that peasants (and others) made.

Rather than an excess of sentimental smallholders, the campaign's most fundamental obstacle was also one familiar to most modern campaigns against aftosa around the world. The virus' frequently mild clinical symptoms, and high rates of recovery made it difficult to convince people that it represented an urgent, even existential problem. Without the "inexorably accumulating deaths and sicknesses" that define human epidemics, aftosa has often struggled for broad public recognition.[34] Countless letters and speeches questioned whether eradication would generate long-term benefits worth the short-term costs. Slaughter often seemed like a "remedy ... worse than the disease itself."[35] Complaints at a fractious public meeting in Tehuixtla between farmers and Mexican officials were typical. A Morelense rancher took to his feet to speak for "small ranchers" in the area: "In 1919 we endured the epidemic of *piojo* (cattle louse), which was most terrible, and now we see that although aftosa in no way compares with that, they are still exterminating all the livestock, and we do not agree with it." Aftosa, another campesino added, "is not as bad as people say." To spur cooperation some politicians then exaggerated the morbidity and symptoms of the aftosa virus, which only

---

[32] Ibid., 37–8.   [33] Kloppe-Santamaria, *Vortex*, 25–6.
[34] Rosenberg, "What is an Epidemic?" 5. On definitions of epizootics, see Woods, "Patterns."
[35] *El Universal*, November 27, 1947.

boosted popular skepticism. The federal deputy for Morelos argued that without action aftosa would wipe out the livestock industry entirely and, quite reasonably, farmers did not believe him.[36] The Mexican government's own propaganda explained the "relatively low" mortality rate of the disease.[37]

In this sense, the character of the virus imposed a familiar general structure on conflicts over eradication, although the Mexican context amplified problems in various ways. As we have seen, aftosa was unfamiliar to Mexican farmers, and its symptoms closely resembled a familiar and relatively harmless ailment known by ranchers as *mal de yerba* and by veterinarians as vesicular stomachitis.[38] Moreover, the clinical symptoms of aftosa were particularly mild among the low-bred "creole," "native" or "*corriente*" livestock that predominated in central Mexico.[39] Many farmers argued that aftosa had been misdiagnosed, perhaps deliberately, and that they already knew how to control it by maintaining clean and dry stables, and applying homemade disinfectants – a combination of lime juice, salt, creolin, honey, and tequila.[40] Corridos sung in the north of Guerrero portrayed the virus as a cruel hoax and aimed to capsize the listing ship of commission expertise: "The real doctors are the campesinos."[41]

As the many theories of shadowy foreign motives make clear, association with the United States further eroded the CMAEFA's legitimacy in many people's eyes. No previous anti-aftosa campaign had been so obviously international. Opposition can hardly be reduced to anti-Americanism, as the all-Mexican Senguio affair attests. The fragmentary images and ideas captured in official sources and the press tell us little about the "speech act" of rumor-mongering: the audience, the intonation, the non-verbal gestures, and the ironic charge that may have accompanied stories.[42] For example, stories about officials digging up slaughtered herds and sending them to feed US soldiers in Korea could have functioned as useful hyperbole, drawing official attention to local maladministration of the campaign, while avoiding the risks of naming particular grafters and

---

[36] Lecuona Ramos to DFS, October 18, 1947, AGN, versión pública: Amelio Robles.
[37] Figueroa Velázquez, *El tiro de gracia*, 44.
[38] Translation of Armando Rodríguez, "Hoof and Mouth Disease in Mexico," CMAEFA, general subject files, box 1, correspondence – misc.
[39] USDA, *Campaign*, 6.
[40] Ibid., 166; various correspondence, AGN, MAV, 4255-2-29B.
[41] Interview with Isidro Ríos Hernández, in Guzmán, *Oxtotitlán*, 118. According to Ríos, this half-remembered corrido was composed by Feliciano Barrera Montes de Oca, member of a family famous for their contribution to the Mexican Revolution in Guerrero.
[42] Ramirez, *Enlightened*, 227.

profiteers – like General Ireta, among others, whose slaughter pits were indeed empty. Still, the US backing and everyday presence clearly raised hackles and fed suspicions that the Mexican government was acting like "a pimp for the gringos."[43] The ejidatarios of eastern Michoacán greeted aftosa officials with a range of shouts and insults, but "above all many cries of 'death' and 'fuck your mother' to the gringos." Corridos also criticized US interference, albeit in a subtler way characteristic of the genre. In Michoacán, one insinuated that the Mexican government had betrayed its people to the United States, thinly disguised behind wordplay and the religious idioms to hand:

> They grabbed my livestock
> And took it to the pit
> And there they shot it for me
> Since it had fiebre aftosa
> When I received the money
> The same thing happened to me as to Judas
> They grabbed the livestock nice and fat
> But turned it into rubbish
> Oh, what pain
> What an ungrateful government
> To destroy all this wealth
> In exchange for another thin gain (*ganado flaco*)[44]

In the wake of the Senguio massacre, the commission sent Xavier Sánchez Gavito, one of its propaganda officers, to survey popular opinion, and he underlined how rural experiences of endemic disease shaped attitudes to aftosa and further increased popular suspicion of US motives:

These people – primitive as they are – always compare animal diseases with those that affect human beings, and arrive at the conclusion that they have lived with sick members of their families and only in a few cases have they contracted the disease. In any case, the old members or the young were those that were hit very hard. The same thing happens with animals ... "Healthy animals are killed because they are carriers of a disease that does not even cause a large percentage of deaths. Would anybody dare to pass a law by which human beings should face the firing squad just because they are carriers of the worst known disease? ... If we let them kill our animals, they (the gringos) would then start killing the 'pintos,' the blind, and the lepers. It is their (the gringos') method of wiping out diseases."[45]

---

[43] Declaration of Juan Rodríguez, soldier, Temascalcingo, February 1, 1949, AGN, DFS, versión pública: Robert Proctor.

[44] Soto Correa, *El rifle*, 121; Meyer, *El sinarquismo*, 235.

[45] Xavier Sánchez Gavito, "Miscellaneous information," c. September 15, 1947, CMAEFA, administrative correspondence, box 5, "Reports, information."

US observers believed that such arguments represented a kind of category error; they muddled human medical questions with the aggregate interests of the livestock economy and merely confirmed the "primitive logic with which the campesino approaches the matter."[46]

Even when people did not contest the campaign in principle – which they often did – the operational nuts and bolts of slaughter made some friction inevitable. Appraisals represented an intrinsically "knotty problem," and encouraged a certain amount of discontent almost by design.[47] The commission gathered data on market prices and offered rough guidelines to livestock appraisers, but it was understood that appraisers needed to exercise discretion, inflating or deflating payments as they guessed the weight of local opposition and the virulence of the outbreak, and navigated the plethora of local standards of livestock breeding. If too little was offered, this tended to fuel non-compliance and opposition; if appraisers were too generous, this would likely create incentives for trafficking and profiteering, and create a host of other problems. By October 1947, prices diverged markedly between some districts, stoking public criticism of inconsistencies.[48] Again, such problems had been and (would remain) very familiar to other animal disease eradication campaigns that involved mandatory slaughter. During the campaigns against bovine tuberculosis in the United States in the 1920s and 1930s – important learning experiences for many BAI staff – appraisers understood that a certain level of discontent with prices was necessary for "optimal" efficiency.[49]

Still, in Mexico the difficulties of stamping out aftosa with slaughter went far beyond built-in wrangling over prices. The aftosa campaign coincided with recurrent droughts that parched central Mexico and wrecked harvests.[50] Some farmers, perhaps those least integrated into commercial markets, may have objected to cash payments as such. Merced Román Castrejón, remembered this problem for peasants around Oxtotitlán, Guerrero: "Sure, they paid us for the livestock, but

---

[46] USDA, *Campaign*, 89. In some ways this back-country thinking was rather up-to-date. In the 1940s and 1950s, international nutritionists and veterinary experts were seeking to "marry food and agriculture," and increasingly pondering analogies between human and animal health. Bresalier, "From Healthy Cows," 120. See also Nash Carter, *One Man*.

[47] USDA, *Campaign*, 45.

[48] See comments on Dr. Levine, by Omohundro, Morelia, to Noyes, October 31, 1947; Noyes to Allen, Coatzacoalcos, January 16, 1948, both in CMAEFA, operations, box 29, Michoacán and Veracruz.

[49] Olmstead and Rhode, "Not on my Farm!" 804.

[50] Gutiérrez, "Cambio," 207–56; Figueroa Velázquez, *El tiro de gracia*, 85–6.

this was not the thing (*el chiste*). What are you going to do with money, if there is nothing to buy?"[51] Still, as we will see, immersion in the cash economy provided no political inoculation against hostility to the CMAEFA. Far more common were complaints that indemnities were inadequate and, especially, that procedures were partial and corrupt. Dr. Manuel Bribiesca, a pediatrician from Zamora, observed the campaign in the Bajío and argued that the poor bore the brunt of it. As a doctor, he understood that the animals of poor and rich both carry the virus, but officials "are killing the animals of poor people and respecting the animals of the rich," further worsening problems of malnutrition.[52] Peasants and small farmers also criticized the slow arrival of replacement mules, which they blamed on official graft and profiteering middle-men.[53] Townspeople in the Bajío had less urgent need of draught animals, but made similar arguments about callous and corrupt officials. The "League of Recuperation of Towns Affected by Foot and Mouth Disease" was founded in La Piedad, Michoacán in July 1947, but claimed to have supporters in towns across the western Bajío. The league complained that commission officials spared the livestock of wealthy and influential men (including cattle belonging to a man from whom the CMAEFA rented property) and that quarantine was similarly skewed against the poor: "If you decide to close the Cavdas bridge due to quarantine why do the 'doctors,' priests and rich bootlickers of the town pass? Do they not carry the disease?" Strictly speaking, the league's criticisms were merely procedural, but the tone was distinctly spiky. If government officials did not stop acting like "semi-god despots," the league would take more direct action since, they added, "WE ARE LIVING IN A DEMOCRACY."[54]

The commission strained to portray itself as an enforcer of impartial rules. Early on, officials in Querétaro exempted one prize dairy herd from slaughter, but Noyes quickly recognized this was a public relations

---

[51] Guzmán, *Oxtotitlán*, 151.

[52] Dr. Manuel Bribiesca, Zamora, Michoacán, to Alemán, July 12, 1947, AGN, MAV, 425.5/2-15A.

[53] Ing. León Carreo Inman, Jefe de la sección de organización agraria, Guanajuato, to state governor, May 14, 1947, AHEG, 3.40 (78), fiebre aftosa, 1947, vol. II.

[54] This league claimed support in Yurécuaro, La Barca, Penjamo, Tanhuato, Zamora, and Ocotlán. Anonymous note from "The League of Recuperation of Towns Affected by Foot and Mouth Disease," La Piedad, Michoacán, August 7, 1947, CMAEFA, operations, box 29, Michoacán. In June 1947, local authorities had banned a seventy-member group from the PAN from leaving La Piedad for Mexico City to complain about electoral abuses. Soto Correa, *El rifle*, 96.

disaster, and urged field officials not to repeat the mistake.[55] Nevertheless, throughout 1947 newspapers spread the muck of campaign favoritism across their pages. In *La Prensa*, a cartoon by Don Yo portrayed *coyotes* on the commission taking bribes and sparing the cattle of rich politicians: "If you don't have money, then your cattle will have aftosa and will die."[56] Allegations of officials directly grafting on the campaign budget, padding slaughter statistics, selling off the contagious hides of slaughtered cattle, and colluding to buy cattle on the cheap were more explosive and slower to reach the press, but they did eventually.[57] There was, then, a widespread recognition of the differential impact of the sanitary rifle, and a shared sense of grievance among poor and marginal groups. This did not hinge on communities' relationship to the cash nexus. Rather, it represented a much broader, shared experiences of official corruption and predation.

Conversely, the alternative of vaccination was well known, and this underpinned much criticism of the slaughter. At the UNAM, Mexico's most prestigious veterinary researchers shunned the sanitary rifle, and their students argued that it was a product of US cattle interests who "forced the theories of its old-fashioned technicians on the weak." An article published in the aftermath of the Senguio massacre in the student newsletter, *La Lanceta*, illustrates the bitter atmosphere on campus:

The students and professors of our school who have been fighting to establish vaccination, today more than ever, let this question rise spontaneously to President Alemán: When, Mr President, will we be able to shove aside Yankee imperialism and vaccinate our cattle? Because of the above ... we dare to make the suggestion that the "little sign" at the Department of Livestock be changed for a more allusive and rhythmical one to go with the age and which could possibly be changed to read more or less the following: AS A CHALLENGE TO THE ENLARGEMENT OF THE NATIONAL LIVESTOCK INDUSTRY, THE MINISTRY OF AGRICULTURE AND LIVESTOCK DEDICATES THESE BUILDINGS TO THE DEMORALIZATION OF THE FEW CATTLEMEN OF THE COUNTRY WHO THROUGH THEIR WORK AND STEADINESS FOUND THE ROAD TO PROGRESS AND IMPROVEMENT. FOR THOSE THAT DARE COME TO THE POINT WHERE THEY COMPETE WITH THE OUTSTANDING LIVESTOCK INDUSTRY OF OUR "GOOD NEIGHBOR,"

[55] Miscellaneous correspondence, summer 1947, CMAEFA, operations, box 29, Querétaro.
[56] July 29, 1947, *La Prensa*.
[57] On bribes, hides, and profiteering accusations, see Figueroa Velázquez, *El tiro de gracia*, 122–3.

WE HAVE A "SANITARY RIFLE" WHICH TAKES CARE OF THE HOPES OF THE BOLDEST.[58]

Such arguments were far from the preserve of an educated elite hunkered down at the university. The general idea that vaccination offered another possible model spread quickly and far in 1947, and many petitions from small farmers, Catholic dissidents, peasant organizations, and commercial ranchers referred to it. In January 1947, a group of cattlemen in Querétaro had already imported four tons of aftosa vaccine, probably from Argentina, although the government quickly seized it and banned further private shipments.[59] Thanks to press coverage and intense discussion within their commercial circles, cattlemen in the Bajío had a degree of knowledge of aftosa protocols that visiting priests and officials found surprising; the better-informed even knew that the US government had used a serum to control aftosa in occupied Italy in 1945, and pointed to the support European experts gave to vaccination.[60] Having lost the 1946 gubernatorial election in Morelos, the campesino leader Rubén Jaramillo survived various attempts on his life, and spent most of the Alemán sexenio in an undeclared, defensive rebellion against the state government – an "armed hiding" – with a core of supporters.[61] In the summer of 1947, Jaramillo further increased his reputation as a "defender of the rural poor" by protesting against slaughter. Like so many others, he also made the case for a biomedical alternative. As Jaramillo argued in a letter to the governor of Morelos, "one does not kill the sick, one cares for them; that is why we have veterinary science."[62]

In Senguio, a welter of different arguments emerge from the sources. Many locals thought that aftosa was an official fabrication, pushed by the United States; others believed that crop-spraying planes might have spread the virus, perhaps at the behest of a "big American firm" eager to sell poor-quality powdered milk.[63] According to press reports, villagers

---

[58] Translated excerpt from *La Lanceta*, September 8, 1947, CMAEFA, administrative correspondence, box 5, "C-220 reports, information." See also interviews in special issue of *Imágen Veterinaria* 1:4 (2001).

[59] Figueroa Velázquez, *El tiro de gracia*, 54. Nevertheless, according to *Novedades*, in March 1947 dairy farmers on the outskirts of Mexico City obtained more vaccine from a Spanish veterinarian, Daniel Cano Vázquez. Ibid., 65.

[60] Clipping of article by Father Ledit, *America*, June 28, 1947, FMDRL, box 1, folder 8; Meyer, *El sinarquismo*, 252–3.

[61] Padilla, *Rural Resistance*, 145.   [62] Ibid.

[63] Soto Correa, *El rifle*, 222, 106; Letter from Adolfo González Robles, Senguio, to Lázaro Cárdenas, transcribed in Soto Correa, *El rifle*, 47.

had also heard news of CMAEFA officials extorting villagers elsewhere in Michoacán and were determined not to suffer the same fate. At the same time, locals contrasted slaughter unfavorably with vaccination. A local agrarista evaded capture for his part in the Senguio massacre, rode through the outskirts of the village at night, and bellowed "stop the massacre of livestock, vaccine or revolution!"[64] While sitting in Morelia's jail awaiting punishment for his part in the massacre, Alejandro Mota scribbled a letter to President Alemán. He demanded the government abandon the "execrable and ineffective" method of slaughter, adopt "scientific methods" guided by "scientific facts based on bacteriology and profilaxis," and follow the example of vaccine-producing countries in Europe like the Netherlands. Alemán's secretary dismissed the letter as a ridiculous post-hoc rationalization for violence, and a "pathetic *j'accuse*."[65] But it is perfectly plausible that the notion of combating aftosa through vaccination or some kind of "medicine" had reached the backwoods of eastern Michoacán.[66]

Such ideas spread through the press, cattle associations, and the pamphlets of the Catholic integralist group known as the Unión Nacional Sinarquista (UNS), but also through the actions of disgruntled Mexican veterinarians themselves. From Guanajuato to Guerrero, commission and state veterinarians openly argued about the virulence and presence of aftosa, sowing confusion among cattle ranchers and local officials.[67] In one dramatic incident, campaign personnel accepted an invitation to dine in the village of Irimbo, eastern Michoacán. A "festive air attended the dinner" and Dr. Chapa, a Mexican veterinarian attached to the commission, stood up to give a speech. Chapa condemned the US-imposed slaughter policy, and claimed that more humane medical approaches existed. According to eyewitnesses, Dr. Chapa "urged cattle owners to fight the program by any and all means. He said he would not blame them if they killed all commission employees as they had killed Dr. Juárez Medina. Warming to the applause, he said he would not blame the

---

[64] Ibid., 233; letter from Adolfo González Robles, Senguio, to Lázaro Cárdenas, quoted in Soto Correa, *El rifle*, 127.

[65] A. Mota, Michoacán, to Aléman, and secretary to Alemán, November 20, 1947, AGN, MAV, 425.5/2-15A.

[66] Pamphlet signed by Benito Malagón, head of Senguio chapter of UNS, Case file 143/1947, CCJM, 160–1.

[67] Governor Castorena, Guanajuato, to Leopoldo Chávez, Comisión de lucha contra la fiebre aftosa, Mexico City, November 4, 1947; Pavia, *Recuerdos*, 77–8; circular, comité regional, October 18, 1947, CNUNS, caja 10, exp. 2719.

people if they killed him. He would be glad to die. The applause was deafening. Several Americans were cheering happily, unaware that they were applauding a maudlin death sentence for themselves."[68] When a bilingual driver alerted them to the contents of the speech, the startled US officials promptly left for Morelia, while "a good number of the near 200 campesinos present gathered around Dr. Chapa at the close of his speech with expressions of agreement."[69]

The polemic over vaccination echoes those triggered by other twentieth-century aftosa campaigns, but the political context and timing of the Mexican campaign made it particularly contentious.[70] Technological advances during the Second World War had raised new hopes for a vaccine among officials and scientists. The experience of endemic disease notwithstanding, by the 1940s Mexican society also displayed a familiarity with vaccination and, in the right circumstances, an appetite for particular vaccines. Indeed, a common criticism of the sanitary rifle recorded in the press, CMAEFA field reports, and dozens of petitions was not only that it appeared disproportionate, but that it contradicted the progress made by modern science. As they had in the United States and the United Kingdom, farmers wondered why, if veterinarians had devised cures for blackleg, rabies, and anthrax, they could not do similar for aftosa?[71] Federico Garcinava from the city of Durango went further still; if the US government could invent something as powerful as the atomic bomb, surely it could develop an aftosa vaccine, or offer a cash prize to someone who could?[72]

---

[68] USDA, *Campaign*, 131–2.

[69] Saulmon, Morelia, to Shahan, Mexico City, November 23, 1947, CMAEFA, operations, box 29, Michoacán. Mexican military officers who heard about Chapa's speech "wanted to do the veterinarian physical harm" and he was soon "transferred." USDA, *Campaign*, 132. According to local historians, Irimbo's municipal president pretended to help the aftosa commission, but secretly did everything he could to oppose it. Soto Correa, *El rifle*, 93.

[70] Olmstead and Rhode, *Arresting*, 115–37; Woods, *Manufactured*, 92–107, 116–9.

[71] UNS open letter June 24, 1947, *Orden*, and petition from ganaderos and dairy farmers of the State of Mexico, Puebla, Querétaro, dairy workers of Federal District, and 26 milk-producing ejidos, both in AGN, MAV, 4225-2-8-1. Throughout 1947, the State of Mexico's cattlemen, ejidos, and worker unions demanded vaccine research. Dozens of ejidos in Veracruz made similar arguments and pressed the government to develop a vaccine or simply import one from abroad. In Puebla, such petitions received support from the state branch of the PRI's official peasant organization, the Confederación Nacional Campesina (CNC). Various correspondence, February-August 1947 AGN, MAV, 4255-2-14, 4255-2-29 and 4255-2-20.

[72] Fernando Garcinava, Durango, to Alemán, April 18, 1947, AGN, MAV, 4255-555, 298.

The 5,000 or so offers the CMAEFA received for new cures for aftosa – which ranged from the vaguely plausible to the downright bizarre – confirm, indirectly, a similar point. Some wrote from abroad, including Michael Hill of Chicago, who promised his own "secret formula" for vaccination. Plenty wrote from Mexico: Juan Silveti, an ex-bullfighter and would-be cacique who had befriended Alemán while working on Manuel Ávila Camacho's presidential campaign, proposed his own method of "hemo-vaccination." In *Excélsior*, Dr. José Najera claimed he could cure aftosa using "vibrations" from a dose of silver salt, water, and "other ingredients." *El Universal* reported Dr. Alfonso Alarcón O'Farrill's claim that aftosa was simply the result of low vitamin C and poor nutrition. The CMAEFA disdained these "quacks" and "crackpots" and rejected them with "more or less polite answers."[73] Still, however cynically composed, these letters assumed a broad official and public appetite for, or at least familiarity with, modern biomedicine that would make their offers plausible. Indeed, officials often worried about apparent overconfidence in the power of vaccination, rather than outright rejection. In private, the CMAEFA hierarchy believed that the vaccine might only offer as little as 15 percent immunity; it could slow non-virulent strains of the disease but not prevent all outbreaks. Fearing demoralization, the CMAEFA kept such concerns from the public and from its own field vaccinators. When the first Mexico-made vaccines were applied in Magdalena, Jalisco, field officials noted that the public reaction was "good," but that campaign propagandists "may even have done too good a job" and failed to warn people of the need for continued vigilance and repeated vaccinations.[74]

Admittedly, the aftosa vaccine still encountered skepticism. According to the Mexican federal agents dispatched to survey opinion in markets and bars, the residents of Mexico City and other major cities – including the "intellectual sectors" – generally backed the vaccination drive and hoped that the US government would continue to support it, but protests continued in more isolated rural areas, albeit on a smaller scale and causing fewer delays than before.[75] The CMAEFA evidently struggled to shrug off its image as a nefarious foreign imposition. New rumors

[73] Sigsworth, "Mexican Epizootic," 86; USDA, *Campaign*, 160–1; *Excélsior* July 27, 1947; Figueroa Velázquez, *El tiro de gracia*, 217; Bernhard, quoted USDA, *Campaign*, 161. Hundreds more can be found in AGN, MAV, 4255-2-35 B.

[74] USDA, *Campaign*, 180, 267.

[75] Iñurreta, DFS, to Alemán, February 4, 1949, DFS to Gobernación, AGN, DFS, versión pública: Robert Proctor.

emerged that US officials were now using vaccine to poison and kill cattle, and possibly people too.[76] According to the US anthropologist Isabel Kelly, these rumors were particularly loud in northern Veracruz, near the commission fence. Around Tajín, locals believed that the fence had been built because the "Mexican government has sold a whole strip of the coast to the gringos," and the aftosa vaccination campaign was part of "a plan of the United States to terminate the Totonac 'race'." (Kelly found that her informant, Nicolasa, was "so alarmed that she wants to clear out with her whole brood – 5 children, of whom the eldest is seven. But the poor woman has no-where to go.")[77] Even before the vaccination drive, in the Sierra Norte de Puebla it was rumored that commission officials – sinister Yankee *"capadores de cristianos"* – wanted to inject poison into livestock and children, sterilize women, and castrate men, part of a Yankee plot against "dark-skinned people (*hombres negros*)."[78] Read figuratively, such stories certainly suggest how farmers associated domestic livestock with family reproduction and social status. They may also have reflected fears of US support for racist positive eugenics and sterilization, topics discussed among Catholic groups from at least the 1930s.[79]

On closer inspection, however, some disputes appear to be about the practice of this particular campaign rather than the principle of vaccination. In late summer 1948, the commission office in Jalisco heard word of concerted opposition to vaccination in the Sierra de Amula around Atengo. An official visited and found that, while the "agreeable" and well-mannered mestizos of the area harbored many "deep rooted objections" to the campaign, most of these stemmed from suspicion of government neglect, corruption, and hypocrisy. Rumors in Atengo echoed fears of sexual enfeeblement heard elsewhere; people heard that the vaccine sterilized female cows, sapped the virility of bulls, and that "anyone drinking the milk" of vaccinated cows "is made sexually weak or entirely sterile." However, few rejected vaccination outright. In ranchers' homes

---

[76] Memo, Luis Palacios, oficial mayor de gobierno, Guanajuato, February 3, 1949, AHEG, 3.40 (78), fiebre aftosa, 1949, vol. II.

[77] I. Kelly, Tajín, to Bertha Harris, Benjamin Franklin Library, Mexico City, May 6, 1948, transcribed in USDA, *Campaign*, 192. Field officials agreed that the "Papantla-El Tajín" area was a hotbed of opposition and hostile rumors. Confidential reports, May 1948, CMAEFA, reports, box 1. For Kelly's later criticism of heavy-handed campaigns against malaria, see Cueto, *Cold War*, 121–8.

[78] Hernández Ferral, Mexico City, to Col. Iñurreta, October 27, 1947; José Matamoros Sánchez, Juez de defensa social, record of trial 21/947, AGN, DFS: versión pública: José Jorge Sánchez.

[79] Elizabeth O'Brien, personal communication, June 2016.

one found "illustrated weeklies or monthly reviews of livestock and agriculture" detailing the latest sanitary techniques, and "quite a number" had already vaccinated their herds against "blackleg and other cattle diseases." In public meetings, ranchers demanded assurances that the campaign would be administered competently. They asked why the campaign had ignored their earlier calls for information and assistance in protecting their herds; others asked, "if the vaccine is effective for only 6 months, does that mean the government is going to leave us to our own fate after that period?" (One of the reported "rumors" in town – that ear-tags the commission used to mark vaccinated animals made them suscep-tible to maggots – proved quite accurate.) More pointedly, ranchers demanded a full explanation of government priorities, asking "insistently why the government did not fight tuberculosis and syphilis – is it because the government is more interested in cattle than human beings?"[80] In February 1949, Mexican officials were briefly worried that the murder of a US livestock inspector in the State of Mexico, combined with the upcoming state elections, might inspire further "acts of agitation and rebellion" against vaccination.[81] A military officer sent to investigate provided reassurance: peasant farmers remained suspicious of the com-mission, not least because many had already had most of their animals slaughtered. However, all the farmers and authorities interviewed con-ceded that vaccination was the best solution to the problem in principle, and promised to support it provided the commission pay for any animals killed by the vaccine – a promise made to them earlier by General Alejo González.[82] In the Nahua-speaking villages of southern Veracruz, argu-ments about administering the vaccine were somewhat different, and boiled down to a dispute about the hated local army detachments. "Juan Grande," the boss of Pajapan, used a translator to make his conditions for accepting vaccination clear to commission officials: "I'll let you vaccinate if you don't bring any soldiers."[83]

While many people criticized the campaign and especially slaughter, actions varied greatly but followed some rough patterns. Even during the slaughter phase, larger cities in central Mexico were generally calm. It is

---

[80] Lic. J. Carillo Manzo, c. August 1948, transcribed USDA, *Campaign*, 217–8.
[81] Memo, Luis Palacios, official mayor de gobierno, Guanajuato, February 3, 1949, AHEG, 3.40 (78), fiebre aftosa, 1949, vol. II; memo, February 2, 1949, AGN, DFS, versión pública: Robert Proctor.
[82] Colonel Maldonado Lara, Estado Mayor de la Secretaría de la Defensa Nacional, to state governor, Guanajuato, AHEG, 3.40 (78), fiebre aftosa, 1949, vol. I.
[83] Testimony of Norberto Chamberlain, USDA, *Campaign*, 246.

unlikely that this reflected eager support for the sanitary rifle. In August 1947, General Corlett concluded that in some ways Mexico City formed the "center" of opposition, since the city's "intelligentsia" – journalists, intellectuals and experts – criticized the slaughter campaign and "this attitude appears to be fashionable."[84] However, larger urban centers – with relatively few livestock, and a greater presence of state authorities – did not offer many incentives or opportunities for active opposition. While the campaign engaged in house-to-house inspections and, later, vaccinations, the CMAEFA reported only a handful of notable incidents of concerted non-cooperation and unrest in larger towns and cities.[85]

The countryside was much more restive. Opposition to the sanitary rifle was extensive, varied, and – like the calls for vaccination – notably cross-class. Although it has largely escaped historical analysis, it should not surprise us that peasant farmers and commercial ranchers big and small found common cause in opposing slaughter. After all, they relied on livestock and many mistrusted the commission and its scientific rationale. If commercial cattlemen in central Mexico were reliant on local and regional markets, and were thus insulated from the disruption aftosa wrought on international trade, peasant farmers were still more so. When ranchers rented out oxen to villagers, or paid ejidatarios a share for fattening calves on their land on a seasonal basis, ties of patronage and economic interdependence cross-cut lines of agrarian conflict. In a little studied process, in the 1930s wealthier ejidatarios began to acquire herds of livestock "to cover the grazing lands on their ejidos," and some started to resemble ranchers themselves.[86] In central Veracruz, cattlemen had deliberately defanged the jaws of agrarismo by cultivating allies among wealthier peasant farmers or former peons.[87] Culturally, the gap

---

[84] Corlett to Anderson, August 26 and September 9, 1947, CAP, "foot and mouth disease."

[85] Along with riots in Ameca, Minatitlán, and La Piedad discussed below, two other exceptions to the trend were reported: in the city of Querétaro on August 22, 1947, when an apparently drunken man attacked a jeep station wagon belonging to the commission and "broke every window ... including two headlights"; and in Tehuacán, Puebla, when two men spotted a commission employee as he was walking home, shouted "that's one of them," jumped out of their car, and shot at the man several times as he ran home. USDA, *Campaign*, 80; Mulhern, Tehuacán, to Noyes, September 30, 1947, CMAEFA, operations, box 29, Oaxaca.

[86] Pavia Guzmán, *Acciones*, 48. On oxen rental in villages in the Bajío and Guerrero respectively, see: Comité Agrario, Acámbaro, Guanajuato, to Alemán, June 9, 1947, AGN, MAV: 4255-2-10 B; Guzmán, *Oxtotitlán*.

[87] Salas Landa, "Enacting." Léonard dates the intensification of economic ties between ranchers and ejidatarios in southern Veracruz to the mid-1950s. Léonard, "Los empresarios."

separating ranchers, peons, and peasants had never been wide or unbridgeable. Some rancheros – ex-Zapatista officers in Guerrero and Morelos – had formerly been subsistence farmers themselves or recently fought alongside them. In any case, as they had during the revolution, many ranchers maintained a plausible grasp of rustic local mores and "country manners."[88]

By far the most common tactic was to gum up the wheels of CMAEFA operations with non-cooperation and evasion. These made up 218 (or 47 percent) of the 465 notable incidents of opposition culled from the sources.[89] This approach presented fewer risks than open confrontation and the campaign's organization offered many points at which cooperation could be quietly withdrawn. On countless occasions, farmers omitted to round-up animals, provide information, dig pits, or meet with CMAEFA staff. Frank Mulhern thought that foot-dragging by Mexican construction workers hired to dig pits was an especially good indicator of local opinion: "when they have to read the instruction book to page 20 before they learn how to stop the bulldozer, it's bad."[90] Hiding animals was so widespread that officials took it for granted and only reported incidents of large-scale and coordinated concealment. (According to José Carmen Soto Correa, in the east of Michoacán "more people took to the hills with their herds than during the Cristero movement."[91]) When faced with poor prices, some farmers conveniently lost control of cattle mid-appraisal and let them run loose.[92] Some of these "weapons of the weak" were rather easy to uncover. One farmer mimicked the green paint that commission veterinarians applied to animals to indicate vaccination, but mistakenly daubed it on his dog and donkey.[93] Other tactics were so subtle they seemed to escape official recognition. In February 1948, field workers along the northern quarantine line in Guanajuato and Querétaro reported

---

[88] See various reports on Colonel Amelio Robles and General Mucio Marín, AGN, versión pública: Amelio Robles; Pavia Guzmán, *Acciones*, 48; Knight, *Mexican Revolution*, vol. 1, 115. On the rural culture shared by ranchers and poor workers and farmers in the Huasteca, see Lomnitz Adler, *Exits*, 165–178. Schryer dates the emergence of a "new breed" of urban, educated, and consciously "modern" rancher to roughly the mid-1950s. Schryer, *Ethnicity and Class*, 151. For a peasant-rancher alliance against federal intervention in the late 1970s, see Buckles and Chevalier, *A Land Without Gods*, 70–123.

[89] See sources cited under Figures 3.1 and 3.2.   [90] USDA, *Campaign*, 89.

[91] Soto Correa, *El rifle*, 91.

[92] For examples, see reports on Bernal, Querétaro, June 1947, CMAEFA, operations, box 29, Querétaro; memorandum from Oscar Flores on incident in Villa Juárez (Puebla), Mexico City, July 9, 1947, CMAEFA, operations, box 29, Puebla.

[93] Scott, *Weapons*; USDA, *Campaign*, 244.

that "campesinos" were systematically taking down posters advertising the campaign with the excuse that they wished to consult the materials more carefully at home; the US section interpreted this as a sign of success rather than subtle subversion.[94]

Opponents of the program also appealed to Mexican officials and politicians for redress. Judicial institutions – notoriously slow-moving and politically puny – were ill-suited to the urgent threat the campaign seemed to pose. Weakened by years of concerted official harassment and repression, in 1947 the UNS was a factionalized and decentralized organization, and its leadership and followers did not speak with one voice on the sanitary rifle. UNS criticism of the sanitary rifle became more prominent after June 1947, after it failed to make headway in state elections.[95] Even so, the UNS leadership backed away from the more aggressive stance urged by some *sinarquistas*, and encouraged members to flood the legal system with injunctions challenging the constitutionality of the decree to slaughter infected animals, distributing a standard formula to affiliates which they could complete.[96] However, the uptake and impact of these measures was limited. Field reports from the commission rarely detected legal obstacles, aside from the occasional commercial dairyman or bull owner contesting fines or underpayments. In December 1947, a group of commercial livestock owners near Querétaro obtained a judicial *amparo* to prevent the commission slaughtering or inspecting cattle, but the Mexican district co-supervisor Dr. Francisco Martínez Garibay quickly "persuaded them to withdraw the injunction."[97] Some lawyers decided they had little chance of success. In Guanajuato, two farmers approached a local "licenciado" to help them claim compensation for their slaughtered livestock, but "he did not want to work with us, and told us that the campaign against aftosa does not permit the involvement of lawyers in any shape or form."[98]

More important than litigation was the lobbying of politicians and bureaucrats. Small towns and villages pleaded with state and federal authorities that their animals – particularly contacts which were not visibly infected – be spared. La Piedad's anti-aftosa league sent a group

---

[94] Confidential weekly report, February 14, 1948, CMAEFA, reports, box 2.

[95] Serrano, *La batalla*, vol. II, 274–5; Soto Correa, *El rifle*, 85.

[96] Vilchis, comité regional, León, to Jesús Rivera, Puruagua, Guanajuato, September 20, 1947, CNUNS, caja 10, exp. 2702; Meyer, *El sinarquismo*, 255–6.

[97] USDA, *Campaign*, 164.

[98] Guadalupe and Antonio Malagón, Apaseo, to President Alemán, July 16, 1947, AHEG, 3.40 (78), fiebre aftosa, 1947, vol. II.

of representatives to meet with Nazario Ortiz Garza and Alemán.[99] In parts of Michoacán and Guanajuato, local UNS cadres aimed to befriend and "get close" to veterinarians, and subtly influence local operations. In one village, they claimed to have minimized slaughter and caused locals to defect en masse from the official *Confederación Nacional Campesina* (CNC).[100] Peasant organizations in Morelos and local authorities in Jalisco alike dropped obvious hints about the kind of concessions that might spur cooperation: the huge investment in aftosa eradication made little sense, they argued, and their real priorities lay in roads, schools, and water.[101] Still, such ploys relied on political, economic, or military resources that most small towns and peasant villages did not possess. The agrarista Manuel Mora always insisted that the people of Senguio had rioted as a last resort. In August 1947 they had repeatedly sought out state authorities and veterinarians to negotiate terms of cooperation, and had even offered bribes to the commission to spare some contact animals, but were rebuffed.[102] Relatively wealthy and politically well-connected, and in tune with alemanismo's business-friendly project, associations of commercial stockmen were in a stronger position, and in the summer and autumn of 1947 a steady stream of delegations met with Ortiz and Alemán behind closed doors and pushed for an end to slaughter. Other businesses hampered by slaughter and quarantine restrictions, such as the Bajío's tanning industries, similarly lobbied the Secretary of Economy for help.[103] Crucially, after November 1947, these groups generally threw their considerable political weight behind the vaccination campaign. In other words, in its closing years the campaign resembled the image of cozy, more or less institutionalized cooperation between business elites and the state, familiar from many studies of PRIismo.

However, the outcome should not be conflated with the process. To shift the campaign towards vaccination, and obtain such control over local CMAEFA operations, commercial ranchers went well beyond polite lobbying. They certainly engaged in public argument. In Michoacán, the

[99] Anonymous note from "The League of Recuperation of Towns Affected by Foot and Mouth Disease," La Piedad, Michoacán, August 7, 1947, CMAEFA, operations, box 29, Michoacán.

[100] "Informe de la discusión al Comité Nacional de la UNS (1947)," in Meyer, *El sinarquismo*, 254–5.

[101] Lecuona Ramos to DFS, October 18, 1947, AGN, versión pública: Amelio Robles; Porter, *Doctor*, 185.

[102] Pérez Escutia, *Senguio*, 288.

[103] Report, November 11, 1947, AGN, versión pública: Javier Altamirano.

dairy interests around Jiquilpan – the heart of ex-President Cárdenas's *cacicazgo* – bombarded the press with complaints that the slaughter campaign was plunging the country into poverty, riddled with abuses, and inspired by US ignorance or shadowy *intereses inconfesables*. After all, they argued, the disease was endemic in South America, but these countries still enjoyed prosperous livestock industries.[104] Open letters from Jiquilpan's cattlemen played an important role in defining the terms of public debate about the sanitary rifle, in part because many people believed that they ventriloquized the views of the "Sphinx of Jiquilpan" himself, Cárdenas. However, a few flashpoints aside, commercial live-stock associations in Michoacán generally steered clear of open confron-tation with aftosa brigades. It probably helped that the CMAEFA succeeded in containing the infection before it spread into the main area of beef cattle ranching in Michoacán's *tierra caliente*.[105] Lying directly in the path of the sanitary rifle, dairy and cattle farmers in the State of Mexico combined lobbying and public criticism with non-cooperation, halting CMAEFA operations outright on at least two occasions.[106]

In Jalisco, the campaign's relations with commercial dairy and beef farmers followed a different trajectory, veering from close cooperation to open hostility. Initially, the CMAEFA's district office in Guadalajara found livestock organizations in the state a great help. In August 1947, CMAEFA officials were disappointed that they had not prevented the virus from following roads and railways into the Ciénaga and Los Altos regions in the east of the state, and by early reports of hostility to the campaign around the town of La Barca. In this context, district headquar-ters accepted an offer from the state's livestock association based in Guadalajara to help staff quarantine lines and act as livestock appraisers alongside US officials. In August and September, this arrangement seemed to work well, and US officials praised the men's "highly commendable" behavior. The men sent by cattle associations knew the terrain, under-stood regional livestock markets, and were "brilliant" at working with ranchers in the flat lowlands around Lake Chapala and the small towns of

---

[104] Romero Méndez, *Ensayos, discursos*, 122–34, 133. In Querétaro, the local press also reported that powerful stockmen sent a delegation to Mexico City to lobby against slaughter prices "as a bloc." *El Día*, November 6, 1947, cited in Figueroa Velázquez, *El tiro de gracia*, 151.

[105] See various field reports, September–November 1947, CMAEFA, operations, box 29, Michoacán. On Cárdenas's reputation for "absolute inscrutability," see Zolov, *Last Good Neighbor*, 15.

[106] See Chapter 2.

Los Altos, mediating disputes, and finding prices that the CMAEFA regarded as fair but not overly generous.[107] With the backing of political patrons in the state capital, these well-to-do mestizo ranchers apparently enjoyed a certain local prestige, and referred to themselves as *charros*.[108] Even news of the Senguio massacre did little to disrupt the campaign in Jalisco. In August 1947, it was the absence of Mexican funds which US officials believed was the "chief source of ill feeling among the people." In September, US field workers reported improved cooperation and smoother operations, as Mexican funds for small animals materialized.[109]

During October and November 1947 the arrangement with Jalisco's charros unraveled. As aftosa began to creep into the central valley and infect valuable herds of dairy cattle and pigs, the charros inflated appraisals or refused to work. As Dr. Hess noted, the charros were "quite influential" and now demanded "concessions because they have sided with the commission."[110] Jalisco's livestock association called meetings in Guadalajara to oppose further slaughter. Federal forces broke up the first meeting causing "a very disagreeable impression among the cattlemen."[111] The second meeting at Guadalajara's bullring went ahead and dozens of stockmen took to the microphone to lambast the campaign. Along with the usual doubts about the severity of aftosa symptoms and calls for vaccination, other arguments had a distinct ranchero flavor to them, focusing on property rights and local autonomy and know-how. Warm applause followed one speaker who argued that low prices imposed by the United States caused people to "protect their private property," an entirely "natural" instinct that superseded "patriotism" or "collective interest." Hardly anyone in Mexico registered their high-grade cattle with the government. Ranchers argued that it was absurd for US appraisers to "pay for dairy and fine cattle as though it were beef cattle, only because they are not registered, acting as though they were in the United States and not in Mexico ... A fine animal is known perfectly by the size of his ears, hair, horns, proportions, etc., which can be ascertained at first glance by one who knows, without the necessity of verifying weight or milk production."

---

[107] Dr. Mau, Guadalajara, to Shahan, August 1, 1947, CMAEFA, operations, box 29, Jalisco.
[108] Ibid.
[109] Guthery, Guadalajara, to Noyes, September 2, 1947; and Dr. Hess, Guadalajara, to Noyes, August 26, 1947, both in CMAEFA, operations, box 29, Jalisco.
[110] Hess, Guadalajara, to Noyes, October 28, 1947, CMAEFA, operations, box 29, Jalisco.
[111] Federico Domínguez L., "Auxiliar de Organización," to Bernhard, Information Division, CMAEFA, Mexico City, November 13, 1947, CMAEFA, operations, box 29, Jalisco.

When CMAEFA and state government officials arrived at the meeting, the atmosphere turned rowdy and threatening.[112]

In their own peculiar way, commission officials in Jalisco also began to butt up against the limited autonomy of the state. Not only were the main stockmen and their charro appraisers – so resourceful in the east of the state – now blocking the campaign. The military zone commander tasked with providing protection and transport, General Ramón Jiménez Delgado, now supported them because, as Dr. Hess noted ruefully, he was a major rancher himself and "also one of them."[113] As a political price for continued cooperation, General Jiménez demanded he be given complete control over the campaign in the state.[114] The commission also began to receive worrying reports that charros had earlier planted their own cheaply-acquired cattle at slaughter operations in the southeast of the state.[115] In mid-November, the commission made a short-lived deal with the head of the livestock association, Mr. Dinacho: it employed new appraisers from out-of-state, while the charros oversaw slaughter operations as joint "chiefs of operations." Dr. Hess reassured his superiors in Mexico City that any local interference in appraisal processes would be punished: "We are watching these men like hawks, the first false move they make we will get rid of them." Within a few days the pact broke down after one charro, Mr. Dinacho's son, interfered in appraisals.[116]

An even more fraught relationship developed between the CMAEFA and ranchers in Veracruz, the most powerful beef ranching lobby in the country. Livestock associations across the state published open letters against the sanitary rifle, invoked a kind of business patriotism, and asked Alemán to consider the "many investments" they had made in land, fodder, and breeding to hasten economic progress in the state.[117] It is easy to understand why ranchers believed such arguments might work. Alemán was a Veracruzano himself, and a reliable ally of ranching

---

[112] Ibid.

[113] Hess, Guadalajara, to Noyes, October 28, 1947, CMAEFA, operations, box 29, Jalisco.

[114] Phone log of call between Hess and Noyes, November 4, 1947, CMAEFA, operations, box 29, Jalisco.

[115] Various phone logs, October 1947, Hess, Guadalajara, to Noyes, October 28, 1947, CMAEFA, operations, box 29, Jalisco.

[116] Hess, Guadalajara, to Noyes, Mexico City, November 18, 1947, CMAEFA, operations, box 29, Jalisco. Cattlemen in Querétaro also demanded they be included in appraisals, but were unsuccessful. Figueroa Velázquez, *El tiro de gracia*, 164.

[117] Uniones ganaderos, regiones norte, centro, y sur de Veracruz, and Liga de Comunidades Campesinos de Veracruz, to Alemán, December 1946, AGN, MAV, 4255-2-29 B. On "business patriotism" in Nuevo León, see Saragoza, *The Monterrey Elite*, 7.

interests. A letter from Dr. Rafael Sánchez, a rancher from Nautla, cast doubt on the disease and, like Guadalajara's ranchers, asserted the prerogatives of private property. Sánchez claimed that his own long experience with livestock had shown him that most animals recover from aftosa in a few months, as with "typhoid" in humans, and that the disease can be cured with improved fodder. The slaughter policy threatened to return ranchers' pastureland to a state of "wilderness" (*acahuales*) within a few months. Even worse, the "rancheros" of Nautla, Tlapacoyán, and Martínez de la Torre feared that the Agrarian Department would pounce and redistribute their empty pastures to peasants, undermining public morality and production. As Sánchez explained, a good work-ethic existed as "a general rule among small property holders" but was "an exception" among agraristas.[118]

Conflict in the south of Veracruz was further aggravated by accidents of geography and timing. The CMAEFA avoided large-scale slaughter in the most populous central region of Veracruz, but decided that herds in the south around Coatzacoalcos needed to be culled. The area's proximity to the southern border of aftosa infection, and international shipping in and out of Coatzacoalcos, made the region a strategic buffer. Throughout 1948, the CMAEFA labored to shift the southern quarantine line north and west from the Tonalá river (the border with the state of Tabasco) to the trans-isthmus railway line between Salina Cruz and Coatzacoalcos (see Figure 3.4). The area's US supervisor, Frank Mulhern, deemed the railway a far more enforceable and secure barrier and argued that the CMAEFA "must push this disease back over the ... railroad, or it will push us into Guatemala."[119] This required slaughtering cattle herds in the broad, hot, sparsely populated, marshy, and malarial lands west of the Tonalá, with few reliable maps and many small settlements accessible only by boats and canoes. These problem meshed with entrenched opposition from the area's organized cattle ranchers, based in Minatitlán, who shared the complaints of ranchers across the state, along with some particular grievances. They demanded to know why their herds should be slaughtered despite the government's well-known shift towards vaccination, wanted to participate in appraisal procedures, and denounced the CMAEFA's efforts to reduce the indemnity prices previously paid elsewhere. (In the neighboring state of Tabasco the CMAEFA had

---

[118] Dr. Rafael Sánchez, Coatepec, Veracruz, to Alemán, June 25, 1947, AGN, MAV, 4255-2-29 B.

[119] USDA, *Campaign*, 169.

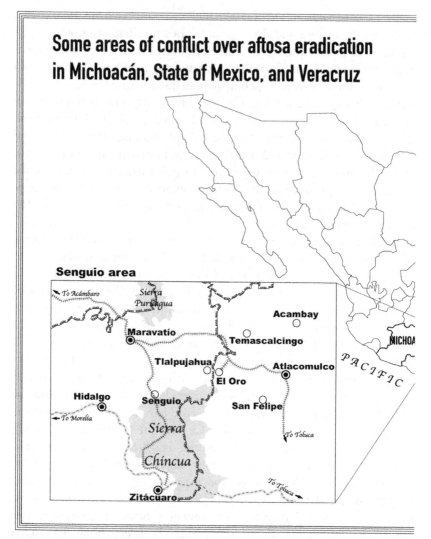

FIGURE 3.4. Some areas of conflict over aftosa eradication in Michoacán, State of Mexico, and Veracruz.

recently paid "four times what the cattle are worth" to tackle isolated outbreaks.)[120] One leading cattleman, Eulalio Vela, also had a lingering feud with state officials who had cut him out of provisioning contracts for

---

[120] Noyes, Mexico City, to Dr. Enoch, Coatzacoalcos, January 7, 1948, CMAEFA, operations, box 30, Veracruz.

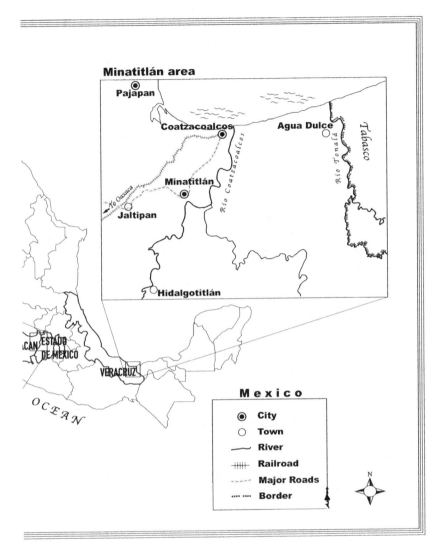

FIGURE 3.4. (cont.)

Coatzacoalcos due to what Vela believed were "personal interests."[121] Others may well have stocked up on cattle on the cheap in expectation of making a literal and figurative killing. Several groups of twenty to thirty

[121] Donato Vidal and Eulalio Vela, Coatzacoalcos, Veracruz, to Alemán, September 6, 1947, AGN, MAV, 4255-2-29 B.

armed men were spotted crisscrossing southern Veracruz on horseback, buying and stealing cattle to take to the slaughter pits.[122]

The men belonging to southern Veracruz's livestock association lobbied and withdrew cooperation, but were not averse to threats of violence. In January 1948, they published an open letter that was quite explicit: "Our patience has a limit and do not blame us if tomorrow there may be acts of violence against those who do not consider our bitter situation."[123] In February, the livestock association put up "very well organized resistance." A public meeting with CMAEFA officials dissolved when ranchers threatened to kill anyone who tried to slaughter their cattle. At another meeting, US officials believed that "it got so bad we were lucky to get out alive."[124] A few days later, the livestock association organized "patrols" to intercept any peasants heading to slaughter pits and turn them back; the same patrols, all "armed," then loitered at the slaughter "trenches" and "stated that if they did not receive the price" demanded by their livestock association "they would put the appraisal crew in the *fosas* with the cattle."[125] Opposition was so coordinated that US officials suspected, and "certain leads" confirmed, that ranchers had their own radio receivers and were "listening in" to commission channels.[126]

Indeed, threats may have translated into action. John López had started work in the CMAEFA as a livestock inspector, but soon gained renown as an effective field worker. Indeed, López seemed to embody the kind of inter-cultural know-how and acumen the commission craved. Born in Guerrero, Tamaulipas in 1898, López later moved to San Antonio, acquired US citizenship, and earned a doctorate in "languages and economics." He could speak Spanish and English, and some French, Italian, and German, and briefly taught police ethics and criminal psychology in the San Antonio police department. In the late 1930s, he

---

[122] Mulhern, Minatitlán, Veracruz, to Noyes, Mexico City, June 25, 1947, CMAEFA, operations, box 30, Veracruz.

[123] Transcription of letter from Unión Ganadera Regional del Sur de Veracruz, in *La Opinión*, February 4, 1948, CMAEFA, operations, box 30, Veracruz.

[124] Shahan, Mexico City, to Simms, BAI, February 17, 1948, CMAEFA, operations, box 30, Veracruz.

[125] Shahan, Mexico City, to Simms, BAI, February 17, 1948, CMAEFA, operations, box 30, Veracruz; Resumé of Conversation with Coatzacoalcos, Shigley, Mexico City, February 23, 1948, CMAEFA, operations, box 30, Veracruz.

[126] Mulhern, Coatzacoalcos, to Noyes, Mexico City, March 30, 1948, CMAEFA, operations, box 30, phone log.

reportedly worked as a priest and as a labor organizer in Texas, before falling out with the famous radical, Emma Tenayuca. López moved to Mexico again during the Second World War, translated for the US railway mission in Mexico, and worked for the US embassy information service "helping establish film libraries in departments of the Mexican government."[127] On 26 March 1948, López was traveling in a canoe along the Coachapa river, one of the eastern tributaries of the Coatzacoalcos river. At a bend in the river known locally as "the witch's cornfield" three men ambushed him and shot him dead. Commission operations immediately ceased, the US section flew its twenty-five strong contingent out of the area, and investigators were dispatched to solve the crime. These included local police, federal spies from the *Dirección Federal de Seguridad* (DFS), and the CMAEFA's own investigation team, led by Colonel Raúl Mendiolea Cerecero – a former police chief from Chihuahua City with a penchant for torture who would be Oscar Flores's right-hand man for decades.[128] After subjecting the three ambushers to "subtle questioning" in Minatitlán's jail, Mendiolea concluded that the men had acted on their own and more or less at random.[129]

Although Mendiolea's US counterpart signed off on the report, other US officials were understandably dubious. The accused men's account of their motives was hardly compelling. They claimed that because they had been drinking heavily – a common excuse used to cover political crimes – they had shot impulsively and "without aiming" and for no particular reason. They vigorously disclaimed any ties with anyone or anything of any political significance: they were mere "*indios*, do not own cattle or lands, and they do not have relations with any cattlemen or persons who sustain any ideology."[130] Juan Gil Preciado of the Mexican Section applied further unconvincing gloss to the official investigation, underlining the accused men's ardent support for the CMAEFA: "Even though

---

[127] This biography is taken from: USDA, *Campaign*, 133–4: Reed, Audit Section, to Gottfried, Assistant Co-Director, Mexico City, April 7, 1948, and "Tina," Mexico City, to Shahan, Co-Director, April 9, 1948, both in CMAEFA, reports, box 2, "Personnel – death of Juan López." López's full name was recorded as John Hernández López, but files indicate that he used his matronym.

[128] On Mendiolea's ties with Flores and, by the 1960s, the drug trade, see AGN, versión pública: Raúl Mendiolea Cerecero.

[129] Mendiolea, Minatitlán, Veracruz, to Gottfried, Assistant Co-director, Mexico City, April 3, 1947, CMAEFA, reports, box 2, "Personnel – death of Juan López."

[130] Ibid. Claims of drunkenness were often used to cover up political murders in the Mexican countryside. Piccato, *Historia mínima*, chapter 2.

they do not own any livestock ... they are of the opinion that the campaign carried out by the commission is a good one, because it is trying to do away with a disease that is killing all the livestock."[131] Reports from López's friend and supervisor, Mulhern, federal spies, and the state judiciary told a different story: large herds of cattle were grazed around Hidalgotitlán near where López had been shot, and their owners, along with the town's municipal president, opposed slaughter; López himself had been aware of one "agitator" in particular, Manuel Sastre Primo, with whom he had argued in the weeks before his murder, and whose uncle and sponsor was a leading cattleman in Hidalgotitlán.[132] The federal spy sent to the scene also believed the murder was part of widespread local opposition, coordinated by "an agitator" that "had been stirring up the cattle owners of the region." Mendiolea was well aware of this version of events: the spy bumped into Mendiolea at a restaurant in Minatitlán and showed him his draft report.[133] The state judiciary and police pursued a similar line. The local judge pointed out inconsistencies in the accused men's stories, and concluded that "some owners and proprietors of these animals were the intellectual authors of this crime and that the accused were paid to commit the crime not telling the names of the persons who are shielding them." Two ranchers in particular caught the attention of state authorities: Lino Colmenares and Tomás Huervo. The latter was known to moonlight as a "professional killer" and had been seen in Minatitlán on the day of murder.[134]

López's murder is revealing of the political dynamics of the campaign in Veracruz, but was unusual. Only one other US citizen was deliberately killed carrying out the campaign; moreover, ambushes and shootings by individuals and small gangs were relatively rare. When other tactics failed, and violence was deployed against the CMAEFA, it was most likely wielded by a crowd of rioters, using pushes, shoves, fists, sticks, stones, knives, and guns to repel or attack commission brigades. The campaign triggered at least forty-one such episodes, an average of about

[131] "Radio Message Received from Prof. Juan Gil Preciado, From Coatzacoalcos, 1 April at 5:00 pm," CMAEFA, reports, box 2, "Personnel – death of Juan López."

[132] Mulhern, Mexico City, to Shahan, April 5, 1948, CMAEFA, reports, box 2, "Personnel – death of Juan López."

[133] Gottfried, assistant director, to Shahan, March 29, 1948, CMAEFA, reports, box 2, "Personnel – death of Juan López."

[134] Investigator 17, Resumé of criminal case 74/948, May 30, 1949; and Mulhern, Mexico City, to Shahan, April 5, 1948, both in CMAEFA, reports, box 2, "Personnel – death of Juan López."

one every six weeks between January 1947 and August 1952. In reality, riots mirrored the general chronology of opposition; roughly half (twenty) clustered in 1947. Riots account for well over half the total number of violent incidents culled from the sources, outnumbering the thirty-four incidents of isolated brawls, knife-fights, and shootings.[135] Field reports hint at other would-be riots that were narrowly avoided, simply because officials heeded warnings about the "attitude of the people" and stayed away.[136] Alongside Senguio, a handful of riots resembled lynchings – that is, crowds used highly visible, collective violence to severely wound or kill officials. In San Pedro el Alto, a Mazahua village near the town of Temascalcingo in the State of Mexico (see Figure 3.4), a crowd chased the US livestock inspector Robert Proctor from the village, stoned and stabbed him hundreds of times, and hurriedly buried his body in the hills.[137] However, most riots stopped well short of maiming, let alone killing officials. Indeed, participants and officials alike often expected such actions to serve as one step in a larger process of "collective bargaining by riot."[138] As the inhabitants of the small village of Amayuca, Morelos wrote to Alemán, they chased the CMAEFA out of town because they believed the brigade should "not come to bother them"; they were not engaged in a "rebellion against the government," but a local "defense of our interests."[139]

A few riots happened in larger towns and cities. Typically several hundred people converged on aftosa brigades in the street, and forced them to retreat. At other times, as in Minatitlán, Veracruz or in the city of Ameca, Jalisco, a crowd barged into a public meeting, shouted down the speakers, and terminated the meeting. La Piedad was a city of some 13,000 inhabitants, a pig-farming center, and sat on a major route shipping livestock into the Bajío. As it chafed under quarantine, a crowd of several hundred confronted General Miguel Z. Martínez, shouted insults and threats, and according to locals, forced him to leave.

---

[135] Author's calculation based on data presented in Figure 3.1.
[136] Report Villa Victoria, Smith, Toluca, to Shahan, August 16, 1947, CMAEFA, operations, box 29, Mexico.
[137] Various reports, February 1949, DFS to Gobernación, AGN, DFS, versión pública: Robert Proctor.
[138] Hobsbawm, "The Machine Breakers," 59. Gema Kloppe Santamaría finds that, while collective lynchings of federal officials declined in the later 1940s, lynching was still widely regarded as a broadly legitimate response to crime and judicial disfunction. Kloppe-Santamaria, *Vortex*, 27.
[139] Amayuca, Morelos, to Alemán, May 29, 1949, AGN, MAV, 4255-2-16.

This dramatic incident passed into local lore, and people celebrated the humiliation of this famously hard-line general, or used it to warn the government of the dangers of ignoring popular demands. One corrido wryly noted the general's reluctance to push the campaign through La Piedad and into the highlands of Jalisco:

> On the soil of the Bajío
> General Martínez says
> We will not move on into Jalisco
> Because it is very cold country.[140]

A complaint sent by townspeople was more explicit: "Remember what was about to happen to General Z. Martínez at La Piedad, for which reasons he has not returned there since? Well if you do remember, assimilate it!"[141]

Most riots happened in villages and pueblos of less than 2,000 people and involved, if not the entire community, a large part of it. As such, these riots resembled the traditional *tumultos* which had long formed a part of communities' repertoires of collective action in central Mexico: localized, defensive, and intended to ward off illegitimate incursions from outsiders.[142] It is unsurprising that such riots took place in relatively small, rural places. Livestock was not necessarily especially numerous, but it was integral: a crucial source of meat, milk and, not least, draft power. Villages were still lightly administered and, along with the consciously anonymous action of the crowd, this made it difficult for the authorities to find individual culprits. As had been the case in the past, riots forced local officials into a tricky political balancing act. Some, like the municipal president of Senguio, counseled against violence, but politically (and sometimes literally) their kept heads down. Others were complicit or, like the aldermen of San Andrés Totimehuacán, Puebla or the local authorities of San Pedro el Alto, helped organize the rioting.[143] Some just conveniently vanished. Once opposition to slaughter grew in Ameca, Jalisco, the municipal president – who owned a large herd of cattle

---

[140] Meyer, *Sinarquismo*, 238.
[141] c. August 1947 plan in CMAEFA, operations, box 29, Michoacán.
[142] Taylor, *Drinking*, 113–51.
[143] Soto Correa, *El rifle*, 129; Ortiz Garza, Agricultura, to Alemán, c. July 1949, AGN, MAV, 425.5/2-20; memo, February 4, 1947, AGN, DFS, versión pública: Robert Proctor.

himself – abruptly left town claiming he needed to visit his sick brother in a neighboring state.[144]

Also long-established was the prominent role played by women. In several places, authorities identified women as ringleaders: Allende, Veracruz; Huaracha and Senguio, Michoacán; San Diego de la Unión, Guanajuato; Puente de Ixtla, Morelos.[145] Whereas the world of elections and formal politics were still associated with men and masculinity, women's participation in such informal mobilizations – and particularly those demanding protection from external harm – enjoyed more public acceptance.[146] It may be that women were seen as offering some additional protection from official reprisals. The commission urged Allende's municipal president to arrest the local woman who led protests, but he refused. Soldiers sent to San Pedro el Alto reported that they had not fired on the rioting crowd because it contained many women, although they also noted that many of the same women "were carrying rifles."[147] When the community of Oxtotitlán mobilized to oppose the sanitary rifle, the men openly carried machetes and the women "carried hidden pistols, so as not to appear malicious (*dar a maliciar*)."[148] Still, gender offered no guarantee of protection. When General Alejo González visited Puente de Ixtla, Morelos, a crowd gathered and one woman taunted him relentlessly, declaring that the pueblo "won't sit here and be shouted at by some *generalito* son of a bitch." The following day General González returned with a vaccination brigade and "they say he almost beat her to death."[149]

Beyond these rough patterns, it is difficult to identify other structural or historical reasons why some towns and villages rioted and others did not. Ethnicity is not a particularly good guide. In some places, riots correlated with pueblos with large numbers of indigenous-language speakers and which generally considered themselves indigenous. This was especially clear in the case of the Otomí- and Mazahua-speaking

[144] US officials were perplexed: "While he is not resisting, there is the possibility that it is passive resistance." Mackery, Guadalajara, to Omohundro, Mexico City, December 9, 1948, CMAEFA, operations, box 29, Jalisco, phone log. For similar cases, see Gipson, *Cow Killers*, 7–9.

[145] Connelly, Coatzacoalcos, to Shahan, October 10, 1947, CMAEFA, operations, box 30, Veracruz; Torres, *Anecdotario* 115; confidential weekly report covering July 25–31, August 7, 1948, CMAEFA, reports, box 1; Pavia, *Recuerdos*, 88.

[146] Taylor, *Drinking*, 116; Joseph, "Rethinking," 149–50; Smith, "Paradoxes."

[147] USDA, *Campaign*, 225.

[148] Bruno Arez Mirando, in Guzmán, *Oxtotitlán*, 176. For similar dynamics in protests over poppy eradication, see Morris, "Serrano Communities."

[149] Pavia Guzmán, *Recuerdos*, 88.

regions where the mountainous southern parts of Querétaro met with the northwest of the State of Mexico. Three of Querétaro's four anti-CMAEFA riots took place in indigenous villages. In the State of Mexico, it was two from a total of four. Field reports sometimes threw around ethnic and racial categories with very little consistency, and have to be treated carefully. However, in this region, they consistently described the strongest opposition stemming from the Otomí- and Mazahua-speaking villages that orbited the larger *cabeceras*. In January 1949, the CMAEFA offered a rough tally: twenty-eight villages around Temascalcingo supported vaccination while nine opposed it, and those "most strongly opposed were Indians who spoke the Mazahua dialect."[150]

And yet, alongside these cases we must also place the twenty-five others (60 percent of the total) where riots took place in communities which were either not conspicuously indigenous or (like the Bajío towns of La Piedad and San Diego de la Unión, or Senguio itself) were consciously mestizo. In Morelos vaccinators noticed that riots took place in some of the most "integrated" and least "Indian" villages in the state.[151] Available sources may underestimate the correlation of riots with indigeneity. Commission and federal officials generally spent less time in isolated indigenous villages, and perhaps missed incidents or deemed them unworthy of attention. Some reports and memoirs gesture vaguely towards opposition in indigenous villages but do not provide enough detail for us to convert these reports into episodes we can tally. Still, while in some regions the pattern of riots was skewed markedly by ethnicity, the overall pattern shows that the tactic of strength-in-numbers enjoyed broad, multi-ethnic appeal.

Ethnicity per se was less important than traditions of conflict with the postrevolutionary state over land, religion, and federal authority in general. In Oaxaca, the most serious communal riot took place more or less where an ethnohistorian might predict: in the heart of the Mixteca Baja at Cacaloxtepec, a region that shared Oaxaca's general traditions of ethnic autonomy, but was distinguished by its conservative resistance to post-revolutionary land reform and secular education. Even by Mixteca Baja standards, Cacaloxtepec was a particularly volatile place. Its peasant farmers held land in an agricultural society, but in 1937 they lost lands to a small group of upstart agraristas, with the connivance of landlords.[152]

---

[150] Report from Leopoldo Telles Cardos, transcribed in USDA, *Campaign*, 223–4.
[151] Pavia Guzmán, *Recuerdos*, 86. The crowd at Senguio included some members of the nearby Otomí ejido of Tupátaro. Soto Correa, *El rifle*, 184.
[152] Smith, *Roots*, 228–9; Benjamin Smith, personal communication, Feb. 2019.

In 1949, the CMAEFA brigades managed to enter the town but trouble started when a solider tried to prevent a goatherder from leaving the plaza with his flock of 125 goats and thirteen cows. The man responded with a blunt declaration of local autonomy: "The people of Cacalostepec [*sic*] are the ones who give orders, and not the Government." A riot then followed a familiar pattern; a crowd gathered at the sound of church bells and the "rolling of a drum"; the crowd beat and disarmed the brigade; an army corporal, a vaccinator, and a nineteen-year-old boy were killed, and the rest of the brigade barricaded themselves into the municipal jail for a day until released by the federal army.[153]

Similarly, it does not seem surprising that Senguio emerged as a flashpoint. The municipality and its surrounding area had long been a conflictive place. By the late 1930s, the municipality's agraristas were ascendant and saw themselves as a vanguard for the whole state. All but one of Senguio's ejidos was granted during the Cárdenas sexenio, and only one hacienda remained untouched by reform. Agraristas – particularly one group of radicals at the ejido Manzana de Guadalupe – were frustrated by the state and federal authorities' turn rightward, and their protection of the region's remaining hacendado. In 1941, after a series of agrarian petitions were rejected, the federal government sent soldiers to occupy the village. In 1945, the town was also known as a base of support for General Miguel Henríquez Guzmán, a cardenista and briefly Alemán's rival for the PRI's presidential nomination.[154] When the aftosa campaign began, local agraristas saw it as one more attack on ejidos, "a farce intended to bury the project of cardenismo."[155] Simultaneously, the municipality was a base for Catholic opposition. During the first and second Cristiada, Catholic rebels found refuge in the surrounding sierra, enjoyed support from surrounding villages, and launched audacious attacks on government forces. In the late 1930s, a small gang of *segundero* Cristeros lingered in the hills, occasionally harassing and assassinating agrarista leaders, while the UNS built up a following among both smallholders and ejidatarios, channeling old Catholic grievances and a more general discontent with the postrevolutionary state. In 1942, hundreds of women from Senguio signed a letter

---

[153] Narrative from USDA, *Campaign*, 243. For a corroborating account from a vaccinating team who were working on the outskirts of the town when the riot began, see Torres y Elzaurdia, *Botas de hule*, 140–4.

[154] Soto Correa, *El rifle*, 35.

[155] Pérez Escutia and Ramón Alonso, quoted in Soto Correa, *El rifle*, 97.

pledging to resist wartime conscription, arguing that it was a tyrannical and godless imposition; among the signatories was Teodora Medina de Guijosa, one of the ringleaders of the 1947 massacre.[156] As the supply of available land dried up, ejidatarios also clashed among themselves.[157] Still, while unrest in Senguio looks preordained in hindsight, local particularities resist easy generalization. Cheek-by-jowl development of agrarista and Catholic forces – and the resulting pointillist political geography – was hardly unknown elsewhere in the state of Michoacán or in other regions of central Mexico.[158] Conversely, we can also point to riots in places which lacked conspicuous form for either agrarian or religious conflict, like the small hamlet of El Chayote, in Aguascalientes. Pre-existing grievances and repertoires surely helped in the organization of resistance, but the aftosa campaign was big and disruptive; protest did not always need to ride on the coat-tails of earlier conflict. In Senguio too, the aftosa campaign had a notable independent effect. While the government and national press blamed the lynching on right-wing sinarquistas, in reality the aftosa campaign fostered a temporary mending of political fences among competing factions of agaristas and sinarquistas; in parts of Querétaro too it had a similar effect.[159]

As important as structural and historical factors was the conjunctural force of the campaign itself as it wended its way across the coasts and central plateau – in particular, the forewarning it gave to some places. The aftosa virus generally spread by following people and goods along main roads and railway lines. Quarantine and slaughter operations thus tended to target towns along these arteries, before spreading out into the surrounding countryside. (Vaccination operations had a different objective and spatial organization, blanketing vast strips of land from north to south in repeated waves.) Those towns and villages that were close enough to these travel hubs to lie in the path of aftosa, but too isolated to serve as bases of slaughter operations, usually had time to prepare for the arrival of the brigades. The brigades tried their best to blend in. After a few months Shahan told commission engineers to remove remaining "United States army markings" from vehicles and paint them in olive drab, which he believed was "a color less distinctive and noticeable to the

---

[156] "325 Madres de Familia," Senguio, Michoacán, to Manuel Ávila Camacho, December 14, 1942, AGN, MAC, 545.2/14-26.

[157] Pérez Escutia, *Senguio*, 77.   [158] Knight, "Popular Culture," 438.

[159] Pérez Escutia, *Senguio*; Soto Correa, *El rifle*, 129–30, 171; Figueroa Velázquez, *El tiro de gracia*, 92, n53.

general public."[160] Still, the campaign's reliance on heavy trucks, diggers, and people carriers, combined with the paucity of reliable roads, made such gestures rather futile. In any case, as in Senguio, the CMAEFA sent officials ahead to gauge infection, meet with local officials, and (quite literally) lay the groundwork for slaughter operations. While the press and fictionalized accounts tended to portray riots as hurried, confused events – with people rushing out of their houses "like ants when you take off the stone from an anthill" – few riots against the sanitary rifle were entirely spontaneous, and several were reported to have been planned weeks in advance.[161] Indeed, it was this which allowed hundreds of people from surrounding settlements to congregate in one place. Officials struggled to determine if piles of boulders blocking roads, or ambushes laid for them *en route* to operations were the work of isolated gangs or the result of widespread collusion, but often concluded the latter. After all, the "huge rocks" blocking roads around Atenango del Río, Guerrero weighed up to half a ton each. In one case in the Huasteca Hidalguense, community support was fairly clear, as the villagers of Tianguistengo appeared on a ridge and stoned the commission brigade on their way up a narrow path, causing one mule driver to tumble over a cliff to his death.[162] In any case, roadblocks and ambushes clearly reflected foreknowledge of CMAEFA movements. Thus, while old rioting repertoires were visible, the peculiarities of the aftosa campaign tweaked how they organized. During slaughter operations, one method communities traditionally used to raise the alarm about unwanted interlopers – ringing the church bells – was often unnecessary. (At San Pedro el Alto, someone did ring the church bells, but this was simply a signal for crowds of people to emerge from the behind the houses, doorways, schoolhouse, and a "line of maguey plants" behind which they had lain in wait.)[163]

Over time, riots probably created a political momentum of their own. News of the events at Senguio reached remote villages in the highlands of Guerrero in a matter of days. Decades later, villagers around Temascalcingo denied ever having heard of the Senguio affair, but this

[160] USDA, *Campaign*, 90.
[161] Rubín, *Ese rifle*, 12; Soto Correa, *El rifle*, 123–4, 133. On "hybrid" riots- communal, localized, but planned – see Fallaw, *Religion*, 131.
[162] Sánchez Gavito report, August 1947, quoted in USDA, *Campaign*, 70; Torres, *Anecdotario*, 217.
[163] Mendiolea report, reproduced in USDA, *Campaign*, 224. The DFS reported a similar chain of events, arguing that the lynching had been "carefully planned beforehand." Memo, February 3, 1947, AGN, DFS, versión pública: Robert Proctor.

is hard to believe; Senguio was only sixty kilometers away, and refugees from post-massacre repression moved through the whole area (see Figure 3.4).[164] Campaign officials were certain that Senguio would inspire imitators. Two weeks later, they gathered a dispiriting list of violent incidents representing probable fall-out from the explosion of protest at Senguio, and worried that the people of Senguio had become "popular martyrs."[165] Federal spies even detained three people accused of distributing subversive corridos about the Senguio massacre. One was printed on paper, and urged people to remember that "our enemy is the nation closest to us." Another was typed on the back of a pack of Alas cigarettes, and warned Alemán that he could easily have suffered the same fate as Dr. Juárez Medina and his escort.[166]

Still, Senguio's effects are tricky to gauge. Given the repression subsequently visited on the village by the army, the stories about Senguio might have acted as a warning as much as an inspiration. Moreover, there are risks in imposing a spurious unity on the dynamics of opposition. Senguio did not detonate the bomb of popular protest on its own; the campaign lit fuses and was undermined by serious detonations elsewhere, some of which had little to do with Senguio. A careful look at the chronology of federal policy and opposition bears this out. In the first half of November, while the Mexican government was finally weighing up whether and how to halt the slaughter, the campaign had long since restarted in Michoacán. Rather, it was in the wealthy heartlands of Jalisco around Guadalajara that it had reached an impasse; this had little to do with the protests of campesinos in eastern Michoacán or elsewhere, and everything to do with the well-organized and rather effective resistance mounted by Guadalajara's large ranchers and dairymen.

The other place where the campaign ground to a halt entirely in September and October was Guerrero (Figure 3.5), scene of the most serious attempt to kick-start a larger rebellion. If the past weighed unevenly on the organization of riots, it was a lot more obvious with plans for rebellion. Guerrero lived up to its reputation as a place resistant to federal authority and punched well above its weight in opposition compared with other states experiencing similar levels of slaughter. More important, the rebels consciously built on old Zapatista networks.

[164] Quintana Rodríguez, *¡Ellos fueron!* 174.
[165] Xavier Sánchez Gavito, "Miscellaneous information," c. September 15, 1947, CMAEFA, administrative correspondence, box 5, "Reports, information."
[166] Case file 143/1947, CCJM, 244, 157–8.

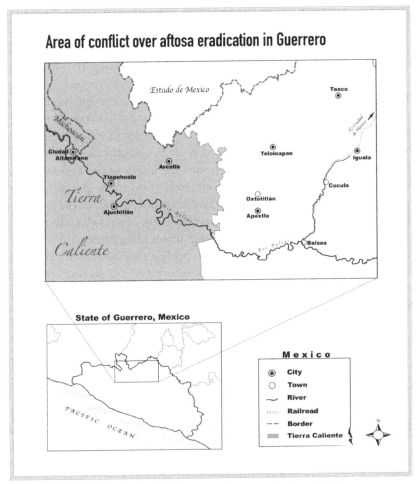

FIGURE 3.5. Area of conflict over aftosa eradication in Guerrero.

According to Mexican agents, plans began at a June meeting in Tenextepango, Morelos, and the main leaders were sinarquista cadres including ex-Zapatista officers General Isaac Marín Parra and Colonel Amelio Robles.[167] Beside halting slaughter, the larger strategy was to

---

[167] Memorandum, Col. Iñurreta, September 24, 1947; and Lecuona, Morelos, to Iñurreta, October 18, 1947, in AGN, versión pública: Amelia Robles. The press also reported that the "improvised General" Cleotilde Herrera was involved, along with a schoolteacher named Urbano Lavín. Soto Correa, *El rifle*, 208.

capitalize on popular anger and "remove Alemán from power."[168] The first objective enjoyed broad support across Guerrero's north, and particularly in the town of Oxtotitlán. Locals formed teams to spy on commission movements from the hills, communicating by blowing a goat's horn or by sending messages with children on donkeys. Hundreds armed themselves to confront brigades, and one blacksmith even forged a crude iron canon.[169] The area's notable livestock-farming families played a leading role; it was they who coordinated opposition, provided material support, and used their ties to friends, families, and business partners to extend support into the towns of the *tierra caliente* and even beyond. According to one testimony from Oxtotitlán, the town's famous dairymen forged agreements with the ranchers in neighboring states to collapse road bridges in the event of a rebellion to prevent the arrival of federal troops. The brother of a leading cattleman, regarded as a "learned man," gathered people to explain that the sanitary rifle was a needless Yankee imposition.[170] On September 23, around 250 men ambushed a passenger train at a junction on the River Balsas. They planned to ride the train as far as the nearby city of Iguala, meet up with around 300 reinforcements from the surrounding hills, and overrun the garrison before moving on to Taxco.[171]

The Balsas attack quickly dissipated, in part due to rapid military deployments and intelligence. While traveling through the state, the commission officials heard that "there is a gang waiting for us at Iguala" and flew back to Mexico City in an army plane from Teloloapan; another brigade, stranded in the sierra near El Cubo, diverted course to Arcelia to wait for another airlift which never arrived, before driving back to Mexico City with a military escort.[172] The rebels on the train clashed with around twenty soldiers and reserve militia at Cocula and retreated

---

[168] Lecuona, Yautepec, to Iñurreta, October 13, 1947, AGN, versión pública: Amelia Robles.

[169] Guzmán, *Oxtotitlán*, 67–8. Most accounts estimate that around 500–1,500 people mobilized to take part in a rebellion in mid-September. Report on Balsas Incident, October 1947, CMAEFA, administrative correspondence, box 5, information reports. One man later claimed as many as 50,000 people gathered in the hills to rebel, which seems unlikely, given the rebellion's denouement. Guzmán, *Oxtotitlán*, 164.

[170] Ibid., 67–8, 124, 113.

[171] Unsigned report to Gottfried, September 26, 1947, CMAEFA, operations, box 29, Michoacán.

[172] Resumé of telephone call from Dr. Digranes, Teloloapan, Guerrero, September 23, 1947; J. W. Amsiejus, "Report Regarding Arrival and Departure From Arcelia," September 27, 1947, all in CMAEFA, operations, box 29, Guerrero.

into the sierra, and the reinforcements at Iguala did not materialize. The road bridges did not fall and the federal government quickly dispatched "eleven truckloads of soldiers" to the area.[173] Plans for a rebellion spluttered on into October 1947, but came to naught. The leaders of the Balsas attack, including Robles, went to Morelos to try to join up with the followers of dissident peasant leader Rubén Jaramillo, and raise support among other ex-Zapatista leaders. They also sent people to the mountains in San Luis Potosí, hoping to build a larger uprising.[174] At this point, Zapatista networks and local knowledge proved a mixed blessing. Many Zapatista veterans were getting old and, in any case, many had been absorbed into the federal government and army. Jojutla's General Alarcón was so frail that he was unable to leave his house, but he considered Alemán a *hijo de tal cual* and promised that the men in his region would fight against the sanitary rifle once the harvest season was over.[175] When Amelio Robles asked Laureano Estrada – whom Robles considered a *revolucionario de los buenos* – to support the rebellion, Estrada temporized and secretly informed General Rodolfo López de Nava, another former Zapatista who was military zone commander in Tlaxcala. General López then passed the information directly to the DFS, which dispatched federal forces to protect Estrada and arrest Robles. Perhaps embarrassed at having been threatened by Colonel Robles (whose transgender identity was well known within the army), Estrada urged the government not to underestimate the task of entering Robles' home village of Xochipala: "We should send at least one hundred men since the village is made up of various stone walls (*corrales*) in a very high location, and its four sides cover a great extension of land."[176] Despite such advantages, federal forces captured Robles in the following days, after which leaders in Morelos backed away from the rebellion. By the end of October, according to DFS informants, any enthusiasm for piecing together a rebellion from this patchwork of ex-Zapatista villages was fading. Significant "agitation" against the campaign continued, but was

[173] Unsigned report to Gottfried, September 26, 1947; résumé of telephone call from Dr. Digranes, Teloloapan, Guerrero, September 23, 1947, in CMAEFA, operations, box 29, Guerrero.

[174] Memorandum, Col. Iñurreta, September 24, 1947, AGN, versión pública: Amelia Robles.

[175] Lecuona, Morelos, to Iñurreta, October 18, 1947, in AGN, versión pública: Amelia Robles.

[176] Aurelio Martínez, Agent 18, to Iñurreta, October 23, 1947, AGN, versión pública: Amelia Robles. On Robles, see Cano, "Unconcealable Realities."

being done "in a passive way by the owners of large quantities of livestock."[177]

Military commanders also drew the rebellion's sting by conciliating the rebels, taking advantage of the local, defensive aims of most of the people involved. In one version of the story, the day before veterinarians were due to arrive in Oxtotitlán, a mysterious bearded man on horseback appeared on the outskirts of town and confronted the men digging the slaughter pits. One of the diggers recognized that this man was Santiago, the patron saint of Oxtotitlán, and hurried to inform the authorities. Hearing the news, General Adrián Castrejón, the commander at Apaxtla, decided to leave Oxtotitlán in peace – or so the story retold for decades goes. Other versions downplayed the saint's role. According to Emiliano Salgado Miranda, the "other part of miracle" occurred at a tense meeting between General Castrejón and a delegation of men and women from Oxtotitlán which took place before the news of Santiago's intervention. At this meeting, the townspeople warned Castrejón of their determination and challenged his nationalist credentials, asking him "why he even fought in the Revolution." (They also reminded Castrejón of a political debt he owed the people of Oxtotitlán who, during the 1910s, had once protected him from federal forces by smuggling him out of town dressed as a woman.)[178] Castrejón suspended slaughter in the area indefinitely and promised not to impose it against local consent, undercutting support for the rebellion. Both stories confirm the circumscribed objectives of rebels. Once Santiago had done his job as a local saint, so to speak, his devotees had little interest in taking the matter further. Afterwards, Oxtotitlán created an annual festival to thank Santiago and commemorate the community's unified defense of its animals. For the first few years of the fiesta, wealthy cattlemen handed out milk to the poor, cut the rental price for oxen, and donated some of their livestock for a feast; each family received two kilos of meat – one of flesh, the other on-the-bone – to thank the people "for their willingness to defend the town."[179] In this way, "the rich livestock owners of the town paid for the favor they had received."[180]

Opposition to the aftosa campaign rarely left such obvious ritual traces or produced such tangible, fleshy rewards as it did in Oxtotitlán. Nor did

---

[177] Lecuona, Cuernavaca, to Iñurreta, October 25, 1947, AGN, versión pública: Amelia Robles.

[178] Guzmán, *Oxtotitlán*, 131. [179] Bruno Erazo Miranda, in ibid., 177.

[180] Lorenzo Arteaga Román, in ibid., 184.

it usually lead to rebellions. Most people used much less risky tactics of non-cooperation, lobbying, and politicking. When these proved impotent, and circumstances permitted, the tactic of choice was to engage in – localized, defensive – collective bargaining by riot. While riots were crucial, centering the Senguio massacre, as many studies do, produces a simplified, distorted picture of the social bases of opposition and, likely exaggerates the cohesion and power of campesino protest. In the crucial weeks when the Mexican government was deciding how and when to halt slaughter, it was the grinding opposition of commercial ranchers – those large owners of livestock mentioned by agents in Morelos and Guerrero, and so prominent in Jalisco – that was the main obstacle for field officials, and which would continue to undermine slaughter for most of 1948 in southern Veracruz.

It was once commonplace to see the 1940s as a decisive turning point when popular power waned and the state and market waxed. As historians have studied this period more closely in the last two decades, old images of a co-opted and compliant society, putty in the hands of the PRI's corporate system are no longer tenable. While many historians recognize the existence of popular protest, work remains to chart its repertoires, unity, diversity, power, and limitations. Most clearly, opposition to the CMAEFA shows the continued salience of those "serrano" traditions identified by Alan Knight: localized, cross-class movements that aimed to resist intrusive, illegitimate interference from the central government.[181] After two decades of postrevolutionary state-building, and the emergence of new forms of class identity and organizing (both against but, from the 1930s, within state institutions), serrano traditions were still politically alive and, at moments of crisis, kicking. The movements that fit into this "serrano" type could take quite different and even contradictory forms, feeding off varied local traditions and experiences. Older repertoires also proved adaptable to new circumstances. Riots were a time-worn tactic in Mexico's central plateau, but could be adjusted to the particular conditions of the aftosa campaign. Just as important, opponents made use of new or newly-relevant institutions: proliferating organizations of commercial ranchers who lobbied, argued, bullied, issued threats and, likely, organized the occasional murder; and the press, enjoying a window of relative postwar freedom and buoyed by a burgeoning readership, which played a key role in disseminating knowledge

---

[181] Knight, *Mexican Revolution*, vol. 1, 122. For an insightful application of this framework to opium-growers, see Morris, "Serrano."

of the campaign and its critics – both outside and, more subtly, within the government. The interaction of these forces produced a movement that was like a disconcerting cacophony of distinct and sometimes discordant notes, rather than a solid, sustained blast of peasant opposition. And of course, such practices endured because, by and large, they could still deliver results: a major reversal of national policy. The case also reminds us of some of the limitations of serrano-style mobilizations. Protests during Mexico's aftosa crisis had many important effects on state institutions, policies, and science in Mexico, the United States, and even beyond. Defensive, cross-class, fleeting and fragmented, they did not create a durable political coalition or radical changes to property and power.

Excavating the broad and varied nature of opposition also offers a way to rethink assumptions of national and regional difference that tend to dominate accounts of Mexican and Latin American history in general. Whether attempted in Mexico, the United States, or Europe, stamping out aftosa with slaughter was difficult and unpopular. It provoked criticism of government overreach, questions about the balance of short-term costs and long-term benefits and, as the twentieth century went on, more public demands for vaccination. Of course, the campaign in Mexico was weighed down by some unusual and important burdens: unreliable, corrupt, or simply overstretched state institutions; a restive countryside with communities well versed in protest and rebellion; an international arrangement which pumped dollars and materiel into the campaign, but further endangered its legitimacy. Still, while the Mexican context aggravated key problems, the basic structure of public arguments connected Mexico's experience to struggles over rural modernization around the world. When farmers, jailed peasants, or veterinarians pondered the mild clinical symptoms of the virus, questioned whether such a broad swathe of the country should suffer for the benefit of a section of the livestock industry, or argued that vaccination would prove a better long-term strategy, they were not peculiar at all, but making arguments common to struggles to stamp out a particularly contentious and counter-intuitive plague.

4

Soldiers, Syringes, Surveys, and Secrets

Encountering Resistance

The village of San Onofre proved "a hard nut to crack." It lay where the State of Mexico borders Michoacán, a mere thirty kilometers over the sierra from Senguio. Officials were certain that news of the massacre had spread and galvanized opposition in San Onofre, although they had no direct evidence. On October 26, 1947, Louis Smith, co-director of the district in Toluca, reported a fruitless month of negotiations. Veterinarians, commission officials, and state politicians had alternately "called on these people, visited with [*sic*] them, talked to them, argued with them, and threatened them with the military, and as yet have been able to inspect but a few of their cattle." Then, in early November, resistance in the town finally gave way and inspections went ahead, although officials remained unsure quite what had tipped the balance.[1]

The commission had different ways to defuse opposition. Some of these were readily acknowledged, as in Smith's missive above: argument and persuasion, threats and military force. Another tactic was also important but rarely acknowledged, even in internal correspondence, lest it stain the commission's image of technical impartiality: co-opting dissent with targeted material inducements, particularly compensation. The commission had a limited supply of political resources – soldiers, pesos, time, rhetorical ingenuity – and striking an effective balance between these tactics was difficult. Doing so required information and knowledge about local conditions that, at the start of the campaign, most commission

---

[1] Louis Smith, Toluca to Noyes, Mexico City, October 26, 1947, transcribed in USDA, Campaign, 130; various correspondence, October–November 1947, CMAEFA, operations, box 29, Mexico, phone logs.

personnel simply did not have, particularly those from the United States. Even when they eventually succeeded in overcoming opposition, as in San Onofre, commission officials were sometimes none the wiser about why they had.

One simple answer to why the campaign succeeded, recognized by almost all the literature on the topic, is that it wisely changed course and adopted vaccination. This was undoubtedly a necessary condition, but not sufficient. A blend of quarantine, vaccination, intrusive inspection, and targeted slaughter still elicited non-compliance and sometimes violent opposition, and required careful implementation. This chapter digs underneath high-level policy to examine subtler political and cultural processes which ran through the campaign as a whole, bridged the shift to vaccination – and informed it – and on which the campaign's success also rested. It explores how officials viewed Mexico's society and landscape; debated and honed the means of repressing, placating, and persuading opponents; and gathered better information about local societies and topographies, and kept tighter control over it. As such, the chapter aims to deepen our understanding of how and why the campaign succeeded, and illuminate one of the central questions of modern Mexican historiography: how the PRI-state consolidated itself and governed the country for so long.

Military force and surveillance had an important place in the aftosa campaign, and not only in snuffing out rebellions in the old heartlands of Zapatismo. A quota of routine military intimidation and force ran through the whole operation. Troops manned quarantine lines, shot cattle, and provided protection and "police power" for the campaign. "Soldier-watchmen" stood guard over the covered slaughter pits, guarded the quarantine fence built across the Huasteca, and shot dead a handful of men who tried to breach it.[2] The commission's normal response to non-cooperation in a ranch, village, or town was simply to impose a military quarantine, erect roadblocks to prevent livestock movements, and disinfect all passing people and goods – an unpleasant and sometimes humiliating experience which the people of La Piedad likened to a "military siege" which "paralyzed" economic life.[3] In most cases the disruption tilted the ground of negotiations in the CMAEFA's favor and induced compliance. The kind of officers Alemán initially appointed to spearhead

---

[2] USDA, *Campaign*, 114, 196.
[3] Municipal president, La Piedad, Michoacán, July 23 and August 12, 1947, to Alemán, AGN, MAV, 425.5/2-15A.

the campaign in the Bajío were telling and not particularly conciliatory choices. Catholics remembered Generals Miguel Z. Martínez and Eulogio Ortiz for the brutal campaigns they conducted against Cristeros in the 1920s. When Ortiz was accidentally killed in an automobile collision at a CMAEFA checkpoint, Catholics considered it a kind of divine retribution.[4] In Cadereyta, Querétaro, people complained that a local cacique, backed by soldiers, forced them to sell him their cattle at desultory prices. They could not sign the complaint, they explained, or "they would grab and kill us, since they are the authorities, and made even worse with the presence of federal troops."[5]

The military's response to attacks on campaign officials and its own forces was localized but ferocious. Once the garrison at Zitácuaro heard reports of the massacre at Senguio, the battalion descended on the town "in a grim mood," seized weapons, and mounted a machine gun in the church tower. For several hours they rounded up, tortured, hanged, and shot dead several dozen men in public view, leaving bodies "piled against the door of the little church." Soldiers raped some local women in front of their families. One witness claimed he heard two officers discussing Alemán's plans to air-bomb the village. When the zone commander General Cristóbal Guzmán arrived from Morelia, he reined in his soldiers, arrested hundreds of people, dispatched flying columns to comb the surrounding hills for suspects, roped at least thirty-nine locals together around their necks and sent them to the jail at Ciudad Hidalgo. (The military later drove another thirty-two suspects to Ciudad Hidalgo, but they had been so badly beaten and tortured by soldiers and federal intelligence agents that the local judge refused to accept them, and they were returned to the village of Senguio). According to press and commission reports, a crowd of soldiers and *soldaderas* (camp followers) descended on the military jail and demanded that the officer in charge allow them to lynch the men and women from Senguio in their cells, but he refused.[6] Eventually, courts sentenced seven ringleaders to life imprisonment and sent them to the prison colony on the Islas Marías. (Some can be

---

[4] Anonymous note from "The League of Recuperation of Towns Affected by Foot and Mouth Disease," La Piedad, Michoacán, August 7, 1947, CMAEFA, operations, box 29, Michoacán; Taracena, *La vida*, 36–7; Figueroa Velázquez, *El tiro de gracia*, 206. For Ortiz's career, see Fallaw, "Eulogio."

[5] Anonymous letter transcribed in Figueroa Velázquez, *El tiro de gracia*, 150.

[6] USDA, *Campaign*, 83; Soto Correa, *El rifle*, 165, 248, 136–7, 134, 138; Omohundro, report on Senguio incident, September 2, 1947, CMAEFA, operations, box 29, Michoacán.

seen as extras on the 1948 film set on the island, starring Pedro Infante.)[7] Just one week after the massacre, the aftosa campaign restarted in Michoacán state, and General Guzmán urged operations to resume around Senguio "to prove to the people that the program would continue." On September 19, while Dr. Juárez Medina's burned-out jeep still stood in the plaza, another CMAEFA crew returned to Senguio and shot 166 cattle.[8]

The people of Senguio paid a terrible price, but later the Mexican government – or at least elements within it – cushioned the blow of terror with some conciliatory gestures. Cárdenas had served as a military commander in the region in the 1920s, fighting guerrillas in the nearby sierra, and had maintained political ties to Senguio ever since; eight of the municipality's nine ejidos were created during his presidency. There is no evidence that Cárdenas himself organized the attack on the CMAEFA, but locals, like most of the Mexican public, were aware he disapproved of the sanitary rifle. As military forces flooded the region, Cárdenas sent a military aide with instructions to moderate the worst kinds of torture – which included hanging one agrarista by a wire wrapped around his testicles. He also sent a military nurse to tend to the wounded, and his wife Amalia reportedly pushed the state governor to improve prisoners' food. Finally, Cárdenas sent his own advisor and military lawyer to help the accused who, after a year, succeeded in getting all but seven villagers released.[9] Such action earned local gratitude, but not unquestioning obedience. In 1948 and 1949, Cárdenas traveled back to Senguio and the surrounding area to urge people to cooperate with the new vaccination drive. A small group of agraristas, who had avoided capture for their part in the massacre took no heed. For the next eighteen months they took refuge in the nearby mountains, harried local authorities, and denounced "traitorous, sell-out alemanismo" ("*alemanismo vendepatrias*"), aided by a knowledge of Mazahua and Otomí, spoken by villages to the east in the State of Mexico.[10] In February 1949, the municipal president of San Francisco de los Reyes, Tlapujahua complained that this group descended on the village to disrupt the vaccination of livestock.

---

[7] Case file 143/1947, CCJM; Soto Correa, *El rifle*, 8.   [8] USDA, *Campaign*, 85.

[9] Soto Correa, *El rifle*, 164, 188–90. Cárdenas's lawyer and advisor, Manuel Hurtado Juárez, began to challenge the reliability and legality of various testimonies in June 1948. Case file 143/1947, CCJM, 77–90.

[10] Pérez Escutia, *Senguio*, 292; Soto Correa, *El rifle*, 127, 207. Decades later, Simón Mora still lived where he could easily escape detention, "in a strategic part of Cerro Prieto, in San Francisco de los Reyes." Soto Correa, *El rifle*, 8.

Simón Mora and Trinidad Vergara shot a "rear-loading carbine" at the municipal president and tried to barge into his house; they then promised to "fuck over" the barracks commander for "going around obeying orders that should not be obeyed," shot up the windows of his home, and shouted that they "were so manly" they would "grab hold of him as if they were his father."[11]

Over time, Cárdenas's solicitude built a new base of support in Senguio, helped discredit the UNS – who publicly denied any involvement in the massacre – and eventually encouraged villagers to recuperate their reputation. In the early 1950s, Cárdenas began to write to municipal authorities in Senguio once more, offering advice on how to petition for federal money to help with schools and sanitation – a mediating role he would reprise on-and-off until his death in 1969. In 1951, the federal government agreed to expand Senguio's access to water from a nearby reservoir, a long festering local grievance. (Some locals wondered if this act was because Alemán felt guilty about his role in the sanitary rifle, but "no one thanked him.")[12] In the early 1960s, as the federal government made a new effort to displace Cárdenas's influence in the region, he visited Senguio and expressed surprise that the recently released Teodora Medina de Guijosa had been in jail for so long.[13] This remark represented the "signal" the village had been waiting for to openly celebrate what they understood to be their role in the aftosa crisis: overturning a nefarious policy imposed by the United States and Alemán to crush Mexico's campesinos. In 1963, Senguio's municipal president wrote to the state government declaring that the area had "overcome its collective trauma" and would now celebrate the role of its campesinos in making Senguio "the tomb of the sanitary rifle."[14] In 1968, Cárdenas visited once more, opened a new sanitation project funded from the Balsas River Commission, and praised Senguio's historical defense of "the rights of the campesinos" by "strongly opposing the caprices of a foreign power, even at the cost of suffering and of lives."[15] In 1969 the village erected a small monument celebrating the patriotic struggles of "the Mexican woman," which everyone understood referred

---

[11] José Trejo, San Francisco de los Reyes, Tlapujahua, February 23, 1949, AGN, MAV, 425.5/2-15A. The people of Huaracha, Michoacán also claimed Cárdenas supported their protests against vaccination. Torres y Elzaurdia, *Botas de hule*, 115.

[12] Pérez Escutia, *Senguio*, 299.   [13] Ibid., 293.

[14] Ibid., 300. In 1961, Cárdenas played a similar conciliatory role in the Mixteca Baja after an abortive Catholic rebellion. Smith, *The Roots*, 280–93.

[15] Cárdenas, quoted in Pérez Escutia, *Senguio*, 343–4.

to Medina de Guijosa. It was placed in the central plaza, renamed in honor of Cárdenas.[16]

The Mazahua villagers of San Pedro el Alto, State of Mexico, who lynched a vaccination brigade and killed the US livestock inspector Robert Proctor, saw similarly harsh collective reprisals but benefited from no such political connections. The villagers roughed up but spared the lives of three soldiers escorting Proctor. Bizarrely, after Proctor had been chased from the village, a crowd surrounded the soldiers and forced them to sing the national anthem and sign a declaration stating that they had not been mistreated.[17] If this was a ploy to avoid reprisals, it did not work. Soldiers of the seventh infantry battalion descended on the town to search for Proctor's body. They tortured dozens of suspects by beating them and hanging them from trees. Villagers saw soldiers marching "three indigenous men" away from the town, and later in the day "they saw the soldiers amusing themselves, cleaning blood from their bayonets."[18] In a gruesome echo of the aftosa campaign, several military executions made spectacular use of livestock. Don Cecilio Pacheco was suspected of having given lodging to one Luciano Gómez Nieto – a sinarquista leader and would-be local deputy for the conservative Partido Acción Nacional (PAN) who lived in Mexico City, encouraged people to oppose the CMAEFA, and hawked a homemade elixir for aftosa concocted by his wife.[19] Soldiers beat Pacheco senseless, passed a rope around his neck, and a horse dragged his body through the town; "those present could never forget the noise that the bones of Don Cecilio's skull made when they bounced against the stones."[20] Later, soldiers found another elderly man leading a mule, questioned him, stripped him naked, and "beat him until he passed out":

Then they lifted him onto an unbroken mule and, very tightly, tied his feet and arms to the animal. They took away the reins and released the mule; they hit him hard on the haunches, and he bolted with the old man on top. The poor old man started shaking and hit the ledges of the stones in the ravines and trunks of trees.

---

[16] Ibid. In 1997, Senguio celebrated the fiftieth anniversary of the massacre. Speeches recalled the town's role at the vanguard of patriotic campesino struggles for justice and sovereignty, and a new plaque recognized Teodora Medina de Guijosa by name: "the heroine of the events of aftosa." See Soto Correa, *El rifle*, 225.
[17] Declarations of Sargento Hernández Rodríguez, Juan Rodríguez, Juan Arturo Campos, February 1, 1949, AGN, DFS, versión pública: Robert Proctor
[18] Quintana, *¡Ellos fueron!* 169.
[19] Various reports on Gómez Nieto, 1949, in AGN, DFS, versión pública: Robert Proctor.
[20] Quintana, *¡Ellos fueron!* 156.

The captain and his soldiers, amused, watched as the beast was lost among the streams and canyons. The old man lost parts of his body, mutilated in each blow against the edges of the rocks, until they lost sight of him.[21]

After the initial frenzy of reprisals, the military chained the entire village together and marched them to the municipal *cabecera*, Temascalcingo, locked them in the town's gatehouse and theater, and imposed "martial law" on the municipality for a month.[22] Each night, soldiers took a handful of locals outside to beat and torture, and cries of anguish echoed around the streets; by the end of the operation, soldiers may have killed around seventy people.[23]

General Francisco Urbalejo led the operation, and townspeople remembered him explaining the geopolitical and racist rationale for such outright terror quite clearly. The Mazahuas of San Pedro el Alto had foolishly created an embarrassing international incident and, besides, Proctor's life could not be compensated even by "five hundred lives of this dirty rabble."[24] As in Senguio, it was rumored that Urbalejo wanted to bomb San Pedro from the air and resettle the population elsewhere, but another general "from Querétaro" arrived and opposed this strategy.[25] As a local historian notes, such episodes left no archival traces, and exist only in "the minds of the old people of the village."[26] Decades later, villagers told stories of soldiers systematically raping indigenous women and girls from San Pedro and the surrounding area. Asked whether these stories could be confirmed, Don Tomás, who had participated in the lynching, was indignant: "So, it could well be. But the thing is, who do you expect is going to talk about that?"[27]

US section officials were aware of the brutal aftermath of lynchings at Senguio and San Pedro but glossed over them in reports. The US section's report on the aftermath of the riot in Cacaloxtepec, Oaxaca was also distinctly euphemistic. When the federal army retook the town, the colonel in charge did not merely throw a dozen instigators into the municipal jail, as US officials reported. He summarily executed them.[28] Stories about these operations passed through the US section, shocking some field officials. John Hidalgo remembered hearing that the Mexican army would deal with troublemakers "ruthlessly," and "would take the men

---

[21] Ibid., 170.   [22] Ibid., 158.   [23] Ibid., 157; Torres y Elzaurdia, *Botas de hule*, 91.
[24] Quintana, ¡*Ellos fueron!* 158.   [25] Ibid., 185.   [26] Ibid., 159.   [27] Ibid., 185.
[28] USDA, *Campaign*, 242; Torres y Elzaurdia, *Botas de hule*, 144.

that were known as resistors or leaders of the village and they would shoot or hang two or three of them."[29]

Still, the campaign could not and did not rely on military force and terror alone. As we have seen, military officers were unreliable, either due to their corruptibility or skepticism of campaign policy. The lower ranks suffered poor conditions and low morale. In Veracruz, troops deserted after tents and rations failed to arrive. Some soldiers refused orders to shoot cattle; more prosaically, disgruntled and poorly paid soldiers simply opened quarantine lines up in exchange for bribes.[30] In any case, the military remained small and overstretched. Given adequate warning, it could dispatch truckloads of troops to inflict collective punishment or – as in Iguala – extinguish small fires of rebellion. But an army of around 45,000 soldiers could not blanket the rugged tableland and tropical coasts of central Mexico and impose an unpopular policy, in part because it was already embedded in rural policing across the entire country.[31] Where soldiers were made available, the commission often struggled to find the means to transport them away from main roads and railheads. For this reason, some brigades sought ingenious ways to inflate the appearance of soldiering strength. In Xoxocotla, Veracruz a mere thirty-six soldiers were available to "command a great mountain-rimmed bowl." The brigade posted nine soldiers in each mountain pass with orders to "march and countermarch so they could be seen from the valley below." According to the Arizonan livestock inspector Norberto Chamberlain, villagers believed that 300 soldiers had descended on the area and "the effect was astonishing." Whereas previous brigades had only found seventeen animals, now they inspected some 3,000.[32] Still, such ruses could hardly be replicated across the country. In theory Mexico's 60,000 strong militia of *defensas rurales* could more than double the number of available troops, but these forces remained unreliable. In Guanajuato, they helped to police quarantine lines, arrested several bands of livestock smugglers, protected vaccination teams, and even reported suspicious outbreaks of

[29] John Hidalgo interview, *Aftosa International*, 16.
[30] Gillingham, *Unrevolutionary*, 123; Padilla, *Rural Resistance*, 243; Soto Correa, *El rifle*, 81.
[31] Rath, *Myths*, 115–43. Even after the attack at Senguio, soldiers relied on commission jeeps and trucks, since "the local military does not have vehicles to transport their own soldiers." Omohundro, report on Senguio incident, September 2, 1947, CMAEFA, operations, box 29, Michoacán.
[32] USDA, *Campaign*, 276.

animal disease.[33] Elsewhere, they appear only sporadically in archival sources, and mainly as sources of opposition. In Michoacán, the defensas rurales took part in a major riot at Cocucho and helped foment opposition across the district of Uruapan. On Guerrero's *costa grande* the militia was manned by owners of large herds of cattle and were "the ones which actually raise trouble for the vaccination operations."[34]

Moreover, field officials quickly learned that deploying soldiers could be needlessly costly. One of the most persistent dilemmas confronting field workers was whether to take soldiers with them on forays to rural communities. Squads of soldiers offered protection and, sometimes, a certain amount of local know-how. On the other hand, using soldiers for protection often meant waiting for opaque and unreliable military institutions to deliver transport and provisions. Without these, the military commandeered local resources, antagonizing surrounding communities, much as they had in the 1920s and 1930s. In Querétaro, the soldiers and soldaderas stationed on quarantine lines seized forty head of livestock a day to feed themselves.[35] More important, the very sight of soldiers clearly angered some farmers, and officials worried that the presence of soldiers simply ensured that "bullets were more apt to fly."[36] As we have already seen, some communities were emphatic on this point. In June 1947 hundreds of cattlemen from Sahuayo, Michoacán visited the hotel where CMAEFA officials stayed. As many as could fit barged into one bedroom while "the balance stood out in the hall." These men "laid down the law in no uncertain terms: that they would not continue to accept appraisal value they were being given, and they resented deeply the fact that soldiers were present at the appraisals."[37] It was difficult for commission officials to be sure exactly what triggered the riot in the village of Allende, Veracruz but they believed that villagers "don't seem to be so mad at the aftosa crew as they seem to be mad at the soldiers." At least, it was the soldiers at whom the crowd hurled insults,

[33] Various correspondence, AHEG, 3.40 (78), fiebre aftosa, 1947, vol. II; 1948, vol. I; 1950, vol. I.
[34] Report by David Ortiz Martínez, c. September 1949, CMAEFA, general subject files, box 10, "Guerrero c-11."
[35] Figueroa Velázquez, *El tiro de gracia*, 167. On the uneven development of military logistics and the persistence of soldaderas into the 1950s, see Rath, "Modernizing."
[36] Del Villar and del Villar, *Where the Strange Roads*, 100.   [37] USDA, *Campaign*, 47.

threats, and rocks.[38] The commission left the matter of military escorts to the judgment of local Mexican officials but, slowly, there was a drift away from a reliance on military force as opposition slackened and field workers honed other techniques which made them less necessary. Military officers remained crucial in many places, but often more as political mediators rather than simple conduits for force and terror.

Indeed, military officers and government officials sometimes dangled promises of future material assistance to recalcitrant farmers – credit for restocking and breeding, tax breaks, roads, or schools. In Guerrero, General Castrejón promised the federal government would reward cooperation with dozens of breeding bulls to help farmers restock and improve their herds.[39] In response to petitions from local and state authorities, the federal government funneled bracero contracts to areas devastated by the sanitary rifle.[40] The CMAEFA also found that road-building, in certain areas, could help dissolve opposition. Surveying possible quarantine lines between Ameca, Jalisco, and the Pacific coast of Nayarit, the US livestock inspector Lee Gates found "very few" locals interested in a fence, but "all are very interested in the road." Cheap loans of diggers and steam shovels to local politicians to dredge irrigation canals could have a similar effect, although the US section was initially reluctant to accede to requests.[41] Some state governments decided it was still necessary to sweeten the pill of vaccination by handing out iron plows and other modern agricultural tools to cooperative villages.[42] While the

[38] Connelly, Coatzacoalcos, to Shahan, Mexico City, October 10, 1947, CMAEFA, operations, box 30, Veracruz.

[39] Clippings from local Iguala newspaper *Alborada*, November 9, 1947, Guerrero, CMAEFA, administrative correspondence, box 5, "C-270."

[40] For petitions from Guanajuato, see various correspondence, March and June 1947, AGN, MAV, 4255-2-10 B; AHEG, 3.40 (78), fiebre aftosa, 1948, vol. I. The state governor of Michoacán (and probably his counterpart in Guanajuato also) allocated more bracero contracts to districts affected by slaughter, although individual selection remained in the hands of municipal authorities. García Maldonado, "Regulating Bracero Migration." A similar policy existed in Querétaro. Figueroa Velázquez, *El tiro de gracia*, 192. For a literary depiction of a farmer forced by the sanitary rifle to seek a bracero contract, see Rubín, *Ese rifle*, 114.

[41] Lee Gates report from Ixtlán, Nayarit, March 1948, quoted in USDA, *Campaign*, 184; Various correspondence, March–April 1948, CMAEFA, CMAEFA, reports, box 2, "Engineering"; various correspondence, Shahan, Mexico City, to Flores, March 16, 1948, and Shahan memo, April 13, 1947, in CMAEFA, operations, box 29, Guanajuato.

[42] Figueroa Velázquez, *El tiro de gracia*, 228.

commission struggled to harness the military, it also made various, largely successful overtures to the Catholic Church. The Alemán administration clearly benefited from warmer relations with Mexico's archbishop who, in 1949, issued several encyclicals urging cooperation. Mexican officials were well aware that priests remained local powerbrokers in their own right and, as we will see, tried various techniques to engage with them. According to General Corlett, in the summer of 1947 Oscar Flores placated at least one recalcitrant village in the Bajío by handing the local priest 2,000 pesos to "fix up" the church.[43] In the montaña region of Guerrero, state veterinarians ingratiated themselves with Church and villagers alike by driving priests to take services in a commission jeep.[44]

By far, the most important material inducements the commission could use were indemnities for slaughtered animals. Sometimes field officials, weighing local attitudes, topography, and the virulence of the outbreak, opted to carefully nudge up prices. Such adjustments to local conditions could produce results. In a valley near Teotitlán del Camino in Oaxaca, farmers initially rounded up only fifty-two head of cattle for slaughter. Mulhern went ahead with slaughter, but asked the appraisers to inflate prices a little. The following day, the municipal president assured Mulhern that he would now be able to bring down a further 2,000 cattle hidden in the surrounding hills.[45] At other times, trenchant opposition forced the commission to raise prices. Chastened by the murder of John López, in southern Veracruz the commission handed over negotiations with ranchers to General Alejo González and southern Veracruz's seasoned zone commander, General Mario Rosado Morales. In Minatitlán, the generals cut a deal with cattle associations and promised that they would be allowed to appoint their own appraisers to the commission. US officials had not been consulted and refused to support this arrangement which they believed would massively inflate prices and leave then exposed to public and congressional criticism. The US section also pushed for a new and more determined officer to replace General Rosales. However, the Mexican section backed the military plan, and vouched for Rosado's deep knowledge of the region and its people. If another General arrived, Mexican officials insisted unofficially, he "would get into trouble because of too-forceful methods, or would act

---

[43] Corlett report, September 1947, CAP, box 7, foot and mouth. On the role of local priests in coordinating and legitimizing the lynching of public teachers and Protestants in the 1930s and 1940s, see Kloppe-Santamaría, *Vortex*, 48–50.

[44] Pavia Guzmán, *Recuerdos*, 90.   [45] USDA, *Campaign*, 128.

in sympathy with people in a manner comparable with that of General Rosales."[46] Faced with Mexican intransigence and recognizing the strategic importance of the area, the US section agreed to restart slaughter operations around Minatitlán with local cattlemen as de facto appraisers, provided the Mexican government paid the salaries of these men, but the campaign still faltered. US appraiser Pat Grattan reported on a typically tense operation at Otapa. Cattle owners "cut the animals back on us" and had them counted twice. They insisted that ten animals be kept back to be slaughtered and eaten that evening, but then opened the corral gate and "starting running the cattle in different directions through the jungle." When Grattan tried to charge the cattlemen for these animals, "the representative told us then that if we didn't pay for the animals we lost, the brigade would not leave the fossa [sic]." Grattan wisely "talked it over with the rest of the brigade" and decided to pay for the lost animals: "There were nearly 100 farmers at the fossa [sic], and we had only a 10-soldier escort."[47] By November 1948 the commission abandoned plans to cull herds remaining in the area between the isthmus railroad and the Coatzacoalcos river, and introduced vaccination to the area.[48]

To reduce the need for the *palo* of military force and the *pan* of indemnities, the campaign also sought to persuade people to cooperate. Half a dozen officials in the CMAEFA's information office prepared press releases, leaflets, films, posters, and radio spots. They also helped General Alejo González make a film, *Outbreak!*, which explained the damage that aftosa would do to Mexicans' capacity to feed their children, described the history of US slaughter campaigns against aftosa in the 1910s and 1920s, and showed US and Mexican commission officials working as equals in a shared patriotic endeavor.[49] The commission tried to tweak propaganda for local tastes and different parts of the ideological spectrum. Someone in the commission penned a corrido which debunked the idea that aftosa was a type of *mal de yerba*, praised generous slaughter indemnities, and promised that in the future the government would

---

[46] Confidential Report for May 9–15, 1948, CMAEFA, reports, box 1.

[47] Grattan report, transcribed in USDA, *Campaign*, 208.

[48] Ibid., 215. At the same time, the commission sent out a small team of claims adjusters "armed with cash, authority and receipt-and-release forms" to mop up any lingering discontent over prices and fines, avoiding entanglements with the courts. Lord, CMAEFA, to Mynatt, USDA, October 23, 1948, CMAEFA, reports, box 2, "legal counsel."

[49] *Outbreak* (1949), NARA, RG16, Series: Public Information and Training Motion Picture and Television Productions, 1773, 16-P-1028.

distribute improved breeds across the land.[50] The dairy and pig farmers of León organized extensive quarantine measures to protect their herds and, with commission approval, raised funds by organizing a *coleadero* – a rodeo where cowboys competed to trip a bull by its tail.[51] While the campaign was still based on the sanitary rifle, Mexican officials told the UNS newspaper, *El Sinarquista*, that vaccination was tainted by association with communism, since the Soviets had stolen the most advanced techniques when they invaded Germany at the end of the war.[52]

The arrival of vaccination provided attractive new themes with which to work. Through 1947, CMAEFA officials puzzled over how to frame and visualize the campaign. Slaughter operations lacked edifying imagery, and the policy could only be explained by conceding its origins abroad, principally in the United States.[53] Striving for a light-hearted tone, one official sketched a cartoon about a farmer shooting his confused cow in the head, but it was never published.[54] With the advent of vaccination, commission propagandists were able to associate the campaign with more familiar icons of medical science and development: the be-suited, mestizo scientist conducting research in a laboratory, or patiently explaining his knowledge of the disease to peasant farmers by candlelight. (Quack vaccines, by contrast, were portrayed as driven by interests that were literally bestial and filthy.) Representations of the campaign's technical authority shifted abruptly away from the proven experience of slaughter towards pure, laboratory-based scientific knowledge (see Figures 4.1, 4.2, 4.3). This shift elided much of the grisly reality of vaccine production, which also involved industrial-scale slaughter of livestock. Still, these images did not so much mold public opinion as reconcile with it, echoing many of the arguments already made by opponents of the commission's slaughter program. Just to underline the shift in mood, by

---

[50] "Corrido de la aftosa," CMAEFA, General Subject Files, box 1, entry 6.

[51] Association Regional de Charros de León, to Governor Nicéforo Guerrero, Guanajuato, September 10, 1947, AHEG, 3.40 (78), fiebre aftosa, 1947, vol. I. León had some 10,000 dairy cattle in 1947, and townspeople and businesses contributed some 40,000 pesos to the city's quarantine measures. General Z. Martínez, Irapuato, Guanajuato, to state governor, February 4, 1948, AHEG, 3.40 (78), fiebre aftosa, 1948, vol. I; various correspondence, comité de lucha, León, to state government, 1948, AHEG, 3.40 (78), fiebre aftosa, 1948, vol. VII.

[52] Figueroa Velázquez, *El tiro de gracia*, 71–2. For more on the impact of the Cold War on animal disease research, see Chapter 6.

[53] For early discussion of these problems, along with mild symptoms of disease, see weekly report, July 31, 1947, CMAEFA, reports, box 1.

[54] This cartoon, and several other drafts can be found in ABB, N82–3B, Heflin papers.

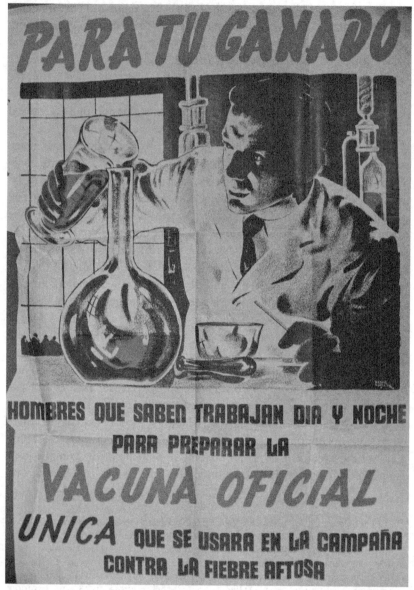

FIGURE 4.1. Campaign poster *For Your Livestock, Knowledgeable Men Work Day and Night to Prepare the Official Vaccine,* c. 1949. ABB, N82-3A, Heflin papers. Archives of the Big Bend, Brian Wildenthal Memorial Library, Sul Ross State University, Alpine, Texas.

FIGURE 4.2. Campaign poster *Do Not Allow Unofficial Vaccine*, c. 1949. ABB, N82-3A, Heflin papers. Archives of the Big Bend, Brian Wildenthal Memorial Library, Sul Ross State University, Alpine, Texas.

FIGURE 4.3. Xavier Sánchez Gavito and a farmer pose for a campaign publicity photograph, c. 1948. ABB, N82-3A, Heflin papers. Archives of the Big Bend, Brian Wildenthal Memorial Library, Sul Ross State University, Alpine, Texas.

1949 vaccination brigades around Mexico City paid a mariachi band to play while they worked.[55]

It took time to for the widening spray of commission propaganda to douse the country. With most resources dedicated to slaughter and disinfection, propaganda officials – dubbed *informadores* – were initially few and unreliable. In late summer 1947, only four were available for the field. Of these, one failed to liaise with the relevant local authorities and one left thousands of posters moldering in a warehouse.[56] By August 1947, support from other federal authorities began to materialize. The Ministry of Public Education loaned its mobile sound-trucks and film projectors, and distributed leaflets instructing teachers how to "prepare the mentality of communities" for slaughter. Later the National

---

[55] Report, March 1949, CMAEFA, General Subject Files, box 1, entry 6, "Radio contracts."

[56] USDA, *Campaign*, 133; Dr. Francisco Herrera and Dr. James Hourigan, San Luis de la Paz, Guanajuato, to Alfonso Serrano and Samuel Montague, Departamento de Información, Mexico City, September 28, 1948, CMAEFA, reports, box 2, "information, general."

Indigenous Institute helped the campaign to translate pamphlets and flyers into Otomí, Purépecha, and some languages spoken in southern Veracruz and Oaxaca dubbed Popoluca.[57] No less important was a growing discipline within the commission itself. One of General Johnson's innovations was to insist that every employee memorize the campaign's objectives and techniques, and he quizzed drivers, vaccinators, and livestock inspectors when out in the field.[58] The campaign's two-headed administrative structure was itself a kind of propaganda, and procedures were adapted to make the campaign more palatable to the Mexican public. After cattlemen stormed the hotel in Sahuayo where officials were staying, the commission asked US appraisers to take a backseat and Mexican appraisers to handle all face-to-face discussions with farmers. Similar instructions were sent to paymasters and, later, vaccinators.[59]

Field officials believed that posters, pamphlets, radio spots, and procedural choreography were useful to some degree, but no substitute for visiting and talking with communities in person. But this raised other questions about how and with whom they should discuss the campaign. At the beginning of the operation, a common technique was to organize large public meetings to quickly reach as many people as possible. However, this approach had drawbacks. In some cases, the commission failed to single out local notables. The municipal president of La Barca, Jalisco was inclined to support the campaign in late September, but felt "offended" that no US officials called on him individually to request assistance.[60] More serious, officials worried that, without careful planning and preparation, large public meetings could just cement opposition. In Oaxaca, Frank Mulhern grappled for months with what he saw as the dangerous psychology of Mexican crowds. During his early struggles in the Mixteca Baja, Mulhern "learned never to have another public meeting." The people of the Huajuapan district were apparently intensely suspicious, hostile, and stubborn: "All the talking in the world will not change their minds. In fact, the only thing they understand is military

[57] Various reports, August 1947, CMAEFA, reports; "El maestro en la lucha contra la fiebre aftosa," AHEG, 3.40 (78), fiebre aftosa, 1948, vol. II; various pamphlets, CMAEFA, general subject files, box 10, E-1, propaganda.
[58] See minutes of "Conference to elaborate a new working plan for Information Division," June 21, 1948, CMAEFA, public affairs, box 2, "informadores – problems."
[59] New field guidance, transcribed in USDA, *Campaign*, 47, 175, 177.   [60] Ibid., 94.

force."[61] However, Mulhern quickly realized that he lacked the troops to impose the campaign by force, and spent September and October trying to find another approach. The main flashpoint in September 1947 was the town of Teotitlán del Camino, lying on the railroad between Oaxaca and Mexico City. Despite numerous public meetings, the town refused to allow slaughter. Eventually Mulhern managed to peel away several of the more educated notables from the town, including the municipal president who was a medical doctor, and met with them privately. These men then asked the commission to leave the town for a few days, reportedly held another public meeting alongside the local priest, and obtained the town's consent for slaughter.[62] By 1948, Mulhern had converted his experiences into a rough theory of crowd dynamics:

From past experience we know that the true value of a contact man lies in the fact that he can't convince a large crowd but he can convince them if he is able to get them in little groups. Convince them and then have a mass meeting; when they observe that they all feel the same way, then they decide to cooperate. On the other hand, if you don't work on these small groups beforehand, I guarantee you that no matter how great a man is as a crowd sayer [sic], he cannot convince a mass of people to cooperate in the slaying of their cattle.[63]

Numerous other officials in the commission either followed Mulhern's advice or reached the same conclusion themselves.[64] In 1948, J. Carillo, adopted the same technique in Atenco, Jalisco. Given reports of opposition to slaughtering a new outbreak in the town, he decided that:

it would be childish to call a general meeting. I felt it would be wise to destroy these antagonistic feelings among the leaders of public opinion in the town, by talking individually with them. Then, when I was sure of the success of a general meeting, I called all cattlemen and outstanding local residents together and had complete success.[65]

---

[61] Mulhern, Tuxtepec, Oaxaca, to Shahan, Mexico City, August 22, 1947, in CMAEFA, operations, box 29, Oaxaca.

[62] Narrative drawn from: various reports, August–October 1947, CMAEFA, operations, box 29, Oaxaca; Sánchez Gavito, "Report on trip to Oaxaca," c. September 30, 1947, CMAEFA, administrative, box 5, "information reports."

[63] Mulhern, Mexico City, to Shahan, April 5, 1948, CMAEFA, reports, box 2, "Personnel – death of Juan López."

[64] For another report on the importance of targeting municipal authorities, and rural teachers – often considered "the learned member of the community" – see Sánchez Gavito, "Report on Camotlán, Huajuapan district," August 1947, transcribed in USDA, *Campaign*, 67.

[65] Report from Lic. J. Carillo Manzo, c. August 1948, transcribed in USDA, *Campaign*, 218.

Similar ideas shaped efforts to channel propaganda through local mediators. Mulhern and John López designed what they believed was an effective model for persuading isolated communities in the hills bordering Oaxaca and Puebla, which took advantage of films and two figures they believed were "invariably" critical to local opinion: the teacher and priest. Since heavy film projectors and generators could not travel on the "steep narrow paths in the mountains," López set off on horseback and dispatched jeeps to "invite people to come down to the movies" in larger, lower-lying villages.[66] Before the screening, some carefully choreographed introductory events took place:

> We generally get in touch with the village teacher and select some of the little Indian girls and boys to recite poems and sing songs they know. This they do over the microphone, and it makes their parents feel very proud. We get the leading citizen to speak on the microphone, and their parish priest counsels them to comply with the Government. The local teachers say a few words. Most people do not read alike nor do they hear alike; they are more likely to see alike; hence the best method of conveying a knowledge of facts is through the sound motion picture ... The effect is astonishing. The Indians are seated there for hours absorbing everything they see on the screen. It is really edifying to see how, after these night exhibitions, in most places they get together with the municipal *presidente* to form a committee, so they can personally invite the doctor assigned to inspect their cattle ... We generally stayed 2–3 days in each of these villages.[67]

Despite such bursts of optimism, it proved difficult to replicate this model, and officials were normally much less certain about the reception that awaited them in the countryside. The sound-trucks sent into the mountains of Guerrero around Iguala received a rough reception; in Los Sauces the head of the film unit was "threatened with being driven from town if he attempted to disseminate propaganda favorable to our campaign."[68] The commission also received vague reports that the first sound-trucks sent to the outskirts of Guadalajara and San Luis Potosí in late 1947 were "stoned or threatened by the local populace," although reliable information was scarce. In one account, the attack in the *Huasteca potosina* was caused by local opposition to the aftosa campaign; another account claimed that the "crowd wished to see more pictures and expressed

---

[66] Mulhern and López report, c. August–September 1947, transcribed in USDA, *Campaign*, 134.

[67] Ibid., 36.

[68] Digranes, Chilpancingo, to Shahan, September 7, 1947, CMAEFA, operations, box 29, Guerrero.

resentment when the film crew declined on the ground that they had to leave for other commitments."[69]

Aiming to adapt the campaign to local conditions and targeting key mediators was all very well, but it demanded considerable time, information, and an understanding of Mexican society and politics which many officials, particularly from the United States, did not possess. In their everyday correspondence, US officials used sociological categories in haphazard and confusing ways. Sometimes they distinguished between *indios*, campesinos, and peons, and sometimes used them interchangeably. Sometimes they defined campesinos narrowly as peasant farmers, and sometimes used it as a catch-all for all rustic people. Strange non-sequiturs abounded, as when John López described "excellent cooperation from all the authorities, civilians, and campesinos."[70] Sometimes US officials retroactively ethnicized opposition and argued in circles. Once the mestizo ranchers of Ameca, Jalisco got "rough" and made trouble for the campaign, they became "natives."[71] Officials were in a rush, of course, and rarely gave these open-ended categories much thought. Some of the confusion was due to officials struggling to match expectations about backward peasant culture with the reality of broader, cross-class resistance. Mexican veterinarians told plenty of stories about opposition from isolated and ignorant campesinos, but unsurprisingly had a somewhat better feel for rural society. In the 1970s, Grant Wilkins Sigsworth, a US geography researcher, sent surveys to the surviving members of the campaign asking them to explain the main sources of opposition to the campaign. While US respondents tended to blame peasant farmers, Mexican veterinarians shared the blame more evenly between peasant and large-scale commercial farmers.[72]

In Mulhern's unusually prolix and ethnographically-minded reports we see the difficulty officials had in making sense of the social forces blocking the campaign, and deciding which ones should be reported. Mulhern's first reports from Oaxaca described the campaign almost as a joint operation with the state government and big mestizo ranchers: peasant farmers and ejidatarios were "very dubious and don't believe in promises, but the cattle owners and I feel that if we had the mules there to

---

[69] Confidential weekly report, January 10, 1948, CMAEFA, reports, box 1.
[70] USDA, *Campaign*, 165.
[71] Mackery, Guadalajara, to Omohundro, Mexico City, December 9, 1948, CMAEFA, operations, box 29, Jalisco, phone log.
[72] Sigsworth, "Mexican Epizootic," 86, 184–5.

replace animals ... our battle would be half won." However, Mulhern struggled to transpose this simple framework onto other parts of Oaxaca, let alone Veracruz. Noting the trenchant, cross-class resistance of towns in the Mixteca Baja, he began to compare these communities to the peripheries of US society: "This town reminds one of our frontier towns with its town criers and just a limited few can even drive an automobile ... We made large sketches of charts whooping trends of the disease in other countries and the danger of recovered potential carriers but they believe like the people of Missouri and want to see it first." By the time he was based in southern Veracruz, Mulhern struggled to understand why it was so difficult to get big ranchers to agree to slaughter, even when offered prices far above market rates. At first he suggested such men might not be commercial ranchers at all, rarely sold cattle, and so perhaps had no understanding of the value of money.[73] Shortly afterwards, Mulhern came to a more plausible understanding: powerful ranchers were simply bargaining with the Mexican government and wanted to be "paid to cooperate" – a "somewhat political ... Mexican transaction."[74] Mulhern's superiors in Mexico City were not interested in repeating this story of murky inter-elite bargaining to Washington DC, and decided a cultural explanation was more plausible and politic. They repeated Mulhern's unlikely claim that big ranchers "never sold a cow in their lives" and "have no reasonable idea of what cattle are worth," and even suggested – with no evidence from the field whatsoever – that the proximity of a Mexico's nationalized oil refinery at Coatzacoalcos might have helped fuel "anti-Yanqui" sentiments in the area.[75]

To counter these problems, in 1948 the campaign recruited more informadores with knowledge of local conditions, and broadened their remit. Rather than simply distributing propaganda, they were to work in communities, in secret if necessary, test the strength of support and identify key powerbrokers – generals, governors, mayors, priests, *caciques* – and liaise with whomever necessary to smooth the path of the campaign. These men also trained the commission's growing ranks of livestock inspectors to do similar kinds of outreach work. Recruited

---

[73] Mulhern, Tehuacán, to Shahan, Mexico City, August 12, 1947; Mulhern, Tehuacán, to Noyes, Mexico City, September 20, 1947; Mulhern, Coatzacoalcos, to Noyes, Mexico City, February 17, 1948, all in CMAEFA, operations, box 1, Oaxaca.
[74] Mulhern, Coatzacoalcos, to Noyes, Mexico City, February 26, 1948, CMAEFA, operations, box 1, Oaxaca, phone log.
[75] Stoops, Mexico City, to BAI, report for May 2–8, CMAEFA, reports, box 1.

on the basis of personal recommendations, informadores were a hetero-geneous bunch: some were former newspaper journalists, like *licenciado* Sánchez Gavito, or former teachers; others resembled local political fixers and guns-for-hire. In Guerrero, Sánchez Gavito recruited well-connected *políticos*, like former congressman Ernesto Domínguez Pichardo.[76]

The CMAEFA considered the informadores' persuasive powers some-what uneven. In the conflictive area of southern Veracruz they made little impression. The people of Pajapan stripped the first *informador* dis-patched to the area naked, and he "had quite a problem returning to civilization clad in the altogether" until a "policeman in a village came to his rescue."[77] After John López was murdered, the Mexican section barred other informadores from the area, arguing that they would under-mine the authority of the military and that public meetings would only permit the region's dispersed population to plan opposition. Throughout the vaccination drive in central and southern Veracruz, the key policing information and decisions – the location of trouble spots, when to deploy soldiers, how to negotiate with isolated villages in the sierra who still opposed vaccination – were in hands of the General in command of the zone.[78]

Elsewhere, informadores made more of a contribution. In late 1948, Sánchez Gavito arrived in Morelos with instructions to overhaul an ineffective and "incompetent" strategy which relied almost entirely on the army.[79] Sánchez Gavito's approach was not enormously original or detailed, but he knew enough about the area's history of antagonism with the federal army to adapt. In 1949, he organized a demonstration of the vaccine on some herds belonging to the relatives of a local congressman, and distributed handbills quoting the governor's pledge to assume respon-sibility for any damage the vaccine caused. Tellingly, the demonstration "was carried out without the services of soldiers, whose presence annoys the people of Morelos." According to field reports "news of this success spread rapidly through the adjoining areas," and these kinds of lightly-policed demonstrations became one of the campaign's most effective tools.[80] The occasional unplanned and involuntary demonstration pre-sented a minor hindrance. In Regules, Michoacán a man fired bullets at a vaccinator's feet and forced him to drink an entire bottle of pungent,

[76] Porter, *Doctor*, 185–6; USDA, *Campaign*, 227. [77] USDA, *Campaign*, 218.
[78] Doughty, *Gringo Livestock Inspector*, 19–26. [79] USDA, *Campaign*, 220.
[80] Ibid.

viscous vaccine. District co-supervisor Dr. Omohundro checked on the vaccinator the following day; the fluid was disgusting but the vaccinator was otherwise "fine, I guess."[81]

Salvador Herrera Montes, a Mexican livestock inspector who worked for the commission in 1949, based his techniques on ideas about the typical Mexican rural family and the sway of local priests. While at Texcoco in September 1949, he typed up a "treatise on how to obtain cooperation from all segments of the population." For Herrera, each family had "three kinds of people" and each required a specific approach.[82] Men could be best be organized through public "community organizations."[83] Children could be approached through the school, using a combination of friendly jokes and reminders that aftosa threatened many of their favorite dishes: cheese, eggs, *chicharrones,* and even beans refried in pigs' lard. Women, Herrera explained, were best approached through the local priest. This kind of knowledge about rural Mexican society was neither precise nor particularly original. It echoed the stereotypes produced by federal teachers and doctors, who long noted the feminization of the laity and suspected women's blind loyalty to the Catholic Church.[84] Still, it did at least spur officials to liaise with a fairly broad array of local interest groups and collect information about their attitudes. Herrera himself claimed that his techniques produced results. In one case, he told how the men of Tepeyanco, Tlaxcala had planned to ambush and kill two particularly abusive vaccinators who imposed excessive fines and chased locals around "like rabbits."[85] The attack was foiled when one of the ambushers' wives rushed to tell the priest, who then "caught those men by the ears, took them away, and gave them a good scolding." Herrera asked:

> why did that woman squeal on her old man? Because, weeks before, the priest had said from the pulpit several times that the vaccine was good, and that the vaccinators were friends of the people. And why did the priest say such words from the pulpit? Was it a revelation that came to him out of the blue? No! He pronounced those life-saving words because he had been told to say then. And who told him? Juan Anicola, one of our *desinfectadores.*

Impressed with Herrera's achievements, the commission promoted him to official informador and sent him to Puebla to recruit lay inspection

---

[81] USDA, *Campaign*, 254.
[82] Herrera report, c. 1949, reproduced in USDA, *Campaign*, 332. [83] Ibid., 333.
[84] Ibid., 332; Fallaw, *Religion*, 25. [85] Ibid.

teams and liaise with priests there.[86] Indeed, some priests had helped the campaign during the earlier slaughter phase too; in villages across the Bajío they stored parishioners' indemnity funds and credit notes while they waited for the arrival of replacement mules, and vouched for farmers' identities in the absence of documentation.[87] US officials also concluded that local priests were essential to the campaign's success but, at the urging of the State Department, they never mentioned this political debt in public for fear of embarrassing the Mexican government.[88]

In Guerrero state, Sánchez Gavito's work focused instead on brokering agreements between caciques, outlaws, generals, and local politicians. In the late 1930s, "a group of bandits, fleeing from justice in the state of Oaxaca" moved into the Sierra del Gallo on Guerrero's Costa Grande. After burning ranches, "killing a good number of campesinos," and "causing terror everywhere," these thirty-odd so-called *chiveros* acquired "several thousand goats, and move their flocks constantly, seeking better pastures." Nominally led by Concepción Márquez, locals knew that "the man who really controls this group is General Damián Hernández (retired), a wealthy cattleman and owner of several ranches, who lives in Ajuchitlán."[89] Between April and August 1949, Sánchez Gavito met with the state governor and other state officials, traveled across the unmapped section of the sierra on horseback for eight days, and sought out General Salvador González, another retired general based in Coyuca de Catalán, who was on friendly terms with the federal government and wielded influence over General Hernández due to an "old friendship and *compadrazgo*."[90] In August, the informador drove to a meeting with Concepción Márquez "at the foot of the mountainous region of *chivero* country" accompanied by an army captain and lieutenant. Márquez agreed to work for the commission as a guide, promised that his men would help round up animals and provide food for the brigades, assumed responsibility for the commission officials' safely, and signed a written agreement to that effect. Márquez's men even offered to help cut trees and

[86] Ibid., 333.
[87] Minutes of Advisory Committee, May 27, 1947, afternoon session, CMAEFA, reports, box 1, advisory committee, 26, 91.
[88] Johnson, CMAEFA, to Truman, May 14, 1949; and Reveley, State Department, to Nash, undated memo, TP, official file, 395-A, foot-and-mouth disease.
[89] Sánchez Gavito, quoted in USDA, *Campaign*, 226–7.
[90] Sánchez Gavito report, March 15, 1949, in Ibid., 226–7, 228.

brush to create a landing strip for a commission plane to bring in crates of vaccine and ice.[91]

This pact, resembling a formal peace agreement, brought unstated benefits to all concerned. Sánchez Gavito's intrepid work received fulsome praise from the CMAEFA, which believed that he had helped bypass the "military council" from the zone command for an armed confrontation with the chiveros. The pact seemed to confirm Márquez's authority and ability to control his followers, a perpetual concern of local *caciques*. According to Sánchez, the chiveros "gave the ... impression that they want to prove they are peaceful people. They explained their need to stage an armed defense of their rights because of their numerous enemies who are jealous of the large tracts of land under their control."[92] One of his colleagues in the commission believed Sánchez Gavito hammered things up to flatter his own negotiating skills, using exaggerated stereotypes of serrano criminality.[93] Still, even his colleagues admitted that the problems of extending state control over the unmapped sierra were real enough; the previous year, the chiveros had "attacked and defeated" an army platoon and killed "several soldiers."[94]

To hone local tactics and inform overall strategy, the campaign demanded accurate information about livestock and their owners, their movements, and more generally about public attitudes to state intervention. Initially such information was in short supply. Earlier censuses and maps proved unreliable, and people's propensity to hide animals, the opaque nature of peasant land-holding, informal grazing arrangements, and the shifting, ad hoc nature of the "roads" along which livestock traveled made this information hard to obtain.[95] Despite some improvements by the 1930s, authorities' view of the contours of rural property

---

[91] USDA, *Campaign*, 228–9.   [92] Ibid., 228.

[93] Pavia Guzmán, *Acciones*, 32–3. Guerrero's Sierra del Gallo had a widespread reputation for lawlessness; the people of Michoacán's tierra caliente regarded these "hillmen" as "renegades and criminals, men who shot first and asked questions later." Del Villar and del Villar, *Where the Strange Roads*, 105. While compiling his compendious survey of Guerrero, the economist Moisés T. de la Peña also heard tales of the chiveros – "*gente de pelo en pecho,* as they say, who exploit great herds of transhumant goats." He heard that they had arrived not from Oaxaca but from Michoacán after the Cristiada. Such dangers "denied us the pleasure and scientific interest of exploring *la montaña.*" Quoted in Pavia Guzmán, *Acciones*, 32.

[94] Ibid., 34–6; Sánchez Gavito report, March 15, 1949, in USDA, *Campaign*, 226–7.

[95] De la Peña, *Guerrero económico*, 22. On the variability and difficulty of identifying rural "roads" compared to railways, see Knight, "Weight," 233, n100.

and agriculture remained heavily clouded.[96] Much of what the US anthropologist Ralph Beals observed in 1940–1 in the village of Cherán, Michoacán applied to peasants and smallholders across the central plateau: "Ownership of cattle is widespread ... but accurate knowledge of the extent of ownership is impossible because of the tendency to conceal wealth. As most cattle are kept at pasture, usually in the mountains, house censuses are of no value."[97] The costs and productivity of pig and chicken raising were similarly opaque, either because (as Beals believed) peasants never quantified such things or (as seems more likely) they feigned ignorance.[98] Like the *región inexplorada* marked on charts of Guerrero, some areas lacked modern maps; some states, like Guanajuato, had maps, but the commission struggled to secure enough copies, and officials complained that the ones they had did not "show enough of the villages."[99]

In response, commission officials gradually built up a more accurate picture of Mexico's human and animal geography. The commission often relied on local guides, although their reports could be dispiriting. One "Indian scout" sent into the Huasteca to find evidence of unmarked livestock trails relayed the news to his supervisor: "Well, he said people were moving in all directions and that the trails go in all directions, north, east, south, and west ... Indians move all the time, anywhere."[100] The commission also employed three US forestry officials who worked with Mexican counterparts to estimate the potential for wild deer and antelope to transmit the disease.[101] They surveyed dozens of forests in central Mexico, and by May 1948 concluded the risks were minimal. The commission could effectively rely on large sections of forest as barriers – part natural, part man-made – to infection. The "mild" and "even" climate of temperate forest did not encourage wild deer to move, while rural poverty ensured that poor people hunted game and depleted numbers. Antelopes, while "great travelers," no longer had a significant presence in the area of

---

[96] Boyer and Wakild, "Social Landscaping," 96–7.   [97] Beals, *Cherán*, 29.

[98] According to Beals, "it is virtually impossible to secure useful data on labor costs or profits in relation to animals ... probably no-one in Cherán knows how much grain he feeds chickens, or how many eggs a year he gets ... the situation about pigs is little better." Ibid., 68.

[99] Mackery, Guanajuato, to Noyes, Mexico City, September 24, 1947, CMAEFA, operations, box 29, Guanajuato, phone log.

[100] Dr. Connolly, Ciudad Valles, to Mr. Reid, Mexico City, April 19, 1948, CMAEFA, Operations, box 29, SLP, radio log.

[101] Confidential weekly reports from March 1948, CMAEFA, box 1, reports.

most interest to US officials, "the northern boundaries of the infected zone."[102] In December 1947, the commission borrowed the US military attaché's aircraft and surveyed the central plateau and coasts, searching how to thread effective quarantine lines through the landscape. A report from January 1948 shows how the US engineer onboard sought other allies among the rugged topography and existing infrastructure:

> From San Luis Potosí westerly to Zacatecas the line continues through semidesert country similar to that farther east ... From Zacatecas there seems to be no other choice than to use the road through Ciudad García, Tepetongo, and Santa María de los Angeles to Colotlán ... From Colotlán southwesterly to where the line crosses the Rio Grande de Santiago, a distance of 80 or 90 miles, the line traverses a very rough, sparsely populated area ... One alternative would be to run the line westerly from Colotlán to connect with the Rio de Colotlán, follow this river down to its confluence with the Rio de Bolaños, and thence down the Rio de Bolaños to its junction with the Rio Grande de Santiago. This canyon forms a practically impassable barrier for a distance of 80 to 90 miles ... A second possible route would be to stay in the high mesa country to the south of the Rio Bolaños from Colotlán to the Rio Grande de Santiago ... From the Rio Grande de Santiago to the Guadalajara–Tepic Highway there are several alternatives for the line ... About 20 to 30 miles from its mouth the river (Rio de Ameca) opens in to a fertile, tilled valley. The line should be run either along the north or south edge of this valley because it will be impossible from an economic standpoint to keep people or animals from moving from one side of the valley to the other.[103]

After further flights, the commission also struck a deal with the cartographer and one-time inspector for the federal Department of Indian Affairs, Alejandro Wladimiro Paucic, then at work on unmapped sections of the sierra in Guerrero. Despite some "misgivings," Paucic agreed to provide the CMAEFA with "information in exchange for the pilots providing the coordinates of the places he asked for, above all in the *región inexplorada*."[104]

Informadores were also expected to gather useful information and send it back to headquarters. A particularly troublesome state for the commission, Guerrero received more than its share of informadores. These officials wrote reports which reproduced many long-standing

---

[102] Confidential weekly reports from May 1948, CMAEFA, box 1, reports; USDA, *Campaign*, 123.

[103] Mitchell report, January 2, 1948, transcribed USDA, *Campaign*, 155–6.

[104] Pavia Guzmán, *Recuerdos*, 89. This information apparently informed Paucic's first coronographic map of the state, published in 1949. Ibid. Afterwards, the federal Servicio Geográfico carried on paying Paucic to keep his map and encyclopedia of Guerrero up-to-date. López, *Crafting Mexico*, 339, n6.

official stereotypes about the state's geography and "wild" society.[105] One informador, Federico Sánchez, divided the state into four conventional geographic areas (the *costa grande*, *costa chica*, the *tierra fría* of the central highlands, and *tierra caliente*). Each area supposedly offered distinctive cultural and ethnic obstacles to state action, but particularly the coastline – filled with men accustomed to laziness and criminality – and the *tierra caliente*: "the most dangerous area," infested with cattle-rustling, banditry, and blood feuds. Still, amid the geographic cliché and ethnic stereotypes, Sánchez also gathered useful information about attitudes to vaccination, lists of more or less cooperative towns, and some key powerbrokers and institutions in the state. The Church had a real presence in state's central highlands, and was a useful ally; in the other regions priests were few and wielded little influence.[106] Other officials in the Mexican section also honed their knowledge of regional religious tendencies. Whereas priests in Guerrero's montaña were numerous, liberal-minded and useful allies, in Oaxaca's Mixteca Baja they were numerous, powerful, "ultra conservative," and decidedly unfriendly to the campaign.[107]

With the shift to vaccination, gathering information became even more important; because the vaccine's effectiveness was limited, it was crucial to obtain as much coverage as possible. Over four years, CMAEFA inspection teams sketched maps, corrected outdated place-names, identified livestock routes, converted a cacophony of local breeding categories and standards into a rough record, and counted the livestock appraised, slaughtered, vaccinated, born, died, borrowed, sold or strayed in each town and village.[108] In parts of Tlaxcala and Puebla, livestock inspectors and informadores worked with rural schools to produce daily sick-animal reports which they passed to the commission: "The teacher calls the roll every morning and, as each child answers, she asks how their animals

---

[105] Aviña, "We have returned," 121, 241 n74. Some municipalities in Guerrero really did boast very high homicide rates. Gillingham, "Who Killed Crispín Aguilar?"

[106] Lic. Federico Sánchez, "Information Man Supervisor," Guerrero, c. September 1949, CMARFA, general subject files, box 10, "c-11 Guerrero."

[107] Pavia Guzmán, *Recuerdos*, 55.

[108] A few reports, sketches and local censuses which avoided destruction: *Comisión Mexicana-Americana para la eradicación de la fiebre aftosa: Distrito de Huajuapan. Sector de Chalcatongo* (n.p., n.d.), microfilm at Bancroft Library, University of California, Berkeley; ABB, N-82-5A, and N82-3B. On the difficulty of classifying breeds, see various correspondence, Mulhern, Oaxaca City, to Mexico City, July–August 1947, CMAEFA, operations, box 29, Oaxaca.

are."[109] By 1952, repeated waves of inspection produced district maps showing "ranches, haciendas, roads, mountains, streams, waterholes, fences, places where overnight accommodation could be obtained, the number of animals, and the names of owners." The US and Mexican sections considered this work "the most complete job of mapping ever done in Mexico."[110] It allowed officials to create far more effective quarantine lines, and to identify sudden shortfalls in herds and likely areas of non-compliance.[111]

The commission also tightened up control of information about its own plans and operations. By late 1947, officials recognized that "there were too many well-known methods of forestalling slaughter when it was known to be on the way," and the same problem would likely undermine vaccination.[112] Radio communications from field operations to Mexico City now went through "speech scramblers" or were otherwise relayed in secret code, and the US section began to dispatch messages to Washington through diplomatic pouches.[113] These changes, combined with vaccination brigades' relative lightness on their feet, made it easier for districts to strike an effective balance between publicity and secrecy. In 1948, the CMAEFA's Mexican section began the first vaccination drive in Morelos, but were surprised by the degree of continuing hostility among communities. They met with the general in command of Cuautla's cavalry regiment and hashed out a technique akin to an electoral *madrugonazo* – an early-morning raid to surprise local electoral authorities and seize ballot boxes. First *informadores* discreetly probed village opinion. If opposition was anticipated, the army marched by foot and surrounded the outskirts of the village in the early hours of the morning. When the sun came up the soldiers quickly rounded up and vaccinated livestock. Although Sánchez Gavito later sought to reduce the campaign's reliance on the army and develop means of persuading communities, these surprise raids on "little villages" remained a useful fallback option, and the

---

[109] Herrera report, quoted in USDA, *Campaign*, 332.
[110] USDA, *Campaign*, 86. See also, Flores, CMAEFA, to José Aguilar y Maya, state governor, Guanajuato, September 12, 1950, AHEG, 3.40 (78), fiebre aftosa, 1950, vol. II.
[111] Various correspondence, Hess, Tepic, to Noyes, Mexico City, June 1948, CMAEFA, operations, box 29, Nayarit; USDA, *Campaign*, 86–7.
[112] USDA, *Campaign*, 213.
[113] Eakin, *Borderland Slaughter*, 66–7; various confidential weekly reports, April 1948, CMAEFA, reports, box 1.

tactic was repeated elsewhere.[114] During the second wave of vaccinations in Tlaxcala and Hidalgo , crews first announced a big public schedule for vaccination. Where they expected problems they worked by "skipping about the municipio, so as to arrive unexpectedly," or returned to areas previously vaccinated "at night for a surprise clean-up job."[115] Similarly, the commission enforced tight control over diagnoses of disease outbreaks. Samples of virus and tissue were sent to Mexico City, herds showing virulent infection were slaughtered, but not even the field officials learned of "contradictory lab reports," let alone the wider public.[116] From this perspective, the archival bonfire with which Flores destroyed Mexico's share of the commission archive in August 1952 simply represented the culmination of a four-year process of increasing secrecy.

The PRI's ability to hold onto power is surprising. As Paul Gillingham and Benjamin Smith have noted, it is not unusual for a single party to consolidate power after revolution. It is odd for one to do so while overseeing the kind of starkly inequitable development that Mexico experienced after 1940. In many ways, the government's response to aftosa fits Gillingham and Smith's concept of the PRI-state as a *dictablanda*: a "soft authoritarian," pro-business regime whose institutional weakness and low penetration of local societies demanded a complicated blend of democratic and authoritarian rule.[117] As we have already seen, the PRI maintained the flexibility and pragmatism to carefully stymie and eventually side-line the sanitary rifle. Focusing on the day-to-day mechanics of the aftosa campaign underlines the violence that ran through its operations as a matter of course, and the terror meted out to particular communities. But the campaign was not implemented by force and terror alone. It also relied on ad hoc negotiations and inducements, and sought out local mediators of different kinds. The cast of powerbrokers was much wider than accounts of a monolithic corporate party, or a hegemonic revolutionary discourse, would suggest. Indeed, the national party does not emerge in this story as a particularly important and well-coordinated political body. Localized arrangements with caciques, cattlemen, communities, governors, generals, teachers, and, not least, priests were of much more interest to the commission. As we will see in the next chapter, the corporatist institutions of most

[114] Pavia Guzmán, *Recuerdos*, 88.
[115] Torres y Elzaurdia, *Botas de hule*, 99; Sharman report from Hidalgo, November 11, 1949, transcribed in USDA, *Campaign*, 244.
[116] USDA, *Campaign*, 268.   [117] Gillingham and Smith, "Introduction."

importance were associations of commercial cattlemen, but these were very much a political work in progress. This said, the campaign does offer a partial corrective to the new orthodoxy on state weakness. In a pinch, the Mexican state (with ample US support) engaged in an extensive burst of information-gathering, normally regarded as a core dimension of state capacity. But these capacities did not develop in a linear way, and competed with other political objectives. By the end of the aftosa campaign the Mexican section had gathered an impressive body of data on social, epidemiological, and economic conditions that would have been useful to any state aiming to dominate and develop the countryside. In a leak-prone political system, whose factions circulated every six years, the commission's archive posed political risks too, and was promptly incinerated.[118]

---

[118] In 1947–8, negotiations between the US government and Mexico over access to loans for Mexico's nationalized oil industry were disrupted several times by embarrassing leaks of documents. Freeman Smith, "The United States," 193.

5

Making a Livestock State

Looking back over his career as a veterinarian and historian, Edgar Pavia Guzmán decided that 1948 was a crucial year for the nation and "the most important year" of his life. A cash-strapped student veterinarian in Mexico City, in 1946 Pavia accepted a job as a food safety inspector in the state of Guerrero, a region about which he knew next to nothing. With the outbreak of aftosa, Pavia suddenly found himself "the center of attention" in the state capital. He toured the state to plan the aftosa campaign, socialized with politicians of all colors, finetuned his knowledge of the state's geography, and became a close ally of the state governor. In the fateful year of 1948, Pavia married into one of the Costa Chica's most powerful ranching families, completed his veterinary qualifications, secured a well-salaried job on the CMAEFA, and then helped run the campaign in five different states, "running around like a headless chicken" for the next four years. When it was over, he worked at the federal Ministry of Agriculture and then directed a new program of livestock development back in Guerrero. Like many other official veterinarians at the time, Pavia saw himself as part of a new professional generation whom the campaign catapulted from obscurity to prominence.[1] More than this, he believed that the campaign jolted officials and ranchers alike out of complacency, stoked a desire for improvement, and created a "new concept of livestock farming."[2] He was all too aware that ranchers' understandings of progress did not always overlap with those of national and international experts.

---

[1] Pavia Guzmán, *Recuerdos*, 80, 74, 91, 73–101.   [2] Pavia Guzmán, *Acciones*, 36.

By eradicating a major viral obstacle to growth and international integration, the aftosa campaign allowed the livestock industry to embark on three decades of expansion propelled by growing demand and a burgeoning road infrastructure.[3] As Pavia suggested, it was also a watershed in the making of what we could call Mexico's livestock state: the interlocking institutions, policies, laws, political alliances, and ideological assumptions through which the government sought to regulate and modernize this industry.[4] The basic goals that unified this project were simple enough: to boost production, wealth, revenue, and nutrition by converting cattle, pigs, chickens, and goats into commodities as efficiently as possible. Still, the impact of the aftosa epizootic was not entirely straightforward. It offered both encouragement and warnings. On the one hand, by disrupting existing methods of production and consumption, creating new technical capacities, and offering an example of effective state action, the crisis prompted Mexican officials to contemplate more ambitious state intervention. On the other hand, the aftosa crisis offered some unmistakable lessons about the kind of political compromises and alliances – international and domestic – upon which government action would have to rest.

Historians generally argue that the 1940s were a turning point in efforts to modernize and develop the Mexican countryside, as the government moved away from redistribution and support for small farmers, cooperated with international (and especially US) agencies as never before, and prescribed markets, infrastructure, and generic technical and scientific expertise to solve rural problems. For Boyer and Cariño Olvera, these changes amounted to an "ecological revolution" for Mexico – a series of "dramatic changes in the way people conceive and make use of their surroundings and the country's so-called natural resources."[5] The Rockefeller Foundation's Mexican Agricultural Program (MAP), in operation from 1943–65, is usually somewhere at the center of the story. After all, it had dramatic effects: new seeds boosted yields, particularly in those large, commercial, irrigated estates which could fund these innovations; and the chemical fertilizers and pesticides which these seeds demanded poisoned soils, wildlife, and workers alike.[6] Mexico provided the

---

[3] For an overview of beef cattle, see Chauvet, *La ganadería*. For the importance of roads to cattle ranching, see Schryer, *Ethnicity and Class*, 154–5, 160.

[4] On the concept of the "nature state" that emerged to regulate and protect supposedly wild nature, see Graf von Hardenberg, Kelly, Leal, and Wakild, *The Nature State*.

[5] Boyer and Cariño Olvera, "Mexico's Ecological Revolutions," 23.

[6] Sonnenfeld, "Mexico's 'Green Revolution,' 1940–1980"; Warman, *El campo*, 133–6; Fitzgerald, "Exporting"; Wright, *The Death*.

Rockefeller Foundation with a "hub" from which to launch similar initiatives around the world and, by the late 1960s was celebrated as the birthplace of a "Green Revolution" in agricultural output and development.[7] However, there are problems with foregrounding the Rockefeller Foundation and its own rather teleological conception of Green Revolution. MAP initiatives built on a longer history of agricultural research and international collaboration in Mexico – precursors that US experts tended to disdain or ignore.[8] The Rockefeller Foundation and the Mexican state housed varied and sometimes competing objectives, which shifted over time; in its early years the MAP emphasized "peasant-friendly" plant breeding, before shifting to a focus on large agribusiness in the late 1940s.[9] The uptake of new technologies was uneven, a result of conscious policy, the central state's many contradictions and weaknesses, and a host of social and ecological contingencies across Mexico's immensely varied landscape.[10] In many ways, Mexico's project to modernize livestock echoed and at times overlapped with these efforts to modernize crops. By shifting the focus away from the canonical Green Revolution technologies towards the tumultuous campaign against aftosa and its long-term effects, we cannot only explore a neglected aspect of the Rockefeller Foundation's activities. We can also gain a fuller understanding of how and why Mexico's developmentalist state took the shape it did in the 1940s, and what was really new about it.[11]

As was the case across Latin America, in the 1970s a mayor scholarly polemic emerged in Mexico about the costs and benefits of livestock for economic development. Early studies portrayed the Mexican state's stance towards livestock farming in very different ways. For Ernest

---

[7] "Agriculture and the Rockefeller Foundation," Rockefeller Archive Center, Rockefeller Foundation records, administration, program and policy, RG 3.1, series 915, box 3, folder 20, available at *100 Years: The Rockefeller Foundation*, https://rockfound.rockarch.org/digital-library-listing/-/asset_publisher/yYxpQfeI4W8N/content/agriculture-and-the-rockefeller-foundation (accessed February 16, 2021). On changing perceptions of Mexico's experience among development experts, see Harwood, "Whatever Happened."

[8] Cotter, *Troubled Harvest*; Zuleta, "Laboratorios"; Soto Laveaga, "Socialist Origins." For similar arguments in other national contexts, see Kumar, Lorek, Olsson, Sackley, Schmalzer, and Soto Laveaga, "Roundtable."

[9] Harwood, "Peasant-friendly."

[10] The most detailed account of the MAP's operations in central Mexico is now Gutiérrez Núñez, "Cambio agrario." On the uneven effects of new technologies on biodiversity, see Soluri, "Home Cooking."

[11] For another international, modernizing initiative running "parallel" to the Mexican Agricultural Project, see Gómez, "La construcción," 1249.

Feder, a rural economist and UN advisor radicalized by the Cuban Revolution, the PRI state had wholly capitulated to the interests of commercial ranchers and business in general; an alliance of domestic and global capital was not the tail wagging the dog of the Mexican state, "but practically the dog itself."[12] For Paul Yates, another former UN advisor close to the Banco de México, the PRI state was actually a very poor vehicle for livestock interests, characterized by fragmentation, incompetence, blindness and even "latent hostility" towards ranchers.[13] Since the 1990s, a second wave of regional studies has slowly moved beyond the sweeping and polemical style of early works, and deepened our understanding of the interplay of ecologies, markets, new technologies, and branches of the state. This literature remains much stronger on some places and some types of livestock farming than others.[14] Combining this scholarship with new archival research, and Mexico's small but valuable corpus of veterinary historiography – much of it written by veterinarians themselves, who have long seen the aftosa campaign as a major event – allows us to sketch how the campaign boosted state ambitions, remade state relations with international agencies and livestock farmers alike and, despite ample evidence of continuing state weakness, provided new technical, institutional, and political resources to state officials.

Even without the aftosa crisis and campaign, Mexico would surely have built some kind of larger and more ambitious livestock state. In the 1950s and 1960s, governments across Latin America established new research institutions and extension programs for their growing livestock industries, often with international help.[15] The aftosa outbreak was partly a product of the perceived economic potential of the livestock industry, as ranchers positioned themselves for future expansion by bending regulations and investing in expensive breeding cattle. Just as they had earlier, officials at the Ministry of Agriculture aimed to regulate disease and gradually usher farmers away from "traditional" ranching that was "extensive," "primitive," and "empirical"– that is, unscientific – towards

[12] Feder, "The Odious Competition," 495, n59. On Feder's varied career, see Ross, "A Critic."

[13] Yates, *Mexico's Agricultural Dilemma*, 114.

[14] The discussion below focuses on production, rather than marketing and consumption. For an overview of meat marketing, see Lopes and de los Reyes Patiño, "Institutions and Interest Groups."

[15] Wilcox and Van Ausdal, "Hoofprints," 191; Acker, *Volkswagen*.

more efficient, "intensified," modern production.[16] Long before the Second World War, postrevolutionary reformers claimed that traditional diets based on corn and beans were deficient and required more animal protein – a key rationale for livestock developmentalism.[17] Contrary to popular conspiracy theories, the Mexican government's plans to augment milk supply with imports of powdered milk also predated the aftosa crisis.[18] Nevertheless, the kind of livestock state Mexico got – its timing, scope, levels of operation, personnel, and many of its strengths and weaknesses – were decisively shaped by the aftosa campaign. The campaign did not radically change the government's overarching goals for livestock farming. But it made these tasks more urgent, suggested and encouraged new ways to accomplish them, and underlined political pitfalls to avoid.

In different ways, the campaign encouraged more federal efforts to regulate and modernize livestock farming. In part, this was because the aftosa campaign, despite ridding Mexico of the virus, still left a series of other problems that demanded a solution. Slaughter had diminished herds, particularly in southern Guanajuato and Querétaro. Despite corruption and favoritism, the campaign eliminated some prize animals, and halted any attempts to import breeding stock.[19] In the north, the closure of export markets led to severe overgrazing and the depletion of pastures and soils. As the campaign wound down, speculators hoarded cattle in anticipation of an export bonanza which, combined with repeated droughts, did further damage.[20] The campaign also exposed the shaky administrative grip of Mexican officialdom over this national resource. Mexico's relative lack of veterinary experts frustrated the Ministry of Agriculture and limited the campaign's effectiveness. As we have seen, it could have geopolitical implications, weakening Mexico's de facto authority over CMAEFA operations and leaving it prey to US administrative demands. The enormous difficulty officials encountered in

---

[16] Ing. Gonzalo Garrido, Oficina de experimentación agrícola, Comisión del Papaloapan, "Anteproyecto para el mejoramiento de la ganadería," RAC, group 6.13, series 1.1, Mexico Field Office, box 31, "livestock improvement project, January 1953."

[17] Zazueta, "Milk," 85–7, 120. In fact, in the mid-1940s studies by Rockefeller Foundation and Mexican experts had broadly defended "traditional" diets and challenged the need for more animal protein, but Mexican officials cited them selectively and interpreted them "according to their own interests." Ibid., 128.

[18] Ibid., 170.

[19] For example, the slaughter of fifteen prize fighting bulls, "scrupulously improved and developed over 25 years," in Galindo, Querétaro, or some high-grade Holstein cattle in Michoacán. Figueroa Velázquez, *El tiro de gracia*, 127, 197.

[20] de los Reyes Patiño, "En la frontera," 204–5.

inspecting or simply counting the millions of domestic animals which roamed around fields and villages more or less freely underlined other drawbacks with extensive ranching beside low productivity. The same conditions which made it difficult for farmers to corral, tether, vaccinate, feed, or breed their animals also helped make their activities opaque to officials and experts.

The campaign's success also heartened Mexican officials. It suggested that concerted state action could accomplish major tasks in disease control and, perhaps, many other useful things. After all, the campaign left a number of apparently tangible modernizing effects. Most important was the sparkling new animal science laboratory at Palo Alto, with the capacity to diagnose more diseases more rapidly and reliably, and produce more vaccines. A new radio network linked far-flung livestock officials and inspectors, affording "a hitherto unprecedented degree of spatial precision and quick reaction for health measures in Mexico."[21] Across the northern half of the country, a dozen new industrial plants slaughtered cattle and canned meat – technically private operations but underpinned by official credit and technical assistance, and generous US export contracts secured by Mexican diplomatic pressure.[22] Snaking through remote parts of central Mexico were 1,813 km of roads built or repaired by CMAEFA engineers to access operations and embed quarantine lines – a figure representing around 13 percent of the length of all new roads built by the Alemán administration, which itself built 80 percent more roads than its predecessor.[23] Mules, whose speed and supposed efficiency were prominent in CMAEFA propaganda, were less attractive than US and Mexican experts hoped.[24] Delivery was slow and leached by graft. Some villagers were quickly disappointed in the animals, which moved too fast for rocky ground, and proved overly headstrong. Compared to oxen, which fed on grass and corn husks, mules proved expensive to keep, consuming precious grains, and they could not be sold for meat or hide. Still, despite these problems, some communities – with cash to spare, and blessed with better soils and flatter fields – adopted them.[25]

---

[21] Sigsworth, "Mexican Epizootic," 280.   [22] Ibid., 335–56.

[23] Author's calculation based on: *La fiebre aftosa en México*, 78; Bess, *Routes*, 120. On the variable quality of roads and the importance of repairs, see Bess, *Routes*, 8–9, 130. Some state governments also "took advantage" of the campaign to build more airstrips in isolated regions. Pavia Guzmán, *Acciones*, 36.

[24] For examples of propaganda, see Soto Correa, *El rifle*, 71, 75.

[25] According to agronomists working for the state government, around 20 percent of Guanajuato's agricultural land was too rocky to be plowed by mules, but those farming

In particular, the campaign boosted the prestige and power of Mexico's veterinarians. Like Pavia, many regarded the aftosa campaign as a kind of professional rite of passage, and an indication they were ready to play a greater role in national development. Mexico's elite veterinary research scientists, quite reasonably, felt thoroughly vindicated, and some began to envision a larger role for themselves independent of US preferences.[26] Younger Mexican veterinarians involved in the field gathered together and published their recollections of the campaign shortly afterwards. Amid the jokes at the expense of ignorant gringos and campesinos, the purpose was to commemorate veterinarians' bravery and contribution to a grand endeavor and show their readiness for more work.[27] The aftosa commission allowed a number of officials to emerge as important political figures in their own right, with new connections and, in some cases, mysterious new sources of wealth. Oscar Flores, for his part, moved away from livestock matters, becoming governor of Chihuahua (1964–70) and then attorney general (1976–82), but continued to invoke his leadership of the aftosa campaign. In 1976 he pointed to his experience in the aftosa commission to reassure US officials planning another sensitive bilateral commission: the so-called Operation Condor, a brutal joint campaign against marijuana and opium farmers all the way down the Sierra Madre Oriental.[28] As far as livestock was concerned, the key figure was Dr. Lauro Ortega, who worked as Oscar Flores' right-hand man, reportedly ended the aftosa campaign a much richer man than when he began it, and became a political patron to other veterinarians working on the campaign.[29]

As the aftosa campaign wound down, the government entrusted Ortega with the reorganization of the Sub-ministry of Livestock (*Subsecretaría de Ganadería*, SSG). Created only days before the official

---

the rest of the land were enthusiastic about the program. Ing. León Carreo Inman, Jefe de la sección de organización agraria, Guanajuato, to state governor, May 14, 1947, AHEG, 3.40 (78), fiebre aftosa, 1947, vol. II. In Querétaro the state government claimed "many ejidatarios" also adopted mules. Figueroa Velázquez, *El tiro de gracia*, 130.

[26] For a discussion of Mexican experts' new international ambitions born of vaccine research, see Chapter 6.

[27] Torres y Elzaurdia, *Botas de hule*.

[28] "First meeting on narcotics with new attorney general," US embassy, Mexico City, to State Department, December 8, 1976, Special Assistant to the President-Bourne, "Mexican and US Cooperation in Narcotics Control," 12/76-1/77 [CF, O/A 156] [1], box 40, Carter Library. My thanks to Benjamin Smith for providing a copy of this document.

[29] Pavia Guzmán, *Recuerdos*, 94-9; Macías, *México*, 36.

recognition of the aftosa outbreak in December 1946, this new branch of the Ministry of Agriculture indicated the growing importance of livestock, although its first four years of existence were almost entirely dedicated to fighting aftosa. It was not until 1950 that Ortega and other campaign officials gradually put the SSG's National Commission for Livestock Recuperation – first announced by Alemán in November 1947 – into operation, supported by a new fund of five-and-a-half million pesos at the National Agricultural Bank dedicated to livestock, and an initial order of half-a-million pesos' worth of dairy cattle from the United States.[30] After Ortega's leadership, the SSG bought hundreds of breeding cattle, pigs, and sheep abroad, and distributed them to state governments and livestock associations. It also sent some animals to reactivate national breeding posts which had laid dormant since 1946, and to dozens of new provincial Livestock Development Centers, built by the SSG with the support of state governments between 1954 and 1958.[31]

Despite this flagship commission's name, the government hoped to go well beyond recuperation to some pre-epizootic norm. Areas that had suffered particularly from the sanitary rifle received attention from the SSG, but it also channeled breeding stock and technical assistance to areas that had largely escaped slaughter but were deemed strategic to modernization. The Livestock Development Centers were intended to spearhead a new extension drive, showing farmers the latest techniques in breeding, management and nutrition, and encouraging them to grasp new lines of livestock credit opened by the government in 1954. Alongside cattle and pigs, these centers promoted the intensification of poultry farming, identified as a crucial and dynamic sector on the cusp of major technical changes.[32] At the same time, the SSG started to contemplate further campaigns against cattle diseases and pests. In 1954 in Durango, it carried out a pilot project of tick eradication, during which brigades of veterinarians gradually moved through the state, building cattle dips, dousing cattle in arsenicals, and carrying out waves of inspections, much as they had while working for the CMAEFA.[33]

---

[30] Sigsworth, "Mexican Epizootic," 247–50; Ortiz Garza, Agriculture, to Beteta, Hacienda, September 8, 1950, AGN, MAV, 515/6811.

[31] Sigsworth, "Mexican Epizootic," 267–8. By 1959, there were twelve centers focused on cattle, and a further twenty-seven focused on pig farming. Saucedo, *Historia*, 163. For an account of negotiations between the federal and state governments over these centres, see Pavia Guzmán, *Recuerdos*, 100–6.

[32] Sigsworth, "Mexican Epizootic," 323–5; Pavia Guzmán, *Recuerdos*, 105.

[33] Sigsworth, "Mexican Epizootic," 323.

To staff these institutions, and raise the general level of education in veterinary science and animal husbandry, the government began to train more experts. In the early 1940s, around 100 students enrolled annually at the UNAM's School of Veterinary Medicine. By 1954, enrolments had more than doubled, and continued to grow steadily through the 1950s and 1960s.[34] Foreign experts regarded the "well planned, and spacious" veterinary school on the UNAM campus, opened in 1955, as the largest and most modern in Latin America.[35] In 1967, roughly 40 percent of the school's graduates worked in the public sector – mainly in the SSG, as extension agents for official banks, or in parallel agencies run by state governments. Later, veterinarians benefited from the mushrooming of the state bureaucracy under Echeverría (1970–6), and the creation of a dedicated livestock extension service. By 1976, the proportion of school graduates employed only by the state had risen to about two-thirds.[36]

All this heralded a lasting expansion of the role official veterinarians envisaged for themselves in the nation's development. In addition to their core work regulating livestock movements and enforcing sanitary protocols, the SSG's corps of regional veterinarians were now responsible for evangelizing the benefits of modern "technified" and "intensified" production to farmers big and small. They were to give advice on how to obtain official credit, control breeding, and produce "unified" livestock types in particular regions, "eliminate degenerated, dried up, and unproductive animals," improve and rotate pastures, register animals, keep proper business records, "do away with antiquated, antieconomic, and antihygienic methods" and convert farms into "commercial enterprises, not only for subsistence."[37] Intensifying livestock farming in this way would also, in theory, make these economic activities far easier for veterinarians to monitor and administer. Indeed, information gathering was another part of provincial officials' expanded job description. By the early 1960s, veterinarians were expected to spend at least fifteen days a month gathering data about the different economic regions in which they worked and preparing dozens of regional development plans.[38] Provincial veterinarians were encouraged to think of themselves as boosters for the

---

[34] Ibid., 303.

[35] José Santivanez, Ciencias Veterinarias, New York, to Dr. Miller, Rockefeller Foundation, November 27, 1954, RAC, group 1.2, series 323: Mexico, "University of Mexico, Veterinary Medicine."

[36] Mayer and Adler de Lomnitz, *La nueva*, 79–80. On extension services, see Chauvet, *La ganadería*, 134, n5.

[37] New field instructions, c. 1962, DGAG, 99, II, veterinarios regionales.   [38] Ibid.

livestock industry or, at least, understood that boosterism was what their superiors wanted to hear. Dr. Óscar Gutiérrez Becerra ended one field report from Veracruz with a breathless encomium for the livestock industry, "the strongest of all the industries" due to the "combined force of all the Mexican veterinarians."[39]

From the 1950s to the 1970s, the Mexican government also secured continued international support for its efforts to regulate and modernize livestock. The first two years of the aftosa campaign showed the political risks that came with accepting international assistance. However, the campaign's conclusion also seemed to confirm Mexican officials' ability to manage these risks and harness international forces to national objectives. It also shaped the practical details of cooperation in different, sometimes contradictory ways.

Most clearly, the aftosa commission laid the political and institutional (and indeed the architectural) foundation for further cooperation with the USDA on animal disease. The Palo Alto laboratory formed the headquarters for the CMAEFA's much smaller successor, the Joint Commission for the Prevention of Foot-and-Mouth Disease, created in 1952 and manned by a handful of Mexican and US scientists. The first two years of this commission were rather tense, as some Mexican officials sought to circumvent USDA policy and pursue an independent project of vaccine production and international engagement.[40] Once this effort was abandoned, the commission worked quite smoothly. Each year Palo Alto received and analyzed hundreds of virus samples sent in from the Mexican countryside, and archival records from the late 1950s and 1960s reveal little of the infighting so characteristic of earlier.[41] *Fiebre Aftosa*, one of the SSG's propaganda films from the early 1970s, gave pride of place to this commission, emphasized Mexican officials' scientific excellence and practical nous, and portrayed an idealized but not entirely unrealistic account of its work: first, extension agents visited a village, talked to locals and showed a film about the symptoms of diseases; farmers then reported suspicious symptoms to their local authorities, who informed the regional veterinarian; the veterinarian got in his pickup truck, drove to the farm, donned his overalls, inspected cattle, and then

---

[39] Oscar Gutiérrez Becerra, Santiago Tuxtla, Veracruz, to Dirección Fomento Ejidal, Agriculture, March 3, 1960, DGAG, 89, Veracruz.
[40] I recount this episode in more detail in Chapter 6.
[41] Annual catalogs of tests submitted can be found in DGAG, 130, "fiebre aftosa."

dispatched a virus sample by plane to the Palo Alto laboratory in a carefully sealed vial.[42]

The travails of a small group of Franco–Mexican cattle breeders illustrate the Mexican government's new concern with livestock genetics and improved coordination with the USDA over disease. In the early 1930s, the cattleman Juan Pugibet brought a herd of prime Charolais cattle to Mexico from France. By 1951, this "Pugibet herd" was owned by another Frenchmen named Gilly, who wanted to move the cattle across the US–Mexico border to sell to breeders eager for Charolais genes but found his path blocked. The Mexican government now regarded his herd as a "national treasure," essential for post-aftosa recuperation. Gilly eventually managed to smuggle his Charolais into Texas, only for USDA officials to repatriate them a few years later, whereupon the Mexican government seized part of the herd and sent them to the Livestock Development Center in Querétaro.[43] For their part, the USDA argued that this herd had been registered in the State of Puebla, outside of the eight northern states permitted to export to the United States under the post-aftosa agreement. Gilly and his group of aspiring Charolais breeders then lobbied extensively, set up their own breed registry, and received the backing of General Alejo González – the veteran of the aftosa campaign who devoted himself to ranching after retiring from the army. In 1962, they eventually persuaded the US and Mexican governments to allow some Charolais bulls to enter the United States, although competing Texan ranchers then resorted to sabotage: "somehow" the dipping vats at Eagle Pass were spiked with extra arsenic – "enough to 'cook the nuts' on bulls."[44] The Charolais group were wise to this ruse and dodged the vats in question, but sanitary protocols still made it difficult to develop the enterprise. In 1963, they begged the Mexican government to allow them to import Charolais from France via a new Canadian quarantine station but were rebuffed. President López Mateos "wasn't interested" and "wasn't cattle people," while the Minister of Agriculture, Juan Preciado, another veteran of the aftosa campaign, "was afraid of the hoof-and-mouth."[45]

In the 1960s, Mexico's progress in monitoring aftosa encouraged an even more audacious joint campaign against another shared biological obstacle. The screwworm, or *gusano barrenador*, was in fact a fly endemic to most of the warmer regions of Mexico, whose flesh-eating

---

[42] *Fiebre aftosa.*   [43] Ewing, *Ranch*, 173.   [44] Ibid., 213.
[45] Manuel Garza Elizondo, in ibid., 216.

larvae thrived in the cuts and abrasions suffered by cattle and sapped the productivity of livestock farming. The origins of this campaign lay in the experiments of USDA entomologists who sterilized flies by radiation after the Second World War. First in Florida and then across the US Southwest, USDA officials gathered millions of flies at huge plants, fed them on enormous quantities of meat and blood, dosed them with radiation, and then released them at strategic points across the landscape. The costs and difficulties of administering the vast US–Mexico border region eventually encouraged both governments to negotiate a bilateral anti-screwworm commission, created in 1972. This commission gradually steered the campaign southwards through Mexico, and reached the Guatemalan border in 1985. The USDA then collaborated with Central American governments to push eradication down to the Isthmus of Panama, and set up a permanent plant to hold the screwworm border there.[46]

The earlier fight against aftosa underpinned the screwworm campaign in various ways, and this was obvious to officials at the time. In the early 1960s, the USDA asked Mexico to gather and analyze data on the distribution of screwworms across Mexico's northern states. It was the offices of the aftosa prevention commission at Palo Alto which carried out this work. When reports were slow to arrive, Mexico's SSG chivvied officials into action by invoking their "patriotic spirit, shown so nobly already in the campaign against *fiebre aftosa*."[47] The overall US strategy of pushing the border for screwworm southwards closely echoed the aftosa campaigns. So too did many of the logistical and organizational arrangements in the joint commission, where hundreds of field personnel worked in binational teams. Negotiations with the US government over screwworm were drawn-out and sometimes tense, as Mexico sought to reduce financial obligations while obtaining support for national object-ives. They also subtly benefited from personal networks built since the 1940s. Gustavo Reta Pettersson, who led technical negotiations for Mexico, was a friend of the USDA's representative, Dr. Robert Sharman – a CMAEFA veteran who had worked periodically in Mexico since 1948. According to Reta Pettersson, while US senators pushed Mexico to carry most of the costs for the campaign, he and Sharman calmly sat down and worked out a statistical formula for cost-sharing

---

[46] For an overview, see Zhang, "America's Never-ending Battle." See also Scruggs, *The Peaceful Atom.*

[47] Undated circular, Sub-ministry of livestock, to veterinarios regionales, c. 1961, DGAG, 99, II.

based on each country's respective livestock numbers. On this basis, Mexico finally agreed to pay around 20 percent of the costs, rather than the 50 percent proposed by the USDA.[48] To obtain additional resources for its own slow-moving and cash-strapped tick campaign – considered a higher priority than screwworm by Ministry of Agriculture officials – Mexico also wanted to combine it with the screwworm campaign in a single joint commission. While the campaigns remained separate, Mexico obtained an International Development Bank loan to support tick eradication shortly after 1972. The USDA initially wanted to build screwworm-radiating plants on three huge ships to be moored off the Mexican coast for the duration of the campaign. Mexico argued that this was impractical and, much like during the aftosa campaign, successfully pushed the USDA to support permanent technical and laboratory facilities.[49]

   The Mexican government also obtained support from the Rockefeller Foundation for its efforts to modernize livestock. Livestock affairs were not entirely absent from the early years of the MAP. In 1943, the Mexican government was "very keen" to get support for its fight against the disease known as *derriengue* – a virus transmitted by vampire bats, that killed tens of thousands of livestock animals each year in areas adjoining bats' wooded habitats.[50] The Rockefeller Foundation sponsored a visit by a small team of researchers and helped identify the virus as a type of paralytic rabies, in the process working with the man who would later lead Mexico's aftosa vaccine research: Alfredo Téllez Girón. (In addition to being a promising virologist, Téllez Girón was "obviously a white man": a quality the Rockefeller Foundation believed would be useful should he visit a university or laboratory in the US South.)[51] Rockefeller

[48] Reta Pettersson, *Indiscreciones*, 60–74. Reta Pettersson also considered Dr. Saulmon, another CMAEFA veteran who had trained and advised him, as a mentor. Ibid., 72.

[49] Reta Pettersson, *Indiscreciones*, 60–74; Zhang, "America's Never-ending Battle"; Feder, *Lean Cows*, 263; Vargas-Terán, "The New World." In 1962, the anti-tick campaign waged across the northern states of Mexico boasted all of two officials, thirteen inspectors, two pick-up trucks, and eight "mobile tick dips." "Plan estructural y técnico para la realización de campañas sanitarias veterinarias 1963–5," Dirección Sanidad Animal, DGAG, 132.

[50] Harrar, Mexico City, to "FBH," New York, September 7, 1943, RAC, group 1.1, series 323 Mexico, box 15, "Instituto Pecuario, Téllez Girón." In 1943, the disease killed around 20,000 animals, a particularly bad year. Various reports, 1943–5, RAC, group 6.13, series 1.1 Mexico Field Office, box 43, "Agriculture, Derriengue."

[51] Blair Hansen, Rockefeller Institute, to Dr. George Payne, St. Louis, Missouri, September 13, 1943, RAC, group 1.1, series 323 Mexico, box 15, "Instituto Pecuario, Téllez Girón."

Foundation officials also noted Mexico's thinly stretched veterinary services and deficient training in husbandry, but during the Second World War crops were the priority for the foundation and Mexican officials. In any case, in 1944, violent clashes between rival student groups at the veterinary school halted animal research, and then the aftosa outbreak put plans for the MAP to expand research into animal farming on hold.[52]

As the aftosa campaign drew to a successful conclusion, various Mexican officials urged the Rockefeller Foundation to increase its support for livestock research and education, and it gradually did.[53] The Rockefeller Foundation initially preferred to build on its existing work on corn and wheat by helping to map existing grasslands and experiment with different pasture crops and feeds.[54] Of the experiment stations jointly run with the Mexican Ministry of Agriculture, most significant for livestock work would be Cal Grande in the pig-farming hub of La Piedad in the central Bajío region, La Campana in the dry prairies of Chihuahua, and the Cotaxtla station on the tropical coasts of Veracruz.[55] In 1955, the Rockefeller Foundation also agreed to support a small pilot program of research on poultry breeding and disease. It identified chicken-farming as a rapidly changing sector crucial for gains in nutrition. Relatively quick progress in this area, it was hoped, might encourage Mexican research on other species and problems around the country.[56] In the late 1950s, the Rockefeller Foundation decided "the time was ripe" to increase support for Mexican livestock farming and education.[57] First, the MAP's experiment camps in Veracruz and Chihuahua moved from measuring pasture yields to systematic experiments on the effects of

---

[52] Harrar, Mexico City, to Hanson, Rockefeller Foundation, August 11, 1944, RAC, group 1.1, series 323 Mexico, box 15, "Instituto Pecuario, Téllez Girón." Pitched battles at the veterinary school were part of a larger political dispute over leadership of the university. See, Pavia Guzmán, *Recuerdos*, 62–7.

[53] Various correspondence, Jorge de Alba, Hermosillo, to Harrar, Rockefeller Foundation, 1951, RAC, group 6.13, series 1.1 Mexico Field Office, box 17; Ing. Gonzalo Garrido, Oficina de experimentación agrícola, Comisión del Papaloapan, "Anteproyecto para el mejoramiento de la ganadería," RAC, group 6.13, series 1.1, Mexico Field Office, box 31, "livestock improvement project, January 1953."

[54] Stakman, Bradfield, Mangelsdorf, *Campaigns*, 165, 169–71.

[55] Various correspondence, RAC, group 6.13, series 1.1, box 20, "forage grasses and legumes, 1953–1960."

[56] Stakman, Bradfield, Mangelsdorf, *Campaigns*, 171.

[57] K. Turk, "Suggestions for consideration by the Rockefeller Foundation for an expanded animal science program in Mexico," c.1959, RAC, group, 6.13, series 1.1, box 2, "Animal Science."

different pastures on breeds of livestock.[58] Second, the Rockefeller Foundation began to support the government's efforts to train more livestock experts, sending a small grant of $40,000 to a new school of animal husbandry in Chihuahua in 1957, $145,000 to the UNAM's veterinary school in 1959, and several dozen smaller grants and scholarships to veterinary officials and students.[59] In 1962, these initiatives culminated in the creation of the *Centro Nacional de Investigaciones Pecuarias* (CNIP), a Rockefeller-funded program headed by its poultry specialist, Dr. John Antony Pino, but increasingly focused on tropical beef and dairy farming.[60] Just like the continuing collaborations with the USDA, this center was based at Palo Alto, but it also sponsored research at the SSG's regional livestock centers, and its staff periodically advised and taught at the UNAM veterinary school and the Chapingo agricultural college. The most obvious driver of new research was the expectation – shared by Rockefeller and Mexican experts, and many ranchers themselves – that tropical ranching was set to expand dramatically, and so "the greatest immediate return for dollars spent in teaching and research in animal husbandry in Mexico can be derived from expenditures in semi-tropical and tropical animal husbandry."[61]

Alongside these economic trends, the aftosa campaign shaped the Rockefeller Foundation's plans for livestock in different ways. Rockefeller experts regarded the campaign's legacies with ambivalence. They regarded the control of epizootic disease as an indispensable first step in modernization, and believed the campaign had alerted the government to the importance of livestock. However, it was clear by the late 1950s that post-aftosa institutions still left room for improvement. A particular "disappointment" were the SSG's Livestock Development Centers, which were undermined by graft, conducted no original research into breeding, and required stronger "leadership."[62] In April 1961, an

---

[58] Ibid.

[59] Wellhausen, Mexico City to Harrar, New York, January 3, 1957, RAC, group 1.2, series 323 Mexico, box 47, "University of Chihuahua"; various correspondence, 1959–60, RAC, group 1.2, series 323 Mexico, box 51, "University of Mexico, veterinary medicine." With the foundation's sponsorship, by 1964 seventeen Mexican men had obtained US graduate degrees in the animal sciences. Stakman, Bradfield, Mangelsdorf, *Campaigns*, 174.

[60] Ibid.; Cervantes Sánchez, Román de Carlos, López Montelongo (eds.), *La medicina*, 189.

[61] Lewis Holland, "Observations concerning animal husbandry education in Mexico," 1966, RAC, Ford Foundation, box 185, report 004077.

[62] K. Turk, "Suggestions for consideration by the Rockefeller Foundation for an expanded animal science program in Mexico," c.1959, RAC, group, 6.13, series 1.1, box 2, "Animal Science."

outbreak of avian laringotracheitis – a respiratory disease similar to bronchitis – further underlined frailties in disease control. It began in poultry farms around Ixtapalapa, the main neighborhood supplying Mexico City with eggs. The government dispatched veterinary inspectors and a battalion of soldiers, imposed quarantine, and enforced its protocols for this particular disease: the immediate slaughter and incineration of all infected and exposed birds.[63] The parallels with 1947 were obvious and, for a few months, the outbreak threatened to unleash a larger political crisis. Many poultry farmers resented the policy – nicknamed the "sanitary garotte" after veterinarians' preferred method of dispatching birds.[64] Columnists wondered whether slaughter was really a ruse pushed on the Mexican government by the United States to cement Mexico's dependence on US stock and destroy Mexican farmers' own breeding innovations.[65] As in 1947, some officials worried that slaughter would simply cause farmers to hide their animals and smuggle them through the quarantine lines. Students and faculty at the UNAM's veterinary school argued that "slaughter leads no-where," advocated vaccination, and condemned the government for ignoring the lessons of the aftosa campaign.[66] In response, the Minister of Agriculture, Julián Rodríguez Adame, bolstered military quarantine, visited Ixtapalapa in person to hear farmers' complaints, promised to offer fair compensation, and planted stories in the press to discredit criticism. Federal police also visited the veterinary school and even briefly arrested Professor Ernesto Bachtold, suspected of spearheading criticism of slaughter.[67] The government had clearly learned some political lessons of the aftosa campaign. It also used the Palo Alto laboratory to identify the virus, produce a reserve vaccine, and reassure the poultry industry and its own officials that the government was prepared with a mixed strategy should the disease spread beyond quarantined areas.[68] Still, the head of the

---

[63] "Campaña contra laringotraqueitis en Ixtapalapa, DF," report dated July 5, 1961, DGAG, 102.

[64] *Excélsior*, June 27, 1961.

[65] Various clippings, May–June 1961, DGAG, 104, "Laringotraqueitis, protestas." The Ministry of Agriculture itself admitted that its slaughter policy was the result of long-standing protocols and the advice it had received from USDA officials and associations of US poultry farmers. Ibid.

[66] Clipping from *Novedades*, May 30, 1961, in DGAG, 104, "Laringotraqueitis, protestas."

[67] Various correspondence, 1961, DGAG, 104, "Laringotraqueitis, protestas."

[68] Various reports on visit of Secretary Rodríguez Adame to Iztapalapa, June 9, 1961, ibid.

Rockefeller Foundation's livestock research, John Antony Pino, still believed that the affair "had been badly handled," and showed the problems that still beset Mexico's veterinary infrastructure.[69]

Indeed, as far as the Rockefeller Foundation's experts were concerned, the aftosa campaign not only left certain problems in place but actually aggravated them. In particular, by strengthening the authority of Mexico's veterinarians – especially its virological researchers – the campaign helped embed organizational disfunction. Across Latin America, the field of animal husbandry or *zootecnia* – the practical application of advances in breeding, nutrition, sanitation, and other aspects of livestock management – was normally regarded as one (minor) part of the job of either veterinarians or agronomists, and professional rivalry between these *gremios* was common. After agrarian reform boosted the status of agronomists in the 1930s, and the aftosa campaign had a similar effect on veterinarians, in Mexico it was particularly visible. "In no place in Latin America," noted one Rockefeller Foundation official, "is the competition for control of the field of animal husbandry as fierce as it is in Mexico between the veterinarians and the agronomists."[70] Turf wars aside, the Rockefeller Foundation believed that allowing veterinarians to control research, training and extension in animal husbandry was unhelpful. This was seen partly as a problem of under-specialization; animal husbandry was large and complex enough to be considered its own field of expertise, as it was in the United States. It also encouraged a confusion of roles, as veterinarians found themselves responsible for both regulation (of disease) and for economic growth and intensification. Underlaying these concerns, but rarely made explicit, was a certain anxiety among Rockefeller Foundation experts and advisors about the correct balance of public and private power. Veterinarians were, at core, "professionals," and closely tied to the state's regulatory functions; they had a role in modernization, but what Mexico needed in even greater numbers were

[69] John A. Pino, Mexico City, to Ralph Richardson, Rockefeller Foundation, New York, November 28, 1961, RAC, group 6.13, series 1.1 Mexico Field Office, box 49, "John A. Pino."

[70] John J. McKelvey ("JJM"), memorandum on Escuela Nacional de Medicina Veterinaria y Zootecnía, April 14, 1959, RAC, group 1.2, series 323: Mexico, "University of Mexico, Science Institutes, Veterinary Science." In the early 1980s, agronomists still undercut veterinarian colleagues in Jalisco, giving advance warning of livestock disease campaigns to rural communities to earn local support for their own programs. Arce, *Negotiating*, 90.

specialists in animal husbandry – a figure seen as more like a "technically-trained businessman."[71]

The Rockefeller Foundation tried various methods to nudge Mexican training and organization closer to the US model, but found the terrain of educational infrapolitics slow going. In Chihuahua, it was worried that Dr. Rubio Lozano, a veteran of the aftosa campaign and "too powerful a figure" in state politics, would dominate teaching at the new school of animal husbandry he had helped found in 1953–4. MAP officials withheld support until they received assurances from the school that Rubio's influence would be curtailed and were told that $300,000 of federal funding for the school was conditional on the faculty following MAP advice.[72] In 1956, the Rockefeller Foundation invited the new head of the UNAM veterinary school, Oscar Valdés Ornelas, to tour model US colleges and learn about their approach to husbandry. Valdés thanked the foundation effusively for the opportunity to learn about "the Latin American problem in teaching veterinary medicine," but promised no specific reforms.[73] In the late 1950s, the MAP angered Mexico's veterinarians by expanding husbandry training for the agronomists at Chapingo. Adler de Lomnitz and Mayer's argument that veterinary science represented a more internationally-oriented "developmentalist" profession compared to the "nationalist" agronomists would have been news to the Rockefeller Foundation.[74] Agronomists' association with agrarian reform notwithstanding, Rockefeller officials believed that they were a better choice to control the field of husbandry, given their already close ties to the MAP, and agronomists' more integrated understanding of the interrelationship of soil, fodder, and livestock.[75] When Dr. Fernando Camargo was elected to run the UNAM veterinary school in 1960, the

[71] I. D. Wilson, "The Education of Animal Husbandmen," paper given at First Pan-American Congress of Veterinary Medicine, c. 1951, attached to K. Turk, "Suggestions for consideration by the Rockefeller Foundation for an expanded animal science program in Mexico," c.1959, RAC, group, 6.13, series 1.1, box 2, "Animal Science."

[72] Memo of John J. McKelvey interview, Escuela de Ganadería, Universidad de Chihuahua, April 1958, and Wellhausen, Mexico City to Harrar, New York, January 3, 1957, RAC, group 1.2, series 323 Mexico, box 47, "University of Chihuahua, animal science."

[73] Valdés Ornelas, Ames, Iowa, to John Pino, Rockefeller Foundation, New York, April 4, 1958, RAC, group 1.1, series 323 Mexico, box 15, "University of Mexico, Veterinary Medicine, Valdés Ornelas, Oscar."

[74] Mayer and Adler de Lomnitz, *La nueva*, 69.

[75] K. Turk, "Suggestions for consideration by the Rockefeller Foundation for an expanded animal science program in Mexico," RAC, group, 6.13, series 1.1, box 2, "Animal Science."

foundation worried that he would cling to husbandry, resist any expansion at Chapingo, and continue to prioritize the pure research and virology he had honed as head of vaccine production during the aftosa campaign. They refrained from responding to any of Camargo's requests for further assistance, and within a few months he had been replaced by a director more supportive of the foundation's objectives.[76]

When the MAP concluded in 1965, the Rockefeller Foundation was privately rather disappointed with progress in husbandry education. It cautioned the Ford Foundation from continuing similar plans unless it had assurances about control over curricula and, not least, some way to insulate itself from university and student politics. In Chihuahua, Rubio Lozano had died in 1959, but his faction of veterinarians still dominated teaching at the animal husbandry school.[77] Pino's relationship with the UNAM concluded with a furious argument with members of the university senate after they broke what he considered a "moral obligation" to continue funding four full-time professorships in husbandry established by the Rockefeller grant.[78] Eventually, the UNAM's veterinary school found the Food and Agriculture Organization (FAO) a more amenable international partner and, in 1968, signed a five-year agreement which boosted support for graduate training abroad, allowed the school's more prestigious researchers to compete for scholarships, and laid the pathway for the school's recognition as a full faculty.[79] For better or worse, the experience confirmed the ability of Mexican officials to obtain international support, without importing policy prescriptions wholesale.

In 1958, the livestock and agricultural research station at Cotaxtla created a new logo resembling the map of a military conquest. Dozens of arrows emerged outwards from the camp, and spread across the surrounding tropics, launching technical expertise and improvement like columns of soldiers or a salvo of missiles.[80] Forceful images like this pervaded the Ministry of Agriculture's propaganda, but officials

---

[76] G. Harrar, Rockefeller Foundation, New York, to R. Richardson, Mexico City, April 29, 1959; marginal note to McKelvey, on M. W. Allam, Rockefeller Foundation, New York, to F. Camargo, Mexico City, June 25, 1959; J. A. Pino, Mexico City, to Moseman, Rockefeller Foundation, New York, September 22, 1960, in RAC, group 1.1, series 323 Mexico, box 15, "University of Mexico, science institutes, veterinary medicine."

[77] Lewis Holland, "Animal husbandry at University of Chihuahua," July 1965, RAC, Ford Foundation reports, unpublished reports, box 17, 000301.

[78] Memo on interview with J. A. Pino, Mexico City, March 12, 1963, RAC, group 1.1, series 323 Mexico, box 15, "University of Mexico, science institutes, veterinary medicine."

[79] Mayer and Adler de Lomnitz, *La nueva*, 87–88.

[80] Various correspondence, 1958–9, RAC, group 6.13, series 1.2, box 65, folders 734–5.

understood they were illusory. Obstacles to the state-backed modernization of livestock were many, and went well beyond problems of professional jealousies and under-specialization.

For a start, as desirable as livestock intensification was in theory,
other government objectives and agencies pulled in different directions.
Most important, as industrialization and urbanization gathered pace after
the 1940s, the government was particularly concerned to protect the
interests of urban consumers of beef and milk: through prices controls,
and the importation and production of powdered milk. Farmers often
resented these policies which, they argued, limited their ability to accumulate capital and reinvest in the fences, breeds, feed, and other innovations that might modernize their enterprises. In some places, the federal
government sought to curb the power of over-mighty rancher caciques by
investing in competing industrial and irrigation projects.[81]

Unsurprisingly, some veterinarians were on the take, and occasionally
in grand style. According to complaints from Torreón, Dr. Fernando
Salinas used his regulatory power to create a formidable *cacicazgo*,
exploiting the desires of ranchers in the central states to access the US
export market. "Papa Salinas" sold false permits, arranging for trains to
arrive at night to avoid attracting too much attention. To avoid compli-
cations he appointed friends to various other official posts, including his
own son at the district slaughter house and packing plant, and intimi-
dated opponents by boasting of his political support in Mexico City.[82] As
the director of the Livestock Development Center in the poor and
unstable state of Guerrero, Edgar Pavia struggled to create long-term
programs in the face of hostile camarillas and governors who emptied
the treasury or allied with cattle-rustlers. Federal agronomists sent to the
state were also unhelpful, mocking veterinarians' technical ability and
arguing that livestock initiatives wasted resources better spent on crops.
Years later, Pavia also admitted siphoning off funds and produce for his
own veterinary business and farm. The interim state governor gave Pavia
his blessing since, he argued, if Pavia did not take the resources they

---

[81] Yates, *Mexico's Agricultural Dilemma*, 96, 111; Ochoa, "Reappraising"; miscellaneous
correspondence, 1960–6, DGAG, 129, quejas; Lomnitz, *Exits*, 194–5. According to one
Ford Foundation report, Mexico's elite veterinary scientists at Palo Alto were generally
supportive of controls on beef prices and were "quite concerned over the possible social
problems that higher retail meat prices would create with consumers." K. Turk, "Appraisal
of Education and Research in Animal Sciences at Monterrey and Mexico City," February
1967, RAC, Ford Foundation reports, unpublished reports, box 70, report 001853.

[82] Elías Núñez, to Daniel Mercado, Agriculture, December 4, 1961, DGAG, 100, Durango.

would only fall prey to officials from a rival political group.[83] Pavia's case was symptomatic. Professional recognition after the aftosa campaign often cleared a path for entrepreneurial opportunities, and many veterinarians combined official responsibilities with business, founding their own clinics, pharmacies, milk pasteurization plants, private laboratories, and vaccine firms.[84]

Graft aside, federal officials still had very limited resources with which to regulate and propel change. Livestock's share of the Ministry of Agriculture's budget reached 11 percent during the peak of the aftosa campaign, fluctuated between 2 percent and 8 percent for the next decade, and only exceeded its 1940s share again in the mid-1960s.[85] After 1952, veterinarians got a new institutional niche then, but no blank cheque. Likewise, their political authority was highly contingent. In the midst of the aftosa campaign, the federal government banned municipal authorities from serving as auxiliary livestock inspectors, and ordered that all sanitary checks and paperwork be conducted by state and federal veterinarians. At the end of the campaign municipal authorities regained these powers. In theory, federal veterinarians could deauthorize corrupt or inept municipal inspectors but, as one pointed out in a private complaint, they sometimes lacked the political connections and support to do so.[86] Veterinary officials also complained about the disjuncture between their growing job description and their limited transport and pay, and need to moonlight in the private sector.[87] Often provincial officials ignored more unrealistic federal demands. Judging by the remaining archives, few of the regional surveys and development plans veterinarians were supposed to prepare ever materialized. According to an internal report commissioned in 1962, only around half of the SSG's provincial officials submitted regular, adequate reports. A quarter of officials submitted sporadic and vague reports, and the SSG never heard from the remaining quarter of provincial officials at all.[88]

Indeed, the federal government's view of the contours of the livestock economy was very patchy. As we saw in Chapter 4, by the early 1950s the

---

[83] Pavia Guzmán, *Recuerdos*, 106–7.

[84] Saucedo, *Historia*, 15; Pavia Guzmán, *Recuerdos*; Bachtold, "Remembranzas."

[85] Sigsworth, "Mexican Epizootic," 251–2.

[86] Miscellaneous correspondence, Renan Burgos, to Agriculture, 1964, DGAG, 100, Oaxaca.

[87] Miscellaneous complaints, 1960–5, DGAG, 99–100, veterinarios regionales.

[88] Salvador Velázquez Anchondo, to Daniel Mercado, Agriculture, January 16, 1962, DGAG, 99, veterinarios regionales.

CMAEFA had gathered more and better information about livestock numbers, property, routes, and markets than the government had previously possessed. And yet, the lenses through which federal officials viewed the countryside quickly fogged again and remained so for decades. National livestock statistics in the 1960s and 1970s were notoriously unreliable. In 1977, Paul Yates annoyed the Mexican government by publishing a long list of serious and sometimes downright bizarre statistical anomalies, which were particularly pronounced in the livestock census. Without this kind of information, it was very difficult to regulate the livestock industry, let alone carry out more ambitious developmental plans. In the early 1960s, input-output models were "all the rage," and the Mexican government hired British and Dutch economic advisors to gather statistics and analyze general patterns in production. The discrepancies in livestock production figures were so great that the advisors eventually gave up, and generated their own figures using statistical "ingenuity."[89]

Given these limitations, it was clear that any project to regulate, sanitize, and modernize livestock farming required cooperation from Mexican farmers' themselves. The campaign against aftosa underlined this political lesson in no uncertain terms and, in some ways, it also made such cooperation easier to obtain and coordinate. During the campaign, some farmers took matters into their own hands, using home remedies, private veterinarians, and more fencing to protect and control their own herds – even causing a spike in demand for US supplies of barbed wire.[90] But the crisis had also boosted some ranchers' appetite for official assistance, or at least showed it to be a necessary evil. A crucial support base for vaccination, organized ranchers demanded more and better veterinarians to oversee livestock shipments, protect their investments, and allow quarantine restrictions to slacken. Indeed, some complained that the demands of the aftosa campaign caused authorities to neglect other sanitary problems, like derriengue.[91] Some ranchers also used the campaign to build social connections. A branch of the SSG was dedicated to liaising with livestock associations, and one of its first leaders was Edgar Pavia, chosen because of the personal and political connections he had forged to Guerrero's ranching families during the aftosa campaign.[92]

---

[89] Yates, *Memoirs*, unpublished manuscript, PLY, 300–4, 77.   [90] *Campaign*, 183.

[91] Various reports, October 1947–February 1948, CMAEFA, operations, box 29, Guerrero, Jalisco; various correspondence, 1951, AGN, MAV, 950/17619; various correspondence, January 1948, AHEG, 3.40 (78), fiebre aftosa, 1948, vol. I. See also, Sigsworth, "Mexican Epizootic," 286–7.

[92] Sigsworth, "Mexican Epizootic," 285–97; Pavia Guzmán, *Recuerdos*, 80.

William Doughty, a former US marine who joined the commission after a brief stint as a riot policeman in British India in Calcutta, portrayed vaccination and inspection in central Veracruz as a joint operation with the area's big cattle ranchers. These men also befriended Doughty, sought his advice on cattle raising, offered to help him purchase his own lands in the area, and appointed him an honorary member of the local police, credentials and all.[93]

The campaign certainly prompted more farmers to gather in federally-authorized livestock associations. Since 1934, the government had invited ranchers to join these corporate associations to represent their interests to the government. They were concentrated in the cattle-raising heartlands of the north and the Huasteca and, after an early spate of registrations in 1937–8, the formation of livestock associations slowed in the early 1940s. In 1946, the rate at which these associations were formed and their geographical dispersion picked up notably and continued throughout the epizootic.[94] The shift was particularly abrupt in central states like Guanajuato, Querétaro, and Guerrero, where only a handful of local associations existed prior to 1947.[95] Similarly, the crisis "accelerated" changes in the milk industry, encouraging the remaining dairy farmers around Mexico City to create an organization to bargain with the government over fresh milk prices and "cooperate with sanitary authorities as a block."[96]

These associations represented an alliance of convenience between farmers and the state. The aftosa crisis made it much harder to ignore government overtures to join. To gain permission to restock or access credit, ranchers either had to be part of an approved association, or secure its approval.[97] For ranchers, joining a group implied a certain loss of autonomy, since the federal government in principle retained the right to

---

[93] Doughty, *Gringo Livestock Inspector*, 11–35.

[94] Saucedo, *Historia*, 64; Sigsworth, "Mexican Epizootic," 283–5. On the burst of associations formed in southern Veracruz in 1947–8, see Léonard, "Los empresarios."

[95] Guanajuato had no state-wide regional association before November 1947. Luis Palacios, Report on first meeting of comités regionales de lucha contra la aftosa, Guanajuato, November 5, 1947, AHEG, 3.40 (78), fiebre aftosa, 1948, vol. VI. Similarly, 1947 saw the creation of many local associations across Guerrero, including a new regional association covering the north of the state. Pavia, *Acciones*, 32. For the creation of a state-wide livestock union in Querétaro in 1950, and its close ties to state government officials, see Figueroa Velázquez, *El tiro de gracia*, 233.

[96] Zazueta, "Milk," 177.

[97] For restocking rules and farmers' requests for information on how to form associations, see AHEG, 3.40 (78), fiebre aftosa, 1948, vol. I.

deny or rescind authorization, but also promised new kinds of influence. Besides technical assistance and credit, livestock producer associations used the aftosa crisis to successfully lobby for sector-wide tax breaks. They also pushed to control access to the urban meat and milk markets, albeit with less long-term success.[98] It is difficult to know how much the aftosa outbreak weighed on Alemán's decision to strengthen protections for ranchers' property rights, although the timing is certainly suggestive. In January 1947, Alemán sent a bill to the Mexican congress increasing the amount of pasture land that was immune to expropriation, just as his administration made arrangements for the CMAEFA, boisterous meetings of cattlemen took place in Mexico City, and the shots of the noisy polemic over slaughter ricocheted around the cabinet and national newspapers. The newspaper *Excélsior* hinted that the two processes were related, reassuring readers that "although herds will be reduced, pasture land will not be."[99]

More broadly, forming livestock associations also offered a way for stockmen to update their role in the imaginary of Mexican development, casting aside old associations of technological backwardness and tradition, and crafting a new image as progressive forces. Again, Mexican officials invited stockmen to accept this role and view the aftosa campaign as a springboard towards further progress. In 1947, Guanajuato's *Comité regional de lucha contra la aftosa* – a gathering of state and local officials, ranchers, pig and dairy farmers – argued that livestock associations were now "an urgent necessity, not just to make the campaign against aftosa effective, but in a more fundamental sense, so the state and the country can organize the exploitation of agricultural resources technically, scientifically, and rationally ... They will be the best allies to the government in bringing about the economic development of the country."[100] In the 1950s and 1960s, livestock associations across Mexico generally presented themselves as patriotic enthusiasts of state-backed

[98] Luis Palacios, Report on first meeting of comités regionales de lucha contra la aftosa, Guanajuato, November 5, 1947, AHEG, 3.40 (78), fiebre aftosa, 1948, vol. VI; Figueroa Velázquez, *El tiro de gracia*, 231, 234; Castro Rosales, "La aftosa," 229–30. The government exercised a tighter control over meat marketing during the years of the epizootic, but never succeeded in eliminating the complicated system of middlemen that controlled marketing. Lopes and de los Reyes Patiño, "Institutions and Interest Groups."

[99] *Excélsior*, May 30, 1947, quoted in Soto Correa, *El rifle*, 67.

[100] Luis Palacios, Report on first meeting of comités regionales de lucha contra la aftosa, Guanajuato, November 5, 1947, AHEG, 3.40 (78), fiebre aftosa, 1948, vol. VI.

modernization and industrialization. Countless petitions sent to the SSG boasted of the innovations ranchers had adopted, from tick baths to regular veterinary check-ups, and complained about obstacles that undermined national progress, particularly cattle rustling, insecure tenure, and agrarismo.[101] In the Huasteca, building a tick bath on a ranch was a way for "rich ranchers" to show "wealth, importance, and progressiveness."[102] In Chiapas this shift had a sartorial counterpart, as ranchers swapped their "planter's white suit for blue jeans and boots," thereby staking a claim to modernity and "shedding their connection to Porfirian latifundios."[103]

In practice, stock-farmers' attitudes to state-assisted modernization were rather selective. From the late 1950s to the 1970s, Mexican officials, Rockefeller agronomists, and visiting ethnographers all recognized a growing interest in new improved pastures and feeds. Pig and poultry farmers drove a rapid expansion of sorghum and alfalfa. Many beef-cattle ranchers adopted the new grasses promoted by the government's extension campaigns, especially in the Huasteca and in central Veracruz.[104] Campaigns against disease generally received, and indeed relied on, continued support from livestock associations. The new system of aftosa surveillance functioned not just because of improved communications and laboratories, but because regional livestock associations continued to create lay inspector teams – first established during the latter phases of aftosa campaign. The same associations supported the government's plan to combat screwworm with US assistance.[105] Beef and dairy interests also offered political and financial support for the expansion of education, although associations tended to focus on regional schools and colleges, which could specialize in the particular problems of their regions.[106]

---

[101] Various correspondence, 1965–6, DGAG, 129, quejas.   [102] Feder, *Lean Cows*, 212.
[103] Bobrow-Strain, *Intimate Enemies*, 173.
[104] Schryer, *Ethnicity and Class*, 153; González-Montagut, "Factors"; K. Turk, "Suggestions for consideration by the Rockefeller Foundation for an expanded animal science program in Mexico," c.1959, RAC, group, 6.13, series 1.1, box 2, "Animal Science"; various correspondence, 1958–9, RAC, group 6.13, series 1.1, box 20, "forage grasses and legumes, 1953–1960."
[105] Miscellaneous correspondence, DGAG, 103, fiebre aftosa; "Plan estructural y técnico para la realización de campañas sanitarias veterinarias 1963–5," Dirección Sanidad Animal, DGAG, 132; Zhang, "America's Never-ending Battle."
[106] Between 1957 and 1965 seven regional schools had been built, beginning in Veracruz. Sigsworth, "Mexican Epizootic," 260. For examples of support from state livestock associations, see Lewis Holland, "Observations concerning animal husbandry education in Mexico," 1966, RAC, Ford Foundation, box 185, report 004077. For Chihuahua ranchers' support for a regional husbandry school and suspicion of federal veterinary

By contrast, most ranchers had little interest in the state's project of information gathering. Faulty statistics and maps were not primarily the result of official incompetence. Rather, ranchers made "every effort" to "deceive with respect who owns what land and who owns what cattle," reduce their tax liabilities and, most important, minimize the risk of expropriation. In the 1970s, such tactics still confused government agencies and banks in the Huasteca, although the real extent of ranchers' ownership of land and cattle were "public knowledge" locally. Facing these difficulties, officials normally just relied on the dubious figures provided by ranchers' own associations.[107] (Privately some federal officials were resigned to observing livestock farming only in its murky outlines. In 1956, the UNAM's geography department asked officials at the Ministry of Agriculture and the Ministry of National Defense to help produce more accurate maps and statistics, showing a list of hundreds of anomalies and errors in the 1950 census. They shrugged and muttered that any such effort was futile since "it would take 500 years to survey all of Mexico.")[108] Unable to inspect ranches, gather data, or produce and check records, officials struggled to create effective breeding programs.[109] Instead, the officials simply took their lead from ranchers themselves, asked which breeding stock they wanted, and conducted little follow-up research.[110] In some ways this was quite efficient, leaving ranchers themselves to assess which breeds might acclimatize best and suit their business plans. Some unusually diligent ranchers and veterinarians still enjoyed success, but overall this strategy hampered long-term planning and research. In the absence of accumulated information, the SSG's various outposts were free to follow the whims and hunches of changing directors.[111] Tellingly, animal disease campaigns also found ways to skirt ranchers' preference for opacity. In the early 1960s, veterinarians tried to speed up the slow progress made by anti-tick campaigns in Mexico's

officials, see various correspondence RAC, group 1.2, series 323 Mexico, box 47, "University of Chihuahua, animal science."

[107] Feder, *Lean Cows*, 212, 213, 152.
[108] "JJM" and "HMM," diary entry on visit to the Institute of Geography, January 14–18, 1954, RAC, group 1.1, series 323 Mexico, box 15, "University of Mexico, science institutes, geography."
[109] On the importance of record-keeping to intensive animal farming, see Fleishman, *Communist Pigs*, 17–47.
[110] Various correspondence, DGAG, 99, veterinarios regionales, and 87–8, ganadería ejidal.
[111] Lomnitz, *Exits*, 322 n110; Yates, *Mexico's Agricultural Dilemma*, 108, 116–19. For the "complete failure" of a project to acclimatize Holstein dairy cattle to the tropics at Chontalpa, see Reta Pettersson, *Indiscreciones*, 121.

northern states by assuring livestock associations that they would not share the information they gathered with any other agencies, including the Agrarian Department.[112] Technological advances allowed the anti-screwworm campaign to reduce the need for close inspections of ranches or tabulation of livestock. By the 1970s, new hi-tech sensors fanned out across the campo, detecting climactic changes and predicting screwworm breeding patterns and distribution.[113]

Unsurprisingly then, the adoption of intensive technologies and techniques – fences, confinement, investments in genetics and high-calorie feeds – was uneven. Change proceeded fastest and furthest where official overtures meshed with compelling economic incentives, as in poultry, dairy, and, a little later, pig farming.[114] Despite official overtures, and several pilot feedlot schemes supported by the Banco de México in the early 1960s, it was far harder for the government to convince beef-cattle ranchers to intensify further and adopt the costly methods of full-blown industrial animal production.[115] Across Mexico, the biological disadvantages of cattle – which convert fodder into calories much less efficiently than pigs or chickens – combined with price controls made feedlot production an expensive and risky venture. Furthermore, northern cattlemen preferred to keep exporting steers to be finished in feedlots in Texas or elsewhere in the United States. In the early 1960s, federal economists predicted beef shortages within the next decade, and pondered a kind of feedlot protectionism, restricting exports, and redirecting steers to a new national feedlot complex to meet rising demand in Mexico City and other central states. In 1965–7 this plan was much discussed in federal political circles, corporate livestock associations, and among students and faculty in Mexico's veterinary schools. It foundered in the face of opposition from northern cattlemen, and official realization of how difficult it would be to recreate the physical, financial and ecological infrastructures upon which the export trade relied.[116] Rail hubs, trucking routes, financial networks, and cattle breeds adapted to the arid north would all be

[112] Various correspondence, 1960–1, DGAG, 105, 108.
[113] Saulman, USDA, to Charlesworth, NASA, September 14, 1973, NAL, https://www.nal.usda.gov/exhibits/speccoll/items/show/7183 (accessed May 1, 2022).
[114] Yates, *Mexico's Agricultural Dilemma*, 88–115.
[115] Various correspondence, May–November 1961, RAC, group 6.13, series 1.1 Mexico Field Office, box 49, "John Pino A."
[116] For examples, see K. Turk, "Appraisal of Education and Research in Animal Sciences at Monterrey and Mexico City," February 1967, RAC, Ford Foundation reports, unpublished reports, box 70, report 001853.

expensive to redirect or replace.[117]To compensate, the government encouraged the expansion of beef production southwards from the central gulf coast into the tropical forests of southern Mexico.

In principle, the government wanted these tropical ranchers to invest in productivity increases too, but extension agents and development experts struggled to convince.[118] As several studies have shown, by and large this advice remained unheeded, and much of the expansion was extensive or, at most, "semi-intensive" where farmers invested in new grasses, a few tick baths, and some occasional improved breeds, but little else. Some studies have blamed tropical ranchers' devotion to extensive farming on an old-fashioned, even "semi-feudal" mindset, which prioritized the acquisition of land, rents, and political power over entrepreneurial risk taking.[119] Given the long association of landholding with local power, there is surely something to this explanation. David Skerrit even found examples of nostalgic urban investors who bought land in Veracruz precisely so they could imitate the kind of low-risk, extensive techniques they associated with traditional ranching.[120] Alongside these we must place other tropical ranchers who were proudly and consciously modern, embraced innovations that paid but, for similar reasons to northern ranchers, found that further investments were too risky or expensive.[121] Conversely, the engine of extensive ranching in the tropics was fueled by a powerful array of interests and attitudes. Perhaps most important was the widely shared perception among ranchers and political leaders of tropical forests as vast, cheap resources, whose exploitation brought few costs, generated wealth, and potentially extended the frontiers of the state's territorial control; ranchers and some extension agents – particularly those "from rancher families" – did not seem to regard the loss of small, subsistence plots as a serious aggregate cost either since they generated little profit and were, by their standards, inefficient.[122] In the words of southern Veracruz's mestizo ranchers, who tried to bully indigenous ejidatarios into selling or renting their parcels for pasture, "corn and beans are only grown by idiots."[123] The engine of tropical ranching was also powerful because it even posed, for a time, as a kind of quixotic

[117] Sanderson, *The Transformation*, 119–81.   [118] Saucedo, *Historia*, 166.
[119] Bassols Batalla, *Las Huastecas*, 151.   [120] González-Montagut, "Factors," 127.
[121] Schryer, *Ethnicity and Class*, 160.
[122] Bobrow-Strain, *Intimate Enemies*, 166; Arce, *Negotiating*, 85.
[123] Letter from Oaxaca, June 18, 1988, in Gilly, *Cartas*, 133.

solution to social conflict, offering peasant farmers work clearing forests and planting and weeding grasses.[124]

Such was the political rise of commercial livestock farmers and the industrializing fevor of the Alemán administration, initially it seemed like the aftosa campaign might terminate government support for small-scale animal farming on ejidos. The Alemán administration's initial post-aftosa plan – a rambling wishlist of dams, roads, chemical fertilizers, and big agro-industrial projects – suggested as much; its use of bracero contracts to conciliate ejidatarios devasted by the sanitary rifle was another reflection of its vision of their future: flexible wage-laborers rather than small farmers. It is hard to quantify just how many small milk producers were eliminated by the epizootic and sanitary rifle, but larger commercial dairy farmers were sure that very many had been. At the same time, officials targeted big commercial dairy farms and ranches for post-aftosa credit and technical assistance, which they believed would lead to bigger productivity gains. Conveniently, many were also the properties of political allies or party insiders.[125] In the mid-1950s, the Ministry of Agriculture's extension efforts for ejidos focused on crops, especially new corn varieties, and ignored livestock almost entirely. In any case, it remained almost impossible for ejidatarios to obtain official credit for livestock development. Some breeding stock distributed by the National Commission for Livestock Rehabilitation was ear-marked for ejidos, but state authorities sometimes diverted them elsewhere. None of the breeding bulls sent to Guerrero ended up with ejidatarios. Dr. Pavia handed them to his rancher friends during an athletics display while the state governor was distracted by looking at the women athletes' legs.[126]

However, in the longer term the PRI could not ignore the pigs, chickens, cattle raised on ejidos. In 1959, the López Mateos administration adjusted course and attempted to encourage and channel more technical support to ejidal livestock farming. At one level, this shift represented a resurfacing of earlier Cardenista currents of "social landscaping" and a tacit acknowledgment of post-Cardenista neglect. After all, censuses revealed that ejidos still possessed around 35 percent of the nation's livestock, and 25 percent of all pasture.[127] Even where the

[124] Schryer, *Ethnicity and Class*, 155–62.
[125] Informe de labores, comisión para la planeación y recuperación de las zonas afectadas por la aftosa, November 1, 1947, AGN, MAV, 4255-2-38; Zazueta, "Milk," 175; Figueroa Velázquez, *El tiro de gracia*, 162, 225–39.
[126] Pavia Guzmán, *Recuerdos*, 100.   [127] Saucedo, *Historia*, 69.

sanitary rifle had delivered a serious blow to smallholders and ejidos, it had not destroyed ejidal livestock ownership. Some ejidatarios surely gave up and turned to migration and wage labor. Others may well have frittered their indemnity money away on gambling, drink, and women, as many journalists worried they might. (In the summer and autumn of 1947, the national press carried stories of mobile gambling dens and brothels which "have become a true industry ... following in the footsteps of each group eradicating aftosa.")[128] But the census data and the CMAEFA's own fragmentary reports do not bear out such patronizing assessments of ejidatarios' capacities. A few planted horticultural crops to tide themselves over; plenty kept their money and restocked as best they could, but wisely waited until the campaign ended.[129]

However, the proximate cause of renewed federal interest in ejidal stock raising was rural mobilization. In June 1958, Jacinto López's *Union General de Obreros y Campesinos de México* invaded the lands of the US-owned Cananea Cattle Company in Sonora, part of a larger

---

[128] *Excélsior*, cited in Soto Correa, *El rifle*, 80. For a novelized portrayal of these businesses, see Rubín, *Ese rifle*.

[129] Sigsworth, "Mexican Epizootic," 168; Alfonso Suárez Serrano, "Report on Restocking," March 17, 1948, in CMAEFA, reports, box 2, "operations: restocking." The incineration of the Mexican section's archive deprives us of slaughter tallies for each town and municipality. A sample of six municipalities in Michoacán, and a comparison of trends in different states shows the difficulty of using census data to identify the impact of the sanitary rifle on the number and social distribution of livestock. Sahuayo and Jiquilpan, two municipalities hits by slaughter in the north, had dramatically different fates. On average between 1940 and 1950 Michoacán increased its cattle, goats, sheep, and pigs by 27 percent, with ejidos growing at a slower rate of 18 percent; Sahuayo reported a 60 percent decline, with ejidos faring worst, losing 80 percent of their animals. Jiquilpan fared much better, increasing livestock by 53 percent, well over the state average; ejidal livestock grew at 33 percent, while the ejidos' share of livestock declined by 3 percent, about average for the state as a whole. Further east, La Piedad and Senguio both offered stiff resistance to slaughter, but again reveal contrasting economic trends. La Piedad's livestock grew by 101 percent between 1940 and 1950, but ejidos benefited disproportionately, increasing livestock holdings by 204 percent. Senguio's overall livestock grew only 9 percent, well under the state average, but its ejidos emphatically increased their share of livestock, growing 89 percent overall and moving from a 33 percent to 58 percent share of the total. Whereas La Piedad's ejidos increased their holding of the most valuable animals (cattle), the ejidatarios of Senguio lost cattle, but increased other animals. A comparison of ejidal shares of livestock and livestock wealth across states further suggests the highly uneven socio-economic impact of slaughter. Surprisingly, judging by census figures, the proportion of livestock owned by ejidos declined more slowly in states which experienced the heaviest slaughter (Michoacán, Guanajuato) than in those which largely escaped it (Morelos). Author's analysis, based on Secretaría de Economía, *Segundo censo agrícola*, and *Tercer censo agrícola*.

storm of invasions that roiled the northwest. The incoming president quickly moved to defuse the conflict, expropriated the company's land, and rejected US suggestions that it be converted into an international park. The Agrarian Department then divided the estate into seven livestock ejidos, supported by technical assistance and no less than 28,000 Hereford cattle provided by the Ministry of Agriculture.[130] It was also careful to cut out López's allies from this deal, and distributed the ejidos to the *priístas* of the CNC.[131] In speeches and plans, federal officials inverted the meaning of the Cananea ejido, portraying it not as the conquest of popular mobilization but as a model development project, part of the "second stage" of the agrarian reform characterized by more careful technical and economic planning, rather than politics or ideology.[132] The Cananea grant also likely drove home another ecological reality for the government. Much of the land remaining to be distributed was not suitable for cropping. If the government was to continue using land reform as useful political tool, it would need a more coherent policy for ejidal livestock farming.

After the Cananea dispute, the government made louder public commitments to ejidal livestock farming, and the SSG engaged in a burst of action. It created around two dozen other model ejidal livestock farms and producer cooperatives, to demonstrate the viability of such enterprises and, it was hoped, free up official credit from the Ejidal Bank. It also urged provincial veterinarians to take a more active role in social development and prioritize attention to ejidatarios.[133] In a few cases the SSG and the Agrarian Department even revived the old rule that ranches with certificates protecting them from expropriation hand over 2 percent of their calves to neighboring ejidatarios each year. Judging by the hundreds of petitions received by the government this drive to support ejidal livestock enjoyed considerable support. It also ran into many problems, particularly the Ejidal Bank's unwillingness to release credit for such ventures. Urged by members of its women's action committee, the SSG also asked the government to make wives and children of ejidatarios eligible for small livestock loans since they often engaged in small-scale "backyard" raising of pigs and chickens; the Ejidal Bank blocked this initiative too.[134] Still, these projects helped lay the groundwork for a

---

[130] Grijalva Dávila, "El ocaso del latifundio Greene."

[131] Sanderson, *Agrarian Populism*, 157.   [132] Saucedo, *Historia*, 66, 69.

[133] Various correspondence, 1959–1967, DGAG, 87–8.

[134] Memo, J. Rodríguez Adame, Secretary of Agriculture, to López Mateos, and report by Salvador Guerra Aceves, c. 1960, DGAG, 87, "Departamento de ganadería ejidal."

bigger drive to modernize ejidal livestock in the 1970s, propelled by the Echeverría administration's newfound support for collective ejidos, and a growing awareness of rural unrest – a good deal of it caused by the expansion of tropical beef ranching. Under Echeverría, ejidatarios also received a larger share of a public livestock credit, although they were expected to surrender much decision making to a new corps of technical experts installed by the Ministry of Agriculture.[135]

As an effort to push the growth and modernization livestock farming in a more equitable direction, the overall results of these initiatives were not so impressive. A small, ejidal elite of cattle owners tended to benefit from these schemes.[136] According to critics writing a little later, the livestock extension agents of the 1970s could be paternalistic and arrogant, deaf to local priorities and knowledge, and overly credulous about generic technical solutions.[137] However, experiments in ejidal livestock development were an important political resource for the PRI state. Recognizing this, even left-wing dissidents tried to compete with official ventures. After Lucio Cabañas's guerrilla group kidnapped the incoming governor of Guerrero in 1974, they sent the 30,000-peso ransom to an underground movement of former Trotskyists in Morelos and the State of Mexico – known to its members as "the Organization" – who spent it on their own projects to support small-scale goat and pig farming.[138]

In the 1980s, political and economic crises dramatically remade the state's approach to livestock farming. The 1982 economic crisis capsized demand. Even before that, the cattle industry in particular had shown signs of strain. From the mid-1970s demand for beef began to slow, and the expansion of tropical ranching began to reach ecological and social limits. From the late 1970s, waves of ranch-invasions shook parts of rural Mexico, from the Huasteca to Chiapas. The government responded with a combination of repression and the hurried creation of more livestock ejidos.[139] Scholars and activists condemned the state's livestock policy for

[135] Yates, *Mexico's Agricultural Dilemma*, 116–24; Chauvet, *La ganadería*, 134, n5.

[136] Various complaints along these lines from the 1960s can be found in DGAG, 87–8. For secondary accounts of ejidal livestock schemes and social stratification see: Gledhill, *Casi Nada*, 399–402; Buckles and Chevalier, *A Land Without Gods*, 6, 124–167; Camou Healy, *De rancheros*; Mújica Vélez, *Los condenados*, 91–4; Feder, *Lean Cows*, 220–5.

[137] Perezgrovas Garza, *Antología sobre etnoveterinaria*; Arellano, López-Ortiz, Pérez-Hernández, Gerardo Alonso, Torres-Rivera, Huerta, Cruz-Rosales, "La ganadería bovina," 204–8; Mújica Vélez, *Los condenados*, 91–8.

[138] Ulloa Borneman, *Surviving Mexico's Dirty War*, 123.

[139] Chauvet, *La ganadería*, 85–106; Schryer, *Ethnicity and Class*, 282–302; Bobrow, *Intimate Enemies*, 105–30, 138.

eroding basic food production, failing to boost popular nutrition, and driving deforestation – part of a growing disenchantment with livestock developmentalism around the region.[140] In 1989, the Salinas adminis- tration disbanded the SSG, cut livestock producer subsidies, and gutted funding for official veterinary and extension services.[141]

In telling the story of post-Cardenista rural development, historians usually foreground three interrelated processes: the conservative drift in Mexican national politics after 1938, which culminated in the pro- business Alemán administration; a more aggressive drive for industrialization, encouraged by the circumstances of the Second World War; and the creation and application of the new seeds, pesticides, and fertilizers associated with the so-called "Green Revolution." Indeed, in some ways, the aftosa campaign can be seen as a reflection of these earlier changes. Despite Lázaro Cárdenas's obvious interest in livestock farming, it is very hard to image that a such a campaign – based on slaughter, with such an obvious US presence on Mexican soil, and generally indifferent to agrarian tensions and distributional conflicts – could have been waged under his presidency. A product of its time, the aftosa crisis was also a crucial event in its own right, reshaping when and how the state sought to regulate, sanitize, and rationalize the countryside. Of course, like the Rockefeller Foundation's Mexican Agricultural Program, the aftosa crisis did not wipe the slate of national policy entirely clean. Mexican officials' general objectives were hardly new. Closer integration with international and particularly US agencies did not eliminate the leverage of Mexican officialdom, neither in 1947, nor in subsequent negotiations over aid and assistance. Official enchantment with technology and markets did not permanently erase previous traditions of state support for ejidal livestock, which emerged from time to time and, flawed as many initiatives were, provided a way to mediate social conflict in the countryside. Still, five years of sanitary warfare against aftosa decisively shaped when and how general goals to regulate and modernize stock raising were translated into practice, which groups in government were involved, what kind of infra- structures were built, and which international connections were forged. Indeed, changes to livestock policies were probably more abrupt than in

---

[140] Feder, *Lean Cows*; Barkin and DeWalt, "Sorghum"; Barrera and Rodríguez (eds.), *Desarrollo y medio ambiente*. For changing attitudes to ranching and development in Brazil, see Acker, *Volkswagen*.

[141] Bobrow, *Intimate Enemies*, 173–4; Cervantes, Román, López, *Medicina*, 199; Chauvet, *La ganadería*, 133–5.

crops research and extension, propelled as they were by a largely unfore-seen crisis.

Tracing the national impact of the aftosa crisis also opens a useful window onto some of the strengths, weaknesses, and many contradictions of the PRI's developmentalist state. In some ways, this story supports the idea that massive epizootics generally boost state power and surveil-lance.[142] The campaign certainly bequeathed improved capacities to monitor and control certain kinds of disease. However, any state-building impulses were constrained and channeled by the Mexican political con-text and the contentious character of the eradication campaign. Mexico's livestock state displayed many of the fiscal and administrative weaknesses that historians increasingly recognize as typical of the PRI state.[143] While officials' view of microbes was much enhanced, their view of animals and farmers was cloudy at best. For those who worked on it, the aftosa crisis represented a cautionary tale as well as an invitation for state interven-tion. As the state's alliance with livestock associations deepened, this provided a measure of political stability, but also placed limits on the state-backed technological change and planning that was possible. Development has meant different things to different people. This "seman-tic ambivalence" gave the concept broad appeal and ensured "bargaining between competing authorities" to give it specific, if temporary institu-tional form.[144] Rather than a simple boost to the Mexican state's pene-tration of society and territory, the aftosa campaign is better seen as building a new consensus on the practical meaning of national livestock development and, crucially, a loose political coalition of officials, experts, international agencies, and farmers to support it. The debt crisis broke this coalition apart and led to a fundamental reorientation of state policy. Economic liberalization demanded that many initiatives aimed at national development be dismantled, but it also relied on earlier achievements – not least the eradication and surveillance of aftosa, without which the galloping integration of the NAFTA era would have been unthinkable.

---

[142] On epizootics and state formation, see Brown and Gilfoyle (eds.), *Healing*; Olmstead and Rhode, *Arresting*.

[143] Gillingham and Smith, *Dictablanda*; Knight, "The Weight."

[144] Acker, *Volkswagen*, 6, 7. For an overview focused on states and policymakers, see Lorenzini, *Global Development*.

6

Mexico and the Cold War on Animal Disease

In November 1950, Colonel Harry Vaughan, President Truman's secretary, wrote to his friend General Harry Johnson to congratulate him. Despite the CMAEFA's many problems, by combining international cooperation, targeted slaughter, and a locally-produced vaccine in a campaign against aftosa on unprecedented scale, "it looks as if we have found the remedy to eradicate it around the world."[1] Soon after US officials were confident enough to raise such hopes in public. The BAI announced that the campaign could act as a "beacon of light in a new era of livestock disease eradication," teaching other countries that they did not need to merely "live with the disease" but could now "completely remove both the disease and its source."[2] President Truman congratulated the CMAEFA on accomplishing "a heretofore impossible feat," and for showing the world the kind of accomplishments possible under the new Point Four program.[3] In this way, Truman retroactively enlisted the campaign as a precursor for US Cold War development projects around the world, and turned what had been an almighty transborder and intragovernmental tussle over policy and resources into a simple story of the delivery of US aid and technical assistance.[4]

Such announcements met an eager audience. After all, the years after the Second World War were a time of renewed internationalism and

---

[1] Vaughan, Washington DC, to Johnson, CMAEFA, November 29, 1950, TP, box 395, foot and mouth.
[2] Bennett Simms in USDA press release, April 24, 1951, BP, box 5, foot and mouth.
[3] Truman, to General Johnson, draft c. December 1950, HP, box 5, foot and mouth.
[4] On the significance of Truman's Point Four program, see Lorenzini, *Global Development*, 22–32.

scientific optimism. Political leaders, intellectuals, and experts around the world argued that science, technology, and international cooperation could allow mankind to dominate nature and solve human problems.[5] In 1947, the FAO organized its first conference on animal disease in Warsaw and the Polish delegate, Professor Parnass, captured the mood and ambitions of the time. Parnass argued that the *Organization Internationale de Epizooties* (OIE), founded in 1924 and based in Paris, should fuse with the United Nations to create a new animal health organization, which would be "analogical to the World Health Organization for people," and "embrace all the countries of the world for the purpose of assuring the world of a greater production of food, health for its people, and a lasting peace."[6] By the 1950s, US and Mexican veterans of the aftosa campaign were in some demand, as national governments – from Panama to Canada, Yugoslavia to Ecuador, Iran to Syria – and UN agencies like the FAO sought to harness their practical experience and knowledge to new campaigns against aftosa and other livestock diseases.[7]

In the end, Mexico's experience did not lead to the rapid eradication of aftosa. While rinderpest emerged as an "ideal" biological target for the development projects of the FAO, aftosa remained a harder virus to manipulate, scientifically and politically. US breakthroughs in rinderpest vaccine research during the Second World War, rinderpest's concentration in colonial or postcolonial states, and its high and obvious mortality, created an urgent problem located in the developing world to which the

---

[5] J. R. McNeill and P. Unger, "Introduction"; Krige and Wang, "Nation, Knowledge, and Imagined Futures"; McVety, *Rinderpest*, 121–206.

[6] Copy of statement of Professor Parnass, at conclusion of Warsaw conference, c. March 1947, FAO, Animal Production, uncoded files, "OIE, correspondence, minutes." On Parnass's later career, attempts to defect to the West, and US officials' suspicions that he was a communist spy, see Nash Carter, *One Man*, 249–51.

[7] Farland, Panama City, to State Department, April 26, 1962, GAU, Colombia Central File: Decimal File 821.241, Internal Economic, Industrial and Social Affairs, Colombia, Animal Husbandry; Ewing, *Ranch*, 184; Allen, Belgrade, to State Department, May 25, 1951, GAU, Central File: Decimal file 868.241, Socialism and National Unity in Yugoslavia, 1945–63: Records of the US State Department Classified Files; Romeo Ortega, Quito, Ecuador, to Foreign Relations, Mexico, January 30, 1951, AHGE, III/811 (72:861) 21700; Project proposal: control of infectious and parasitic livestock disease, regional Baghdad pact, 1957, GAU, US Missions in Iran, 1950–61, 23/366; Report of the FAO Special Meeting on the Control of Foot and Mouth Disease in the Near East, 1953, FAO, published reports, 17; minutes of joint FAO-OIE committee on food-and-mouth disease, Paris, May 15–20, 1950, FAO, Animal Production, uncoded files, "OIE, correspondence, minutes."

developed world appeared to have a technical solution.[8] Aftosa's frequently mild and hard-to-detect clinical symptoms, its wide array of types and subtypes, and the sheer difficulty virologists had in producing a stable, attenuated form of the virus suitable for a vaccine, limited any country's capacity to mobilize resources and fulfill the hopes Mexico's campaign initially raised. Present in much of Asia, Africa, Western Europe, and in major cattle producers desperate for aftosa-free markets like Argentina, it was harder to conceptualize aftosa control solely as a problem of underdevelopment, and harder still to insulate US policy from accusations (sometimes accurate) of protectionism. Before the Second World War, some US colonial and military officials had fought animal plagues abroad, particularly in the Philippines, but most of the USDA's energies had been directed inwards, towards epizootics and sanitary problems in the mainland United States.[9] Through the late 1940s and 1950s, and seeking to channel new dreams of development, the US government built a series of institutions to govern animal disease around the world. Precisely because it was such a thorny, controversial problem, aftosa was a central concern.

The aftosa crisis in Mexico gave a major impetus to these new institutions, and powerfully shaped where and how they were built. By demonstrating the apparent threat aftosa posed to national security and improving vaccine technology, Mexico's aftosa campaign boosted the international ambitions of Mexican experts, inspired the creation of the new US-led laboratories and multilateral organizations in the Americas – from Rio de Janeiro to Long Island Sound – and reshaped the United States' scientific and military relations with its Cold War allies in Europe. As such, the story challenges the conventional image of Mexico as an object of international history rather than a subject. It joins new scholarship tracing how – for better or worse, acknowledged or not – events in Mexico affected international institutions, and ideas and expertise traveled in multiple directions between Mexico and the Global North.[10] As tempting as it is to describe the aftosa campaign itself as a kind of laboratory for US policy, this flatters the capacity of officials to plan and control the conditions of political experimentation. Still, as the

---

[8] McVety, *Rinderpest*, 125.
[9] Ibid., 36; Doeppers, "Fighting"; Olmstead and Rhode, *Arresting*.
[10] Olsson, *Agrarian Crossings*; Rosemblatt, "Other Americas"; Shepard, "Algeria, France, Mexico, UNESCO"; Flores, *Backroads Pragmatists*; Thornton, *Revolution in Development*.

campaign veteran Robert Anderson declared after decades of work in the USDA, the Mexican crisis was a learning experience and one which helped lay "the foundation" of the USDA's knowledge on disease control.[11]

During the aftosa campaign, the "magnificent" new laboratory at Palo Alto, and the success of the vaccination program encouraged Mexican veterinarians to claim a larger national role and also inspired new international ambitions. After all, officials boasted that it was the most advanced animal disease laboratory in the Americas.[12] The same year that Palo Alto opened, Mexican virologist Alfredo Téllez Girón joined a committee advising on aftosa immunization policies at the OIE – an organization of which Mexico had not even been a member previously.[13] During the campaign Mexican scientists learned new ways to produce vaccines and identify viruses, adapted techniques developed in Europe and South America for use with Mexican animals and climate, and produced new knowledge about them.[14] Indeed, at times US veterinarians, with little experience of aftosa research, had deferred to their Mexican counterparts and entrusted them with sensitive tasks. Asked by the US section whether cattle previously infected with anthrax could be used to harvest the virus for vaccine production, Dr. Omohundro declared that "by golly I could not tell you" and awaited the verdict of Dr. Camargo.[15] It was Camargo too who tested some strange, white spherical objects found floating around rivers near Zacoalco, Jalisco, which locals blamed for spreading the virus, and which US officials worried might be a evidence of attempted sabotage. He crushed up the balls in his laboratory, inoculated guinea pigs with the resulting powder, and found no trace of aftosa virus.[16]

---

[11] Ewing, *Ranch*, 242.

[12] Pavia Guzmán, *Recuerdos*, 78; "Orgullo de México," *Mañana*, September 10, 1949.

[13] Speech by Dr. Carlos Ruiz, OIE, in report on Regional Consultative Foot and Mouth Disease Conference, Panama, August 21–24, 1951, NA, CO 852/1287/3, 29.

[14] For Mexican scientists learning the Waldmann vaccine from Argentine and Brazilian scientists: Tellez Girón, "Iniciación." For visits to Chile to learn the compliment typing technique for analyzing viruses: Confidential report, July 1948, CMAEFA, reports, box 1. For experiments with different cattle breeds and injection methods during vaccine production, see respectively: Confidential report, August 23, 1948, CMAEFA, box 1; Cockerill to Fogedby, December 20, 1956, FAO, Animal Production, miscellaneous correspondence and reports on foot-and-mouth disease.

[15] Omohundro, CMAEFA, to Manly, Valles, SLP, November 12, 1948, CMAEFA, operations, box 29, SLP.

[16] Camargo, Mexico City, to Shahan, "Report on Analysis of Spheres," November 13, 1947, CMAEFA, operations, box 29, Jalisco.

In recognition of Mexico's new standing, in October 1950 Venezuela's military junta invited a party of fourteen Mexican veterinary experts to visit and advise them. An aftosa outbreak was rippling through Venezuela, most likely caused by some recent, controversial imports of beef from Argentina. Headed by Dr. Manuel Chavarría of the SSG, the visitors built a replica of Mexico's vaccination-production system and laboratory, which allowed the government to substantially control (but not eradicate) the outbreak. Interviewed by Venezuela's press, the Mexican group argued that their experience had taught them that Latin American nations needed to collaborate rather just swallow Yankee policy prescriptions, and suggested that, with their help, Venezuela could also produce a vaccine for neighboring Colombia: "We have to show the English and American experts that we Latins can come together and resolve these kinds of problems, however grave."[17] Mexican diplomats probably hoped that such technical assistance would be repaid, in part, with commercial opportunities. Earlier in 1950, Mexico's ambassador, General Otero Pablos, invited Venezuelan veterinary experts to inspect the CMAEFA. He then oversaw cattle shipments to Caracas from northern Mexico, generating "great profits" and "largely displacing" Argentinian imports, and he hoped to organize more.[18]

US officials believed that the Venezuelan mission was part of a larger, unwelcome Mexican initiative. According to the US State Department, at the same time a "faction" of Mexican scientists, with support from officials in the Ministry of Foreign Relations, also planned to make an aftosa vaccine in Mexico for export, putting the country "in the vaccine production business."[19] In 1950–1, the US section of the CMAEFA even worried that two of the last outbreaks of aftosa in Mexico – in central Veracruz in December 1950 and September 1951 – might have been planted by members of this group, eager to extend the campaign and allow "Mexico to export vaccine to Colombia and Venezuela in addition to supplying domestic demand."[20] The USDA argued that allowing

---

[17] Machado, *Aftosa*, 66; "Probaremos a los sajones," undated clipping, personal collection of Dr. Juan Manuel Cervantes Sánchez. On the background to the Venezuela outbreak, and Chavarría's ties to veterinarians in Venezuela, see Freites, "Relaciones científicas."

[18] General Otero Pablos, Caracas, to Foreign Relations, Mexico City, February 15, 1950, AHGE, III/614.2(72:870) 20889.

[19] Randal to Neal, State Department, Secret message, October 19, 1951; Rubottom, to Embassy, Mexico City, February 27, 1951, both in IAMSD, 1950–54, reel 27, 231, 219.

[20] Randal to Neal, State Department, Secret message, October 19, 1951, IAMSD, 1950–54, reel 27, 231.

Mexico to retain samples of the live aftosa virus after the end of the campaign – necessary for any vaccine – was unnecessary and a "constant threat," risking an accidental or politically-motivated leak.[21] In September 1952, the US and Mexican governments confirmed that their campaign had eradicated aftosa, and reopened the US–Mexico border to cattle and livestock products. Continued funding for the CMAEFA's small successor organization dedicated to surveillance came with conditions: Mexico must not store live aftosa virus at the laboratory at Palo Alto, or engage in commercial vaccine production, although the laboratory was permitted to retain some serums it had produced by passing the virus through guinea pigs.[22]

Despite US opposition, in 1953 Mexico's ambitions to produce aftosa vaccine emerged again, this time embodied in the new Minister of Agriculture, Gilberto Flores Muñoz – a former governor of Nayarit and seasoned political insider, who was not shy of confrontation with US experts and diplomats.[23] According to the Rockefeller Foundation, in 1952–3 Flores Muñoz considered himself *presidenciable* – a presidential contender – and was determined to use his ministry to build a political clientele, ignore the foundation's advice, and make a lot of money.[24] Six months after the US–Mexico border was reopened to livestock, the US government closed it again after a reported outbreak of aftosa near the town of Gutiérrez Zamora, in central Veracruz. Flores Muñoz announced to the press that he would reject US advice to slaughter the infected herd, vaccinate thousands of head of livestock around the outbreak, and ban the handful of US joint commission experts who remained in the country from visiting the area. In doing this, Flores Muñoz unnerved the USDA, which argued that the most effective means of countering an isolated outbreak of this kind remained slaughter, and overruled his own Under Minister of Livestock, Lauro Ortega, then co-director of the joint aftosa commission.[25] The head of the FAO, former Under Secretary of

---

[21] Rubottom, to Embassy, Mexico City, February 27, 1951, IAMSD, 1950–54, reel 27, 219.

[22] Palo Alto vaccine production reports, May–July 1950, *Foot and Mouth Disease Scrapbook*, University of Wisconsin library. For more on the Joint Commission for the Prevention of Fiebre Aftosa, see Chapter 5.

[23] On Flores Muñoz's ties to Gonzalo N. Santos, a quintessential regional boss and lynchpin of the ruling party in 1940s, see Santos, *Memorias*, 656–7, 766–8.

[24] Gutiérrez, "Cambio agrario," 193–4.

[25] Belton, State Department, memo of conversation with Ambassador Tello, June 2, 1953; Minneman, Mexico City, to State Department, June 15, 1953, both in IAMSD, 1950–54, reel 27, 236, 246.

Agriculture Norris Dodd, also wrote to Flores Muñoz pleading with him not to depart from a careful combination of vaccination and targeted slaughter – the template created by the 1947–52 campaign which had been "so successful" and was respected by "responsible veterinarians around the world."[26] The dispute was not helped by a "clash of personalities" between Flores Muñoz and Noyes, the acting co-director of the commission, who declared that he "would prefer to leave Mexico than accept vaccination as a means of stamping out the outbreak."[27]

After a few weeks, the State Department and the US embassy stepped in to mediate the conflict, and did so quite skillfully. First, they removed the abrasive Noyes and flew in experts who were more conciliatory and less opposed to vaccination.[28] US Ambassador Francis Wright met with Flores Muñoz and received assurances that the government's public promise to avoid slaughter, and the press articles lambasting the United States "for expecting Mexico to kill its cattle" were only for public consumption and were written by Mexico City newspapers whose access to information Flores Muñoz "strictly" controlled.[29] The Mexican government initially argued that the decision to vaccinate was taken to avoid popular unrest in Veracruz, although the US experts were dubious that this was the main concern.[30] In any case, Flores Muñoz privately admitted he wanted to use the outbreak to "try out" making and administering a vaccine within Veracruz itself (thus skirting the restrictions agreed for Palo Alto), but promised Ambassador Wright that if this did not work, and new outbreaks were discovered, Mexico would simply revert to slaughter. However, Flores Muñoz argued that "he could not say this publicly" nor give assurances in writing, but would informally allow US members of the joint commission to remain in the area and conduct inspections. The US ambassador believed this arrangement was "the most that we can hope for on that phase of the matter" and suggested that it

[26] Copy of telegram from Dodd, FAO, Rome, to Alemán, July 7, 1951, IAMSD, 1950–54, reel 27, 254.

[27] Ambassador White, to Mann, State Department, July 9, 1953, IAMSD, 1950–54, reel 27, 258; Memorandum of conversation between Assistant Secretary Cabot, State Department, and Ambassador White, June 5, 1953, IAMSD, 1950–54, reel 27, 244.

[28] Mann, State Department, to Ambassador White, July 20, 1953, IAMSD, 1950–54, reel 27, 255.

[29] Ambassador White to Mann, State Department, July 9, 1953; Minneman, Embassy, to State Department, July 1, 1953, both in IAMSD, 1950–54, reel 27, 258, 249.

[30] Assistant Secretary Cabot, State Department, memo of conversation with Ambassador Tello, June 2, 1953, IAMSD, 1950–54, reel 27, 237.

might be best to de-escalate the row, ignore press criticism, and observe carefully as Flores Muñoz's project took its course.[31] US officials hoped that northern cattlemen would again pressure the government to resolve the dispute and reopen the border. At the same time, they worried that these interests might not be as influential as they were before the aftosa epizootic. After all, Mexico planned to use tariffs to limit livestock exports anyway, to cater to domestic demand, and new industrial plants made stockmen less dependent on live cattle exports.[32]

Having established some diplomatic latitude to develop a vaccine, Flores Muñoz confronted a still more serious obstacle. In August 1953, US officials in Veracruz reported, with some relief, that the SSG had either not found a way of imposing quarantine or making a reliable vaccine. Five herds of cattle around Gutiérrez Zamora reported outbreaks, and were quietly slaughtered. Local farmers suspected the vaccine had been somehow sabotaged, while US inspectors believed that hurried Mexican scientists had been unable to attenuate the virus sufficiently for use in the vaccine.[33] In any case, prior to his meeting with President Eisenhower in October 1953, President Ruiz Cortines aimed to draw a line under the affair and assuage US concerns about aftosa – a problem Mexico's diplomats considered second only to US–Mexico migration in "sociopolitical" importance.[34] Ruiz Cortines's diplomatic aides advised him to minimize the risk of infection and argue that Mexico's livestock industry was really "two industries" – one in the north exporting to the United States and one in the center oriented to Mexico City – which were "almost completely independent." They also suggested he offer to only authorize cattle exports from the northern states, to reassure the USDA and dovetail with Mexico's policy of protecting domestic supply.[35] The offer was accepted, and in March 1954 both

[31] Ambassador White to Mann, State Department, July 9, 1953, IAMSD, 1950–54, reel 27, 258.
[32] Belton, Mexico City, to Assistant Secretary Cabot, June 12, 1953, IAMSD, 1950–54, reel 27, 245.
[33] Various reports, 1953, Campaña contra la fiebre aftosa, AGN, DFS, versión pública; Ambassador White to State Department, August 20, 1952, IAMSD, 1950–54, reel 27, 263.
[34] Memo, "Asuntos pendientes con Estados Unidos," c. September 1953, AHGE, B/226.2 (72:73) "53" 31.
[35] Memo, "Problema de la fiebre aftosa," c. September 1953, AHGE, B/226.2 (72:73) "53" 31.

governments declared that aftosa had been eradicated once more, and the US–Mexico border reopened again to the livestock trade.[36]

The dispute over the Gutiérrez Zamora outbreak confirmed the political and technical obstacles to making a reliable aftosa vaccine in Mexico, and revealed the State Department's role in smoothing conflicts over animal disease, growing since 1948. During the outbreak, the USDA invited the former ambassador Walter Thurston to replace Noyes as the new US co-director of the joint commission.[37] (It had briefly considered reappointing General Johnson, but the State Department warned that, while Johnson had delivered administrative "drive" to the 1947–52 campaign, he "did not contribute to the smooth operation of the commission" and was roundly disliked in Mexico.)[38] After 1954, Mexico's independent pursuit of an aftosa vaccine ceased and, as we saw in the previous chapter, Mexico generally opted to support US sanitary campaigns and negotiate for an advantageous position within them. This strategy allowed for progress on overlapping objectives like aftosa and screwworm control and, within limits set by US policy, it also magnified Mexico's scientific authority within Central America. With the support of Mexico, the USDA's long-term strategy was to create a secure aftosa and screwworm-free zone across Central America, using the Isthmus of Panama as a geographical barrier and Palo Alto as a hub for surveillance. In the 1960s, Palo Alto became the designated laboratory for a Central American system of animal disease surveillance and control created – with US support – by the *Organismo Internacional Regional de Sanidad Agropecuaria* (OIRSA). In addition to analyzing samples, the laboratory hosted regional conferences, helped to train Central American experts, and sent Mexican veterinary advisors to Central America.[39]

The aftosa crisis in Mexico demonstrated to US officials the vulnerability of the US–Mexico border to animal disease, the enormous economic and political costs involved in improvising a response to a major epizootic, the improved if imperfect knowledge of the virus and vaccination that was available, and the need to revamp US policies in response. The clearest illustration of this change in South America was the Panamerican

---

[36] Machado, *Aftosa*, 51.

[37] "Background Information for a Meeting with President of Mexico," October 19, 1953, FRUS, 1952–4, American Republics, vol. IV: https://history.state.gov/historicaldocuments/frus1952-54v04 (accessed June 2019).

[38] Memo, Assistant Secretary Cabot, to Morse, Undersecretary of Agriculture, June 4, 1953, IAMSD, 1950–54, reel 27, 240.

[39] Various reports, 1960–1968, AGN, DGAG, box 131, "OIRSA."

Center for Foot-and-Mouth Disease (PANAFTOSA), a new animal disease laboratory in Rio de Janeiro created in 1951. It was funded in large part by the US Point Four program of technical assistance channeled through the Organization of American States and the Panamerican Sanitary Bureau (PASB), and also received support from the Brazilian government. Rather than leaving South American governments and veterinarians to their own devices, the US government decided that more effective control and surveillance in the south – by whatever means – could help prevent the spread of animal disease further north. The Rio laboratory could serve as a first line of defense, use South America as a vast living archive of different virus strains, and provide a site to refine vaccination techniques. It received virus samples from across South America for testing and typing, began to map different strains, gathered statistics about veterinary capacities in different states and regions, published occasional reports in the bulletin of the PASB, trained visiting veterinarians and advised national governments on appropriate systems of aftosa control. Since aftosa was already widespread in Brazil, the United States placed no restrictions on storing live aftosa virus and creating some facilities for vaccine production. However, the PASB still expected vaccine production in South America to remain primarily a private commercial venture – as it had since the 1920s – albeit now supported by PANAFTOSA's advice and assistance.[40]

From a US perspective, the location in Brazil had much to recommend it. The USDA officially blamed Brazilian exports of high-grade cebu bulls for causing Mexico's aftosa outbreak, and US diplomats probably considered PANAFTOSA a useful way of helping to smooth over the resulting tensions. As the Mexican vaccine was developed, US officials were careful to keep Brazil – and Dr. Silvio Torres specifically – involved, "for the promotion of general goodwill, if nothing else."[41] Along with Argentina, Brazil had one of the most developed centers of veterinary expertise in the region and (unlike Argentina) was a major geopolitical ally. For its part, the PASB had a track record of working on infectious diseases in Brazil; its leader, Frederick Soper, started working there in the 1920s on Rockefeller Foundation public health campaigns, earning the nick-name "the Commander."[42] Whereas in Europe the FAO oversaw

---

[40] Palacios and Seoane, *Informe sobre la aftosa*, 1–12.
[41] Shahan, Mexico City, to Simms, BAI, March 5, 1948, CMAEFA, reports, box 2, procurement and property, phone log.
[42] Cueto, *The Value of Health*, 73.

animal disease, in Brazil it took a minor and diminishing role and the PASB took the lead.[43] The Brazilian location may have made the project somewhat more palatable to US ranching interests and their congressional allies. Many ranchers in the US Southwest feared one day having to compete with cheap, disease-free South American meat, but above all with the high-quality beef of Argentina.[44]

Indeed, the PANAFTOSA project undercut Argentina's own efforts to bolster its authority over all things aftosa. Desperate for new export markets, Argentina was eager to substantiate its argument that aftosa vaccination was viable and that vaccinated cattle – perhaps accompanied by official vaccine passports, if necessary – were suitable for export to aftosa-free zones.[45] To this end, in May 1948, Argentina enticed Otto Waldmann, the German scientist known for developing the first effective aftosa vaccine ten years earlier, to travel to Buenos Aires and set him up in an official aftosa laboratory.[46] Argentine officials also saw Mexico's eventual pursuit of vaccination as a crucial diplomatic opportunity, and sought to strengthen ties to Mexico's livestock officials. If the United States tolerated or even supported vaccination in Mexico, they reasoned, it could hardly use vaccination as a reason to block Argentine imports. In 1947–9, Argentina dispatched scientists to advise the Mexican government, invited the heads of the Mexican section of the CMAEFA to Buenos Aires, and then tried to organize its own Interamerican organization – based in Buenos Aires, and without US participation – to support aftosa vaccination. When Oscar Flores visited Buenos Aires in November 1948, his many commitments and "hasty" departure apparently ensured that he was unable to sign up. Despite repeated subsequent invitations, Mexico politely declined to join.[47] Argentine diplomatic overtures were useful to

[43] This unusual arrangement is explained in Murdock, PASB, Washington DC, to Manuel Tello, Director, SSA, December 28, 1950, SSA, SubA, box 57, file 3. Initially the FAO agreed to fund a small number of field operation costs, and PASB covered the larger costs of laboratory work, but by 1955 this arrangement was "getting out of line" and FAO funding shrank further. Kesteven to FAO, March 23, 1955, FAO, Animal Production Division, uncoded files, memos by minor staff, foreign trips.

[44] Comments by Brock, Minutes of Advisory Committee, May 27, 1947, afternoon session, CMAEFA, Reports, box 1, "Advisory committee."

[45] For a Mexican view on the push for exports, see Quijano, consejero comercial, Mexican Embassy, Buenos Aires, August 14, 1948, AHGE, III/510(82-o) "48"/.1-R.

[46] Various reports, Boyle, Buenos Aires, to Cabot, Ministry of Agriculture, November 1948, NA, MAF 35/620; "Otto Waldmann, German Chemist," October 4, 1948, CREST, CIA-RDP82-00457R001900380002-2.

[47] Carlos R. Desmarás, Argentine embassy, Mexico City, to Nazario Ortiz, Agriculture, February 7, 1949, and various correspondence, 1949–50, AHGE, III/342.5 (82)/19888.

Mexico while it tried to challenge the sanitary rifle, but less so once its own vaccination program was established. The batches of vaccine Argentina actually sold to Mexico in 1948 proved disappointing, while closer ties to Argentina risked antagonizing the United States more than was necessary.[48] Eventually, Argentina abandoned the effort to create its own multilateral organization to support aftosa vaccination, and applied to join the FAO shortly before the PANAFTOSA laboratory was opened in 1951.[49]

France and Britain initially responded rather coolly to the PANAFTOSA project. The Paris-based OIE was generally focused on Europe, and seems to have made little effort to engage with the new institution. Britain, with colonial territories in the Caribbean and Central America, and a long history of livestock imports from South America, took more interest. However, British veterinary authorities hesitated to establish close ties to the new laboratory. The UK government already gathered quite extensive information on animal disease in South America, particularly aftosa. The British embassy in Buenos Aires had a permanent post for a veterinary inspector, whose job it was to monitor sanitary conditions in Argentina, track the development of the plethora of private laboratories working on aftosa vaccines, and write occasional reports on neighboring countries in the Southern Cone.[50] For nearly two decades, the Pirbright laboratory in Surrey had received virus samples from British colonies, Argentina, Brazil, and many other countries. Owing to its geographical reach, and the UK government's uncompromising policies towards aftosa, Pirbright established itself as one of the leading authorities on the aftosa virus in the world, "a sort of museum of types of virus against which many . . . countries check the type involved in an outbreak from which they may suffer."[51]

Ian Galloway, head of Pirbright, questioned why these established networks should be disrupted, and feared that PANAFTOSA would

[48] By the end of 1948 it had become clear that the Argentine vaccine shipped to Mexico was ineffective against pigs and goats, and much of it had been spoiled in transit. Confidential reports, July 1948, CMAEFA, reports, box 1.

[49] Various correspondence, Dodd, Rome, to Argentina, 1951, FAO, uncoded files, Dodd correspondence.

[50] Various reports, Boyle, 1937, Rio de Janeiro, NA, MAF, 35/857.

[51] "MFD," note for minister, c. 1952, NA, MAF 255/112. On Pirbright's international network, see various correspondence, 1946–51, NA, MAF 35/620, MAF 35/621, MAF, 35/464.

simply produce a "duplication" of work or, worse, competing findings that could easily become politicized. He also sensed that the southward expansion of US government agencies into the regulation of animal disease across the Western Hemisphere represented a challenge to Pirbright's authority, and feared becoming a "satellite of a newly formed galaxy with a multiplicity of aims and counsels."[52] Colonial officials in British Honduras and Jamaica also urged caution. Rapid air links meant it was preferable to send a flask of sample virus (and receive policy decisions) along existing networks. British Honduras also worried that the protocols the USDA promoted via PANAFTOSA would prevent them importing breeding stock from any country infected with aftosa, no matter what quarantine safeguards they created. These rules might prevent them from importing stock from Britain during isolated outbreaks there, and could force them to import animals from "dollar sources."[53] In any case, it made little sense to commit British resources to the center when it was going to be generously funded by the US Point Four program. In 1951, British officials decided to offer the laboratory, which they saw as largely the product of US policy, vague rhetorical support for the sake of "lip service," but little else.[54]

However, PANAFTOSA was hardly a unilateral imposition of US power and knowledge. The laboratory was also an attractive proposition to Brazil's government, ranchers, and veterinary experts. Brazil supplied land and existing facilities and contributed an initial investment of half-a-million dollars to construct laboratory facilities. In return, it received US technical assistance and investment, and recognition of its regional leadership role.[55] US support for research and possible eradication also carried the vague promise of future unimpeded access to US and UK markets. PANAFTOSA provided a major stimulus for Brazil's own nascent project of aftosa research and control, which had begun in 1943 in Rio Grande do Sul under the leadership of Silvio Torres. At the start of the Mexican campaign Torres's relations with the USDA had been strained. Having arrived to advise the Mexican government in January 1947, he warned of the impracticality of slaughter due to the scale of the

[52] Galloway, Pirbright, to Metivier, Ministry of Agriculture, Trinidad, September 25, 1951, NA, CO 852/1287/3.

[53] Governor, British Honduras, to Secretary of State for Colonies, December 20, 1951, NA, CO 852/1287/3.

[54] Memo, Simmons, April 24, 1951, NA, CO 852/1287/3.   [55] Machado, *Aftosa*, 74.

epizootic and Mexico's low level of education and administrative weaknesses, but condescending USDA officials had ignored his warnings that imposing slaughter might provoke another "revolution."[56] Torres now interpreted the change in the USDA's stance as a vindication of his own ideas and research, welcomed the advent of PANAFTOSA, and participated in its programs and events.[57] Indeed, PANAFTOSA represented a compromise in US and South American perspectives on aftosa. Importantly, the advice dispensed by PANAFTOSA was more flexible and open-ended than the BAI's position before 1947. For experts in the Americas and Europe, the aftosa campaign in Mexico had shown the viability of a third "Mexican model," between the traditional two options of eradication via "stamping out" or amelioration via vaccination.[58] Countries should consider which mix of quarantine, inspection, slaughter, and vaccination was best suited to them, taking into account a host of contextual factors. PANAFTOSA insisted that the ultimate decision whether to vaccinate or slaughter lay with local officials in member states. As in Mexico, the Rio facilities initially set up for aftosa control also branched out into research on other animal diseases which South American nations deemed significant to national development.[59]

As such, the project exemplified larger trends in the PASB of which it was part. From 1947 to 1960, the PASB grew rapidly in size and engaged in a growing range of ambitious projects, changing its name to the Panamerican Health Organization (PAHO) in 1958. Through the 1950s it offered prestigious scholarships to Latin Americans to study medicine and veterinary science at US colleges, and one of PANAFTOSA's roles was to help recruit suitable candidates for these programs across South America. Frederick Soper and a handful of officials at the PASB were increasingly concerned with the connections between human and animal health, and saw the PANAFTOSA project as a useful way to stake out an area of expertise they called veterinary public health: a field encompassing zoonotic diseases and epizootic diseases like aftosa that undermined

---

[56] *Anais da I conferência de febre aftosa*, 55.

[57] *Anais do Segundo Congresso Panamericano.*

[58] Dr. Yasin, in minutes of joint FAO-OIE committee on food-and-mouth disease, Paris, May 15–20, 1950, FAO, Animal Production, uncoded files, "OIE, correspondence, minutes."

[59] Copy of paper by Dr. Benjamin Blood and Dr. Ramón Rodríguez, "PANAFTOSA," in report on Regional Consultative Foot and Mouth Disease Conference, Panama, 21–24 August 1951, NA, CO 852/1287/3.

production and indirectly damaged human health.[60] And yet, as Marcos Cueto has argued, there was more to the Bureau than one-way Americanization. Soper was very keen to avoid accusations of imperial meddling, and jealously defended Bureau autonomy from other US agencies. He carefully recruited ambitious, young professionals from Latin America and reduced the dominance of US personnel; under Soper, PANAFTOSA was jointly run by a Chilean and US veterinarian. Soper encouraged Bureau staff to see themselves as apolitical experts in progress, relatively autonomous from any national government.[61] Cueto also argues that the Bureau's experience in public health campaigns in Haiti from 1950–4 fostered a greater sensitivity to different national contexts and popular culture.[62] For those involved in veterinary medicine and PANAFTOSA, it is clear that the decisive learning experience had happened a few years earlier, during Mexico's aftosa crisis.

Such compromise did not guarantee success, but eventually the PANAFTOSA project bore fruit. Early hopes that the Mexican campaign could be a new model for eradication elsewhere in the America were soon frustrated. In the 1960s all the national eradication drives attempted in South America – in Argentina, Ecuador, Uruguay, Venezuela, Colombia – failed, undermined by political instability, popular opposition, and unreliable live vaccines produced in private laboratories, which easily spoiled in storage and provided immunity for only a few months. Political support from the United States was also wavering. The Kennedy administration incorporated aftosa control into the Alliance for Progress' package of rural modernization, but faced renewed criticism from US beef-cattle interests on this score, and stable funding from the Organization of American States was uncertain.[63] However, in 1969 the PAHO took over both the funding and operation of PANAFTOSA, and in 1972 it became the headquarters of the *Comisión Sudamericana para la Lucha Contra la Fiebre Aftosa*, a new multilateral body which provided financial support, and planned control policies and information-sharing across national borders. As a result of improved coordination and slowly improving oil-based vaccines, in the 1980s and 1990s Chile, Argentina, Uruguay and Brazil gradually controlled and eradicated aftosa through a mixture of slaughter and vaccination.[64]

---

[60] Nash Carter, *One Man*, 163–6.   [61] Cueto, *The Value of Health*, 95–108.
[62] Ibid., 110.   [63] Machado, *Aftosa*, 77–107; Nash Carter, *One Man*, 168.
[64] Woods, *Manufactured Plague*, 135.

The aftosa outbreak in Mexico also reshaped policies and institutions much closer to Washington DC. The United States had long seen public calls for more research on the aftosa virus, but these were generally resisted by officials who deemed it unnecessary, uneconomic or dangerous. The outbreaks of the 1910s caused some scientists, ranchers, and members of the public to wonder why the advances made by the BAI controlling other animal diseases with vaccines could not be replicated with aftosa. The outbreak in California in 1924 again led to more calls for research. In response, the USDA sent a committee of three scientists to Europe to investigate the possibilities of vaccination. However, the committee concluded that vaccination was unviable and slaughter remained the cheapest and most efficient policy for the United States, isolated as it was from areas of endemic infection. The BAI stood firm behind its slaughter protocols and argued that the virus was simply too dangerous and contagious to risk further research in the mainland United States.[65]

By the 1940s, various new forces had emerged within the US state that pushed for further research, not only abroad but in US territory. The experience of the Second World War deepened US official understandings of food production as a matter of national security, and fed a new interest in how animal diseases could potentially disrupt the mobilization of resources.[66] Since the late 1930s, US military and intelligence services worried about other states – principally Germany and then the Soviet Union – weaponizing aftosa for germ warfare, and secretly developed their own germ warfare program with the UK and Canada. When the German scientist Otto Waldmann announced that he had produced the first reliable aftosa vaccine in 1938, this was particularly troubling, since it raised the possibility of other countries being able to inflict the virus on enemy territories while protecting their own.[67] At the close of the Second World War, US and UK military intelligence hurriedly gathered information on German aftosa research facilities on the Island of Riems in the Baltic Sea, and the US Army organized several vaccination campaigns in occupied Europe, desperately sourcing vaccine from suppliers across the continent.[68] By the war's end, these concerns began to filter into policies in the Western Hemisphere. In 1944, the US military sent a small team to

[65] Corner, *A History of the Rockefeller Institute*, 196.
[66] McDonald, *Food Power*, 19–47; Collingham, *The Taste of War*.
[67] Woods, *Manufactured Plague*, 87.
[68] Various correspondence, 1946–7, NA, FO 943/560; WO 219/1317; WO 208/3973.

survey animal diseases and veterinary services along the proposed route of the Panamerican highway.[69] Some scientists and politicians believed that the new context of global military mobilization and virological advances demanded more sustained government investment in aftosa research and vaccine development. The Rockefeller Institute offered discreet support to vaccine research on aftosa, although Nelson Rockefeller himself was not eager to involve himself publicly in such a contentious campaign and, with the aid of his secretary, he concocted an excuse to decline an invitation to congressional hearings on aftosa.[70] Charles Duckworth, assistant head of Agriculture for the State of California, never believed slaughter was viable in Mexico and urged major livestock producers – including the Wyoming rancher Elmer Brock, former head of the American National Livestock Association – to change their approach. Instead, Duckworth advocated a program combining innovations in vaccine storage made during US campaigns against rinderpest in the Philippines, and more recent Swiss techniques of "ring vaccination" – isolated slaughter of infected herds encircled by repeatedly vaccinated and inspected animals.[71]

Prior to the Mexican epizootic, however, these forces could not dominate aftosa policy. Even during the Second World War the US government refused to endorse aftosa research on US territory. Instead, it devised a tripartite agreement with the UK and Canada to divide scientific labor on germ warfare. On the desolate Grosse Ilse in the gulf of St Lawrence in Quebec, US scientists focused on rinderpest and Canadian scientists on various poultry diseases; UK scientists worked on aftosa at Pirbright. Even then, according to US Secretary of Agriculture Clinton Anderson, aftosa research received relatively little support and focused on pure research on typing and epidemiology rather than vaccination. In February 1948, as the Mexican campaign stalled, Anderson described the wartime arrangements in a furious private letter to the editors of the *Farm Journal*, and argued that US beef ranching interests and their allies

---

[69] Nash Carter, *One Man*, 73–119; Steele, "Veterinary Survey."

[70] Anderson to Farm Journal, January 1948, CAP, box 7, foot and mouth; Rockefeller, to Abbey, February 2, 1948, and draft telegram to House Committee on Agriculture, January 28, 1948, RAC, group 4, series III 4 L, box 80, "foot and mouth disease."

[71] Duckworth, to Mitchell, Albuquerque, January 3, 1948, and handwritten note from Pancho Scanlan, to Shahan on Hotel Genève letterhead, c. January 1948, CMAEFA, reports, box 2, advisory committee. Trigg, BAI, to Mitchell, Bell Ranch, New Mexico, August 21, 1947; Mitchell to Secretary Anderson, August 17, 1947; and Duckworth, Sacramento, to Mitchell, August 13, 1947, all in CAP, box 7, foot and mouth.

in Congress – "chiefly Kleberg" – had quietly sabotaged any advances on aftosa:

The War Department set up three projects (there were many others, but I refer to three). This was very hush hush during the war and still may be hush hush, but I am damned if I am going to let the Department of Agriculture get pounded much longer on Foot and Mouth without washing a little family linen in public … I assume you know that we had developed the greatest collection of germs to spread diseases over the world. People said that we had enough diseases in bottles to wipe out the world in a few weeks, as did some other countries, but the War Department said it would be foolish to concern ourselves with counter offensives on disease warfare for humans and not guard against the possibility that someone could introduce disease into our livestock population that would just as quickly bring us to our knees as human diseases would do … The money was set up , everything was all ready, the virus men were available, but the work never got done. Why? You might do a service if you printed the true answer to that. I have listened to the excuses. When you call the people in who should have started it, it is like that verse in the Bible: "And they all with one accord began to make excuses." You know the answer and so do I. If we develop a vaccine that wiped out foot-and-mouth disease, we couldn't keep Argentine beef out of the United States. There is no other reason why the work was not done, and the same group of cattlemen who stopped that work would not now allow us to develop a vaccine if the disease were not in our own neighborhood.[72]

Anderson's letter also underscores how the wartime research by Richard Shope – head of the Rockefeller Institute and US germ warfare research – in creating a new vaccine for rinderpest fueled optimism that similar breakthrough was at hand with aftosa: "It will not take years and years and years … Shope was close to the answer in his work on rinderpest. Starting where he left off, six months might give us a very good vaccine."[73]

Around the same time Anderson wrote this explosive letter, the US government changed tack. In February 1948 Anderson at the USDA and the US Army briefed Truman on the need for a US-based research facility, and Truman signed a request for funding.[74] In May 1948, Shahan, co-director of the CMAEFA and one of the BAI's senior researchers, was ordered back to Washington to help make preparations for the US laboratory he would later direct, assisted by US Army Colonel Don

---

[72] Anderson to Farm Journal, January 1948, CAP, box 7, foot and mouth. Anderson never received a reply, and it is possible that he decided against sending this letter.

[73] Ibid.

[74] Various correspondence, February–November 1948, TP, Presidential Secretary Files, box 161, foot and mouth.

Mace, a germ warfare expert who had observed the Mexican campaign.[75] Deteriorating US–Soviet relations – the factor emphasized by most historians of germ warfare research – was doubtless central to these new plans.[76] The US Army Chemical Corps, whose budget had already mushroomed in 1947, would surely have pushed for new research regardless of the crisis in Mexico.[77] In 1948, the British secretly evacuated the German germ warfare and aftosa specialist (and Rockefeller Institute alumnus) Eric Traub from Soviet-held eastern Germany, and in early 1949 Traub arrived in the United States, a beneficiary of Operation Paperclip, and advised the US government on aftosa research. While the Argentines harbored Traub's mentor Waldmann, British intelligence reported that Traub was the real scientific prize and that Waldmann, in his sixties, was increasingly restricted to administrative work.[78]

However, the Mexican epizootic helped shift the balance of forces in favor of those US scientists and politicians – like Anderson – who wanted to develop research on aftosa (and other animal diseases considered dangerous, including rinderpest) on US territory.

Most obvious, it provided a useful public rationale for renewed and US-based germ warfare research. The USDA presented aftosa research as the primary objective of any new facility, with vague suggestions that it could also branch out into defensive research on other dangerous diseases. Indeed, as the US government scouted sites and endeavored to get a laboratory built, some critics argued, quite accurately, that the Trojan Horse of aftosa research contained wide-ranging military research. In February 1949, an anonymous letter to the *Providence Journal* condemned plans for a US animal disease laboratory, arguing that defensive research was a "mere cover" for a "festering center of biological warfare set down in our midsts," intended to "harbor the most deadly, hard to control and destructive agents of plague and disease known to immoral science."[79]

---

[75] Carrol, *Lab* 257, 48–9, 53–4. Other US military officers who assisted the Mexican campaign included a Colonel Brown, sent to assess Swan Island as a possible laboratory site in October 1947, and head of the US army veterinary corps, Dr. Kelser. Dr. Jacob Traum, of the University of California, also observed the Mexican campaign before being recruited to work at Plum Island. Monthly reports, October 1947, CMAEFA, operations, box 29, Querétaro; various confidential reports, October 1948, CMAEFA, reports, box 1.

[76] P. Millet, "Anti-Animal."   [77] McVety, *Rinderpest*, 177.

[78] Hunt, *Secret Agenda*, 344; various correspondence, 1945–6, NA, WO 208/3973.

[79] Anonymous letter, *Providence Journal*, February 3, 1949, in BP, box 5, foot and mouth.

However, the Mexican epizootic provided more than convenient window-dressing for the new policy. While BAI officials used to argue that US geographic isolation was similar to that of the British Isles, the Mexican crisis discredited that idea. As Anderson realized, it was this new sense of vulnerability, above all, which convinced key figures in the livestock industry that the time had arrived for virus research on US soil.[80] Moreover, the vaccination program in Mexico dramatized the US government's dependence on foreign laboratories and researchers whose control by US officials would always be negotiated and incomplete. Kleberg's group of Texas ranchers opposed vaccine research for as long as possible, but by March 1948 even they proposed a vaccination program of sorts in Mexico, albeit one in which US authorities strictly controlled and administered all the vaccine. The BAI considered these conditions utterly impractical and politically unviable.[81] The Mexican campaign showed both the political necessity of cooperating with host governments on animal disease research, and the "extreme difficulty" of dictating the terms of cooperation. In the BAI's judgment, "only the extreme exigency of the eradication program" in Mexico "kept the two forces working together with reasonable harmony."[82] The experience of the 1953 Gutiérrez Zamora outbreak, and Mexico's efforts to shake off US control and produce and export a vaccine, only confirmed these problems.

In response to the failure of slaughter in Mexico, the USDA created a "long-term" plan for aftosa research on US soil, and a "short-term" project of collaborative research with European laboratories. In early 1948 the USDA dispatched scientists to laboratories in Denmark, Holland, and Switzerland. The arrangement helped the BAI learn from laboratories it believed knew most about making and administering aftosa vaccine.[83] It also helped the USDA and the FAO gradually strengthen their authority over aftosa policies, and veterinary science in general. In the early 1950s, "two blocs" had emerged in Europe regarding aftosa policy.[84] The FAO, closely allied with the US government,

---

[80] Minutes of Advisory Committee, May 27, 1947, afternoon session, CMAEFA, reports, box 1, advisory committee, 80–90.
[81] Various correspondence, Shahan to Anderson, March 1948, CAP, box 7, foot and mouth.
[82] Secretary Anderson, USDA to Simms, BAI, December 12, 1947, FMDRL, box 2, file 32.
[83] Various reports on European program, 1948–50, FMDRL, box 1, file 3.
[84] C. P. Quick, minute, July 6, 1955, NA, MAF 252/48, 27.

promoted the same kind of policy advice dispensed at PANAFTOSA, which had emerged from the crucible of the Mexican campaign. The competing bloc was led by the Paris-based and French-influenced OIE, an organization which saw itself as an institutional counterweight to US authority channeled through the FAO.[85] The OIE's stance had also transformed in the postwar years. Until 1950, it was a strong advocate of aftosa vaccination, presenting itself as an alternative to the traditional US and UK adherence to "stamping out"; it was because of this that Mexico had sought to build closer ties with the organization. After vaccination failed to control major outbreaks in France in 1950–2, the OIE's director Professor Gaston Ramón abruptly turned against vaccines and promoted extensive slaughter as an essential component of control.[86] British and US officials believed Ramón exaggerated small differences in approach to defend the OIE's autonomy; by the mid-1950s, the OIE's approach to aftosa differed only in emphasis from the "mixed methods" promoted by the FAO.[87] The USDA's European research program likely encouraged loyalty to the FAO, and evidently encouraged some European scientists to criticize the OIE. All the countries involved were founding members of the FAO's European Commission for the Control of Foot and Mouth Disease, founded in Rome in 1954 to share information and coordinate policy. At the FAO's 1955 conference on aftosa control, the OIE stance was criticized. The delegate from the Netherlands teased Ramón, suggesting that even Agatha Christie would be hard pressed to discover the difference between its aftosa protocols and those of the FAO.[88] After 1955, the FAO and OIE established a loose cooperative agreement on aftosa, and tensions between the blocs abated.

Nevertheless, US officials argued forcefully that the European program was only a temporary fix. Much could be learned and accomplished, but the US government could never control the military security or research priorities of laboratories abroad. These would always depend in part on

[85] Speech by Dr. Carlos Ruiz, OIE, in report on Regional Consultative Foot and Mouth Disease Conference, Panama, August 21–24, 1951, NA, CO 852/1287/3, 29. On OIE and FAO turf-wars around rinderpest, see McVety, *Rinderpest*, 150–2.

[86] Various reports on foot and mouth disease policy in France and Switzerland, 1953–4, NA, MAF 387/23; Torres Bodet, Paris, to Foreign Relations, March 24, 1955, AHGE, III, 368(44) 25286.

[87] Wahlen, FAO, in Proceedings of Foot and Mouth Disease Conference, FAO, Rome, June 14, 1955, MAF 252/48. See also, various correspondence, 1950–3, FAO, Animal Production branch, uncoded files, OIE.

[88] Van der Lee, transcript of plenary session, proceedings of FMD conference, FAO, Rome, June 14, 1955, MAF 252/48, 5.

the "consent of the governments concerned" and the interests of national farm organizations.[89] While the new laboratories in Mexico and Rio de Janeiro focused on surveillance and branched out into a variety of programs aimed at modernizing livestock production, the argument for the US laboratory rested on a more militarized notion of national security. As knowledge of virus and vaccine techniques spread, the US government could not afford to fall behind in its understanding of how to defend itself from germ attacks, still less farm this work out to foreigners, or be blocked by narrow cattle ranching interests.[90]

However, the project for a US laboratory still faced long delays and resistance. Between 1948 and 1950, the USDA surveyed several possible sites in Washington State, Rhode Island, and New York. Some congressmen condemned the plans and vowed to block research in their states, while others pushed hard for the project. In July 1949, the head of the Democratic committee in Maine called the USDA "to say that if we will put the foot-and-mouth laboratory there, he will guarantee to carry the state in the next election."[91] While the US Army was impatient to establish a laboratory as soon as possible, the Navy apparently dragged its feet. When the USDA tried to survey possible laboratory sites in Rhode Island Sound, Navy officers dodged appointments and exasperated USDA officials; the head of the BAI decided that the prospects of Navy support for the laboratory were "unpromising to say the least" and decided that "contacts at a higher level will be required."[92] The US government invited Ian Galloway, who had overseen British aftosa research during the Second World War, to advise on the laboratory plans. Galloway was strongly in favor, but warned that the island location, favored by the USDA, would bring unforeseen practical difficulties. Based on his experiences in Britain and visiting the German laboratory on Riems, research on an island could work for a short time, but quickly the isolation sapped morale and caused researchers to "develop nomadic tendencies."[93] Despite such concerns and considerable opposition to the project voiced in town-hall meetings and local newspapers, in 1951 the US government eventually settled on an old military base on Plum Island, in Long Island

[89] Osteen, Chief of European Mission for Research on Foot and Mouth Disease, Report, May 31, 1950, FMDRL, box 1, folder 3.

[90] Carroll, *Lab 257*, 41–70.

[91] Memo from "Wes," USDA, to CFB, July 28, 1949, TL, BP, box 5, foot and mouth.

[92] Simms, BAI to Secretary Brannan, May 2, 1950, BP, box 5, foot and mouth.

[93] Galloway, Report on Progress and International Collaboration, December 12, 1947, NA, MAF 117/107.

Sound, and determined that the USDA would run the laboratory in partnership with the US Army Chemical Corps. Still, the USDA recognized that refitting the decayed facility and designing the elaborate security and waste disposal systems would take several years. The Plum Island laboratory did not open until 1954.[94]

To compensate for delay, the US government also renewed and bolstered the old wartime alliance with aftosa researchers at Pirbright. Ironically, aftosa research at Pirbright was itself the product of struggles in the UK very similar to those around Plum Island. In 1912, an early attempt to conduct research in British India failed because local cattle breeds showed few clinical symptoms and some developed immunity to strains of the virus. Research with animals on a disused warship moored off the coast at Harwich proved impractical. Slaughter during the 1922–4 epizootic provoked such a wave of criticism that the British Ministry of Agriculture grudgingly allowed for the establishment of permanent aftosa research at Pirbirght, but retained tight control. Thereafter Pirbright scientists found themselves in an awkward relationship with the public. Many British famers and citizens assumed that the ultimate goal of research was to produce a viable vaccine to replace slaughter, but the government remained firmly wedded to stamping out any UK outbreaks and prioritized typification and epidemiology. Scientists were encouraged to downplay the possibility of a vaccine even as they reported research findings to the public.[95]

Similar awkwardness colored Pirbright's international work. The laboratory emerged from the Second World War as one of most prestigious animal disease laboratories in world, and also seems to have been perceived by many governments as enjoying some independence from US agencies, perhaps more than it really had. When the CMAEFA invited Galloway to advise the Mexican campaign in 1947, he experienced some of same difficulties faced at home in reconciling his public defense of slaughter policies with his scientific authority and desire for increased knowledge of the virus. At first, Galloway believed that slaughter was probably the best method to adopt in Mexico, and defended it in public. At the same time, the reports he wrote on the strains of the virus sent to him from Mexico hinted at the possibility of other approaches. Galloway wrote that the Mexican strains had allowed for very promising "immunization tests" and asked Mexico to send more samples to him so he could

---

[94] Carroll, *Lab 257*, 44–5.   [95] Woods, *Manufactured Plague*, 68–80.

continue research on these strains. Some Mexican officials interpreted Galloway's reports as tacit support for their vaccination plans.[96] In mid-1947, as the difficulties of the slaughter program became obvious, Mexico also approached Pirbright for independent advice and asked for permission to send two scientists to visit. Galloway and his colleagues initially agreed to the request, assuming that it had received the backing of the USDA and State Department, but then found out that both agencies had not been informed and disapproved of the visit. Placed in an awkward position, Pirbright settled on a diplomatic fudge: it decided to receive the two Mexican scientists, provide a perfunctory tour, and restrict discussion to laboratory techniques, hoping not to anger the USDA. Much to Galloway's relief, when the two Mexicans arrived they were very tight-lipped anyway, and uninterested in broaching larger geopolitical or policy questions.[97]

Despite its international standing, increased US support for Pirbright came at an opportune time for the institution. In 1947–8, the laboratory faced a tightening budget, struggled to deal with all the viruses it accepted for analysis, and confronted critics who could see little use for the facility in peacetime given its lack of progress (or even hostility) towards vaccination. In 1948, the USDA included Pirbright in its short-term European research project. While the other European laboratories which received US assistance tended to focus on their own immediate concerns with vaccination and disease control, research at Pirbright remained better suited to military purposes, focusing on the virus itself, its strains, the rapid detection and mapping of virus strains, the study of their behavior, and means of diffusing the virus; this may explain why the USDA dispatched veterinary scientists to European laboratories, but it sent a physicist to Pirbright.[98] In 1950, the US government asked the UK to engage in further expansion of Pirbright for the purposes of joint germ warfare research on aftosa and other diseases. The UK Chiefs of Staff

[96] Galloway, "Summary of Further Information to Date 9 June 1947 on the Mexican Virus (MP) with Special Reference to Vaccination Experiments," and unsigned memo of July 31, 1947, both in AGN, MAV, 4255-2-35 A.

[97] Pirbright Monthly Reports, 1947, National Archive, NA, MAF 240/77. Venezuela invited Galloway in 1950 and he briefly accompanied Mexico's team of veterinary scientists. Machado, *Aftosa*, 66.

[98] Various reports on European program, 1948–1950, FMDRL, box 1, file 3. On the renewal of US collaboration with Pirbright during the Mexican crisis, see report on 1953 meeting, NA, WO 195/12458. For experiments with balloons and rockets to diffuse animal germ agents, see Millet, "Anti-Animal."

were delighted with the request, and considered it an important way of improving US–UK relations, given the continued problems the Truman administration faced establishing a laboratory on US soil.[99] The British Ministry of Defence and Ministry of Agriculture proposed a seven-year expansion program; after further US encouragement, in 1951 plans were accelerated, funded in large part by US loans secretly channeled through the Ministry of Defense.[100] In turn, Pirbright helped the USDA assemble its own germ stockpile. Maurice Shahan, the former head of the CMAEFA, spent six months of 1953 secretly gathering viruses for the new lab at Plum Island. After obtaining rinderpest from a top-secret US Army project in a jungle in Kenya, he traveled to Pirbright, met up with Colonel Mace, handed Galloway a US treasury check for $5,000, obtained pig and cattle tissues infected with six types and sixteen different strains of aftosa virus, and then returned to New York on a US Navy freighter.[101]

Pirbright scientists, led by Galloway eagerly embraced cooperation with the United States, although the project was not without problems. The laboratory expansion ran five years behind schedule, hampered by infighting among the various agencies and officials involved, only some of whom were aware of the military dimension of the work. Officials at the Ministry of Agriculture regularly expressed bemusement at the levels of secrecy surrounding aftosa research.[102] In 1952, Ernest Gowers, who chaired a committee of inquiry into aftosa research, described the situation to the ministry's parliamentary secretary:

> You ought to look at the Pirbright problem personally. The scientists there are splendid people doing splendid work. But the system of control is just chaos ... the governing body itself is quite incapable of controlling Galloway [who has] been charged (so he says) with highly secret work which he cannot possibly tell his governing body about because they have not been passed by MI5![103]

Along with problems of secrecy, expansion at Pirbright also heightened long-standing tensions between competing understandings of its role and purpose. The British government's unwavering support for slaughter in yet another aftosa outbreak in 1951–2 became even harder to justify juxtaposed to the ostentatious investment in Pirbright, and news of

[99] Unsigned memo, August 23, 1951, NA, DEFE 10/30. See also NA, DEFE 5/33/544, DEFE 4/47/156.
[100] On funding, see various correspondence, 1951–2, NA, MAF 250/163.
[101] Carroll, *Lab 257*, 66.
[102] Farrell, to Miss Terry, c. March 1952, NA, CO852/1287/3, 142.
[103] Cited in Woods, *Manufactured Plague*, 89–90.

innovations in vaccination in Europe and in Mexico. Managing these tensions apparently placed Galloway, an able scientist but prickly man and limited administrator, under considerable strain, and officials began to worry about his psychological wellbeing.[104]

Once Plum Island was opened in 1954, it gradually took a larger share of biological warfare research, but Pirbright remained prominent.[105] Military investment and further integration into US security policy benefited Pirbright in the long term. In 1957, the FAO nominated it the "World Foot and Mouth Disease Reference Laboratory," whose authoritative library of strains remained essential for eradication projects and military purposes alike. This secured the laboratory's position as a major scientific hub in the new network of US-sponsored laboratories and interlocking multilateral commissions dedicated to surveillance and control in the Americas and in Europe. Indeed, Pirbright scientists often visited and sometimes administered other points in this network. In 1957, Dr. William Henderson, a veteran researcher at Pirbright, accepted the PASB's invitation to lead PANAFTOSA, held the post in Rio de Janeiro for nine years, visited most countries in South America, and advised them on the collection and testing of virus samples and control techniques.[106]

Historians of Latin America's Cold War have recently put considerable effort into dismantling what Tanya Harmer memorably dubbed the "historiographic Monroe Doctrine": the tendency to emphasize US influence on the hemisphere, and downplay other regional and international connections.[107] Following the trail of the aftosa virus and the expertise surrounding it offers a useful way to contribute to this effort. A recalcitrant virus with many types, with an "insidious" capacity to spread and remain undetected, aftosa nevertheless had its political uses and, like rinderpest, demanded the creation of new institutions and knowledge.[108] As experts recognized at the time, in the early Cold War the problem of aftosa was internationalized as never before, and the US

[104] Cabot to Ministry of Agriculture, c. 1952, NA, MAF 240/565.
[105] Balmer, "The Drift of Biological Weapons Policy." For the continued interest of the Central Intelligence Agency in animal diseases and germ warfare into the early 1960s, see Nash, *One Man*, 247–69.
[106] Obituary of Sir William Henderson, *The Guardian*, December 19, 2000.
[107] Harmer, "Review." For a broader discussion of this shift, see: Harmer, "The Cold War in Latin America"; Field, Krepp, and Pettinà (eds.), *Latin America and the Global Cold War*; Lorek and Chastain (eds.), *Itineraries of Expertise*.
[108] Galloway, "Summary of Further Information to Date 9 June 1947 on the Mexican Virus (MP) with Special Reference to Vaccination Experiments," AGN, MAV, 4255-2-35 A.

government decided to build a new global veterinary infrastructure to govern the virus: to gather information about it, to understand how it spread and mutated, and learn how it could be controlled, eradicated, and weaponized.[109] This infrastructure was not homogenous. Publicly acknowledged research for the purpose of surveillance, defense, and economic development in Central and South America coexisted with a well-funded and highly secretive transatlantic program of germ warfare. Labor was divided among laboratories in Mexico City, Rio de Janeiro, Pirbright, and Plum Island, but they were part of an interconnected system, receiving US money, sharing certain kinds of information about the virus and vaccine, and feeding the libraries of virus strains amassed at Pirbright and, later, Plum Island. These arrangements reflected the US government's enormous power and its wide-ranging notions of national security, but also incorporated some of the interests and ideas of national governments and scientific experts in the Americas and Europe.

Mexico's aftosa crisis shaped this infrastructure and helps explain when, how, and why it was built. Some Mexican experts hoped that the aftosa campaign would allow Mexico to emerge as an independent exporter of aftosa expertise and vaccine, but the hostility of the USDA, northern Mexican cattle interests, and the technical difficulty encountered in manipulating the virus frustrated this project. Nevertheless, it provided Mexico with new scientific capacities and a broader role in Central America. The aftosa crisis also undermined US officials' and farmers' sense of geographical protection from aftosa, demonstrated the enormous costs of polices of aftosa control that were reactive, based on slaughter alone, and guided by narrow US beef-cattle interests, and offered a new kind of eradication policy. In turn, it pushed the USDA to catch-up with the latest vaccine techniques developed in European and Latin American laboratories, even as it exposed the dangers of relying solely on foreign laboratories for aftosa research, and helped establish aftosa as the public face of secret germ warfare research on US soil. For better or worse, the conflicts unleashed and lessons taught by Mexico's aftosa epizootic reverberated across Latin America, into supposedly domestic US institutions and, indirectly, reached across the Atlantic and reshaped relations with Cold War allies.

---

[109] Duckworth, "Cooperación internacional en vasta escala."

Afterword

In the end, what is the best story to tell about the campaign against aftosa in Mexico? For those who carried it out, the experience often seemed rather bizarre. Officials remembered countless confrontations with suspicious villagers with strange, bewildering customs. The apparent cultural gulf separating the campaign from rural folk, sometimes lead to danger and bloodshed; sometimes it led to strange juxtapositions and comical misunderstandings. In hindsight, many of these stories do not seem so strange at all, but straightforward expressions of urban prejudices, and modernizing experts' well-documented habit of lumping together obstacles into a single object they called tradition.[1] Still, in terms of scope and cost, the campaign was truly unusual. And some incidents were ineluctably weird. No matter how you look at it, there is something odd about a jeep driving around the hills and valleys of Oaxaca with a giant poison-filled syringe strapped to its bonnet; or boxes of ice parachuting down onto the slopes of the Sierra Madre del Sur; or a cowboy gulping down a viscous vaccine of ground-up cow-tongue suspended in aluminum hydroxide solution at gunpoint.

If the story still seems a little weird today, that may also be down to our expectations about what a story about livestock animals should or can be about. Neither the bucolic imagery surrounding dairy farming, nor the increasingly sterile and disembodied way that meat is marketed, nor even

[1] Mitchell, *Rule*, 223–4.

the animal rights movement's emphasis on the cruelty of slaughter, really prepares us for all the roles livestock play in this story: as vectors of disease; sources of food, draft power, and fertilizer; participants in household and subsistence farming; commodities in international markets; technologies for vaccine production and breeding; and unwitting conscripts in plans for germ warfare. If this story seems strange, this is partly because historians still have work to do connecting animals to the production of scientific knowledge, the development of capitalism, and the formation of states – that is, showing how animals were shaped by, and themselves shaped the processes that made the modern world.

Putting weirdness to one side, it is also possible to tell part of the story in the "tragic idiom" often reserved, quite rightly, for the history of US interventions in Latin America during the Cold War.[2] In the countryside, bitterness about the sanitary rifle lingered for a long time. Decades later, people remembered it as a feeding frenzy of corruption and profiteering, overseen by Oscar Flores and a "bunch of cheats."[3] As we have seen, by the 1960s the people of Senguio felt comfortable celebrating the patriotic resistance of campesinos and their village's role as "the graveyard of the sanitary rifle." Others, like the villagers of San Pedro el Alto, just remembered the episode as a source of senseless waste and violence. In the 1960s, a marijuana farmer in Michoacán discussed his trade with a military commander and argued that it was a form of revenge against the "gringos" for "what happened in '47."[4] In Inchamacuaro, Guanajuato, the family of a campesino accidentally shot during a slaughter operation sought to avenge his death by dynamiting the presidential train when it passed through the state, but the bomb failed to explode on time.[5] Mexico's veterinary experts celebrated their victory over the disease, but also mourned their losses, unveiling a plaque at the veterinary school commemorating the lives tragically lost during the campaign. While the campaign was remembered intensely in a handful of places, many participants in the drama – veterinarians, cowhands, or villagers – complained that the general public quickly forgot about it. For their part, Mexican and US officials learned important lessons from the campaign but were in no hurry to encourage ongoing public discussion and scrutiny. Mexico's share of the paper archive went up in smoke, and other

---

[2] Friedman, "Retiring the Puppets," 622.

[3] Interview with Andrés Héctor Quezada Lara by Myrna Parra-Mantilla, 2003, "Interview no. 988," Institute of Oral History, University of Texas at El Paso.

[4] Maldonado, *Los márgenes*, 349.   [5] Soto Correa, *El rifle*, 78.

kinds of potentially embarrassing traces literally stayed buried. In the late 1950s, a couple of Mexican businesses offered to dig up the now virus-free slaughter pits and convert the remains into bonemeal. Perhaps wary of more scandalously vacant animal graves, the government declined.[6] Fifty years after the campaign ended, veteran Mexican officials still engaged in bizarre distortions. Dr. Ernesto Bachtold insisted that the lynching at Senguio was the only episode of violent conflict in the entire campaign.[7]

As we have seen, the campaign opened up the path to a new phase of state-assisted livestock development in Mexico. However, we know too much about the costs and failures of that process to be too sanguine about this outcome. For all the debate over disease control, Mexican officials never really questioned the idea that national progress demanded ever-growing production and consumption of meat, milk and eggs. And yet, by the late 1970s it was clear that most of the gains in production were consumed by the urban middle and upper classes and remained out of reach for Mexico's poor majority. That is, the political economy of livestock skewed in much the same way as the PRI's overall model of national development.[8] Officials were aware of some of the social costs of extensive beef ranching, but were rather blithe about the destruction of tropical forests and had limited power or will to restrain it. The costs of more intensive animal farming – pollution, animal welfare, biodiversity loss, increasing dependence on antimicrobial technologies – were rarely considered at all.[9]

Still, in political terms, reading the story as a tragedy seems incomplete. There was certainly something inflexible, scientifically authorized, and "high-modernist" about the first year of Mexico's aftosa campaign. The US government imposed a slaughter policy on the commission which then struggled mightily to make rural Mexico legible and compliant.[10] Expert and popular demands for vaccination and research – informed by other Latin American and European models – show how the crisis also produced a competing scientific modernism with what might be called a bifocal perspective: in Scott's terms it was lower – more amenable to local (or at least subnational) sociopolitical and epidemiological contexts – but also much higher – promoting and celebrating the production of

[6] Various correspondence, 1954–7, AGN, DGAG, 130, fiebre aftosa.
[7] Bachtold, "Remembranzas." [8] Sanderson, *The Transformation*, 147–50.
[9] For a rare Mexican case study, see Pérez Espejo, *Granjas porcinas*.
[10] Scott, *Seeing Like a State*, 4.

laboratory-based scientific knowledge.[11] As Palmer and Cueto argue was the case in human medicine and public health, the aftosa crisis shows how Latin American societies – with their particular geopolitical location, historical trajectory, and socio political structures – engaged with foreign expertise and produced competing, regionally-inflected modernisms.[12] If few actors in the aftosa drama challenged the core productivist assumptions of industrial modernization, neither the US or Mexican governments could dictate the practical response to this particular crisis. The success of the aftosa campaign rested on secrecy, bribery, force, and sporadic doses of outright terror. It also required an admission, however reluctant for some, of the fundamental interdependence of the United States and Mexico, and the need to address at least some of the attitudes and interests of Mexican society. If nothing else, this story helps us understand the appeal of mid-century visions of development in which governments and experts claimed to able to harness science, technology and state power to forge an inclusive, genuinely national version of progress, countering narrow business interests and ameliorating the harder edges of capitalist exploitation. This vision ultimately proved a myth; but it remained plausible for so long because at times, as at the conclusion of the aftosa crisis, it could approximate reality. Currently, there is no lack of policy problems that cross national borders, nor of walls and other kinds of physical barriers posing as quixotic solutions. In that context, we can be forgiven for looking back at the politics of the aftosa campaign, for all its waste and violence, with some wistfulness.

---

[11] For an argument for "low modernism" in the US New Deal, see Gilbert, *Planning Democracy*, 60–79.

[12] Cueto and Palmer, *Medicine and Public Health*, 3–4.

Bibliography

ARCHIVAL SOURCES

Mexico

Archivo Comité Nacional de la Unión Nacional Sinarquista (microfilm), Biblioteca del Museo Nacional de Antropología y Historia (CNUNS).
Archivo General de la Nación (AGN).
    Dirección Federal de Seguridad (DFS).
    Dirección General de Investigaciones Políticos y Sociales (DGIPS).
    Fondo 215, Dirección General Agricultura y Ganadería (DGAG).
    Ramo Presidentes: Miguel Alemán Valdés (MAV), Manuel Ávila Camacho (MAC), Lázaro Cárdenas (LC).
Archivo Histórico del Estado de Guanajuato, Secretaría General de Gobierno (AHEG).
Archivo Histórico de la Secretaría de la Defensa Nacional (AHSDN).
Archivo Histórico Genaro Estrada, Acervo Histórico Diplomático (AHGE).
Casa de la Cultura Jurídica, Morelia, Michoacán (CCJM).
Personal papers of Professor Juan Manuel Cervantes Sánchez, Facultad de Medicina Veterinaria y Zootecnia, Universidad Nacional Autónoma de México.
Secretaría de Salubridad y Asistencia (SSA).

United States

Foot and Mouth Disease Research Laboratory, National Agricultural Library, Maryland (FMDRL).
National Archives and Records Administration, Maryland (NARA).
    Confidential US State Department Central Files, Mexico: Internal Affairs, 1945–9, 1950–4, microfilm (IAMSD).
    Record Group 17, Bureau of Animal Industry, Commission for the Eradication of Foot-and-Mouth Disease (CMAEFA).

Rockefeller Archive Center, Sleepy Hollow (RAC).
Sul Ross University, Archive of the Big Bend, Aftosa Papers (ABB).
Tannenbaum Archive, Columbia University (TA).
Truman Presidential Library
    Clinton Anderson Papers (CAP).
    Charles Brannan Papers (BP).
    Kenneth Heckler Papers (HP).
    Truman Papers (TP).
University of Wisconsin, Special Collections

Europe

Food and Agriculture Organization, Rome, Italy (FAO).
National Archive, Kew, United Kingdom (NA).
Paul Lamartine Yates Papers (PLY).

Digital Archives

CIA CREST archive (CREST).
Foreign Affairs Oral History Project, The Association for Diplomatic Studies and Training, Arlington, VA (FAOHP).
Foreign Relations of the United States, Office of the Historian, State Department (FRUS).
Gale Archives Unbound (GAU).
George S. Messersmith Papers, Special Collections, University of Delaware Library, Newark, Delaware (GMP).
Institute of Oral History, University of Texas at El Paso.
USDA National Agricultural Library, Special Collections (NAL).

Periodicals

The Atlantic
Excélsior
Imágen Veterinaria
La Prensa
Mañana
Novedades
El Universal
Washington Post

OTHER PRIMARY SOURCES

Aftosa International Roundup. n.p., 1985.
Anais da I conferência de febre aftosa: realizada na cidade do Rio de Janeiro D.F., de 5 a 11 de setembro de 1950. Rio de Janeiro: n.p., 1950.
Anais do Segundo Congresso Panamericano de Medicina Veterinària, realizado em São Paulo Brasil de 3 a 10 de abril de 1954: Proceedings of the Second Panamerican Veterinary Congress, April 3–10, 1954. São Paulo: n.p., 1950.

Bachtold, Ernesto. "Remembranzas del brote de fiebre aftosa en México." *Imágen Veterinaria* 1:4 (2001), 9–13.

Bedford, Sybille. *A Visit to Don Otavio: A Mexican Journey.* London: Eland, 1982.

Burnaman, J. H. *A Week in the Wilds of Old Mexico.* n.p., 1931.

Cárdenas, Lázaro. *Apuntes: una selección.* Mexico City: Universidad Nacional Autónoma de México; Centro de Estudios de la Revolución Mexicana Lázaro Cárdenas, 2003.

CMAEFA. *Comisión Mexicana-Americana para la eradicación de la fiebre aftosa: Distrito de Huajuapan. Sector de Chalcatongo.* N.p., n.d. Microfilm at Bancroft Library, University of California, Berkeley.

Del Villar, Mary and Fred del Villar. *Where the Strange Roads Go Down.* New York: Macmillan, 1953.

Dillmann, C. *Manual del ganadero mexicano.* Mexico City: Imprenta y Litografía Española, 1883.

Doughty, William D. *Gringo Livestock Inspector.* New York: Vantage Press, 1962.

Duckworth, Charles U. "Cooperación internacional en vasta escala: una realidad demostrada en el control de la fiebre aftosa." *Boletín de la Oficina Sanitaria Panamericana* 31:3 (1951): 244–7.

Eakin, James. *Borderland Slaughter, A Love Story: Chronicle of the US-Mexico Campaign to Eradicate the Hoof-and-Mouth Virus.* Buenos Aires: E-libro. net, 2002.

Fernández, Rubén and Guillermo Quesada Bravo. *El problema de la fiebre aftosa y las últimas investigaciones científicas que sean realizado al respeto.* Mexico City: Publicistas e Impresores "Beatriz de la Silva," 1947.

Gilly, Adolfo, ed. *Cartas a Cuauhtémoc Cárdenas.* Mexico City: Ediciones Era, 1989.

Gipson, Fred. *The Cow Killers: With the Aftosa Commission in Mexico.* Austin: University of Texas Press, 1956.

Gruening, Ernest. *Mexico and Its Heritage.* New York: Century Co., 1928.

La fiebre aftosa en México. Estado actual de la campaña. Mexico City: Secretaría de Agricultura y Ganadería, 1951.

Pavia Guzmán, Edgar. *Recuerdos incompletos de un pasado feliz.* Self-published, 2011.

Porter, James A. *Doctor, Spare My Cow!* Aimes: Iowa State College Press, 1956.

Reeves, Frank. *Hacienda de Atotonilco.* Yerbanís, Durango: Atotonilco Livestock Co., 1936.

Reta Pettersson, Gustavo. *Indiscreciones de un médico veterinario zootecnista.* Mexico City: G. Reta Pettersson, 2012.

Romero Méndez, Salvador. *Ensayos, discursos y poemas.* Mexico City: Página Seis, 2020.

Rubín, Ramón. *Ese rifle sanitario: semi-novela.* Imprinta Insurgentes, 1948.

Santos, Gonzalo N. *Memorias.* Mexico City: Grijalbo, 1986.

Secretaría de Agricultura. *Memorias de la Secretaría de Agricultura, 1938–1939.* Mexico City: Secretaría de Agricultura, 1939.

Secretaría de Agricultura y Ganadería. *Fiebre aftosa.* Secretaría de Agricultura y Ganadería, n.d. Film held in the library of the Facultad de Medicina

Veterinaria y Zootecnia, Universidad Nacional Autónoma de México, Mexico City.

Secretaría de Economía. *Primer censo agrícola-ganadero, 1930.* Mexico City: Secretaría de Economía, 1936.

Segundo censo agrícola, ganadero y ejidal, 1940. Mexico City: Secretaría de Economía, 1948.

Tercer censo agrícola, ganadero y ejidal, 1950. Mexico City: Secretaría de Economía, 1955.

Shahan, Maurice. "La fiebre aftosa: una amenaza para los Estados Unidos." *Boletín de la Oficina Sanitaria Panamericana* 32:6 (June 1953): 576–83.

Stanislawski, Dan. *The Anatomy of Eleven Towns in Michoacán.* Austin: University of Texas Press, 1950.

Steele, James H. "Veterinary Survey in Mexico, Central America and Colombia: A Summary." *Boletín de la Oficina Sanitaria Panamericana* 25:9 (1946): 810–19.

Téllez Girón, Alfredo. "Iniciación del brote de fiebre aftosa en México e investigaciones llevadas a cabo durante los años 1946–1952." *Veterinaria Mexicana* 9 (1978): 31–6.

Torres Bodet, Jaime. *La victoria sin alas: memorias.* Mexico City: Ed. Porrúa, 1970.

Torres y Elzaurdia, José Domingo. *Botas de hule. Anecdotario de la campaña contra la fiebre aftosa en México.* Mexico City: Centro Nacional de Investigaciones Agrarias, 1956.

USDA. *Campaign in Mexico Against Foot and Mouth Disease, 1947–1952.* Unpublished 1954 manuscript by Agricultural Research Service, USDA, available at Sul Ross University, Archive of the Big Bend, Aftosa Papers.

SECONDARY SOURCES

Achim, Miruna. "Making Lizards into Drugs: The Debates on the Medical Uses of Reptiles in Late Eighteenth-Century Mexico." *Journal of Spanish Cultural Studies* 8:2 (2007): 169–91.

Acker, Antoine. *Volkswagen in the Amazon: The Tragedy of Global Development in Modern Brazil.* Cambridge: Cambridge University Press, 2017.

Agostoni, Claudia. *Médicos, campañas, vacunas: la viruela y la cultura de su prevención en México, 1870–1952.* Mexico City: Universidad Nacional Autónoma de México, 2016.

Alexander, Ryan. *Sons of the Mexican Revolution: Miguel Alemán and His Generation.* Albuquerque: University of New Mexico Press, 2016.

Alvarez, C. J. *Border Land, Border Water: A History of Construction on the US-Mexico Divide.* Austin: University of Texas Press, 2019.

"The US-Mexico Border and the 1947 Foot-and-Mouth Disease Outbreak in Mexico." *Journal of the Southwest* 61:4 (2019): 691–724.

Alves, Abel. *The Animals of Spain: An Introduction to Imperial Perceptions and Human Interaction with Other Animals, 1492–1826.* Leiden: Brill, 2011.

Arce, Alberto. *Negotiating Agricultural Development: Entanglements of Bureaucrats and Rural Producers in Western Mexico.* Wageningen: Agricultural University, 1993.

Arellano, Lucrecia, Silvia López-Ortiz, Ponciano Pérez-Herrera, José Gerardo Alonso B., José Antonio Torres-Rivera, Carmen Huerta, Magdalena Cruz-Rosales. "La ganadería bovina veracruzana: hacia la sustentabilidad." In *Ganadería sustenable en el golfo de México*, edited by Gonzalo Halffter, Magadalena Cruz, Carmen Huerta, 189–212. Xalapa, Veracruz: Instituto de Ecología, 2018.

Aviña, Alexander. "'We Have Returned to Porfirian Times': Neopopulism, Counterinsurgency, and the Dirty War in Guerrero, Mexico, 1969–1976." In *Populism in Twentieth Century Mexico: The Presidencies of Lázaro Cárdenas and Luis Echeverría*, edited by Amelia Kiddle and María Muñoz, 106–21. Tucson: University of Arizona Press.

Balmer, Brian. "The Drift of Biological Weapons Policy in the UK, 1945–65." *The Journal of Strategic Studies* 20:4 (1997): 115–45.

Barkin, David and Billie DeWalt. "Sorghum and the Mexican Food Crisis." *Latin American Research Review* 23:3 (1988): 30–59.

Barnett, Michael and Martha Finnemore. "The Politics, Power, and Pathologies of International Organizations." *International Organization* 53:4 (1999): 699–732.

Barragán-Álvarez, José Adrián. "The Feet of Commerce: Mule-trains and Transportation in Eighteenth Century New Spain." PhD dissertation, University of Texas at Austin, 2013.

Barrera, Narciso and Hipólito Rodríguez, eds. *Desarrollo y medio ambiente en Veracruz: impactos económicos, ecológicos y culturales de la ganadería en Veracruz*. Mexico City: Fundación Ebert; Centro de Investigaciones y Estudios Superiores en Antropología Social, 1993.

Bartra, Armando. *Los herederos de Zapata: movimientos campesinos posrevolucionarios en México, 1920–1980*. Mexico City: Ediciones Era, 1986.

Bassols Batalla, Ángel. *Las Huastecas en el desarrollo regional de México*. Mexico City: Trillas, 1977.

Bazant, Mílada. "Bestiality: The Nefarious Crime in Mexico, 1800–1856." In *Sexuality and the Unnatural in Colonial Latin America*, edited by Zeb Tortorici, 188–212. Berkeley: University of California Press, 2016.

Beals, Ralph. *Cherán: A Sierra Tarascan Village*. Washington DC: USGPO, 1946.

Berdah, Delphine. *Abattre ou vacciner: la France et le Royaume-Uni en lutte contre la tuberculose et la fièvre aphteuse (1900–1960)*. Paris: Éditions EHESS, 2018.

Bess, Michael K. *Routes of Compromise: Building Roads and Shaping the Nation in Mexico, 1917–1952*. Lincoln. University of Nebraska Press, 2017.

Bobrow Strain, Aaron. *Intimate Enemies: Landowners, Power and Violence in Chiapas*. Durham, NC: Duke University Press, 2007.

Borah, Woodrow. *Justice by Insurance: The General Indian Court of Colonial Mexico and the Legal Aides of the Half-real*. Berkeley: University of California Press, 1983.

Boyer, Christopher and Martha Micheline Cariño Olvera. "Mexico's Ecological Revolutions." In *A Living Past: Environmental Histories of Modern Latin America*, edited by Claudia Leal, José Augusto Pádua, and John Soluri, 23–44. New York: Berghahn Books, 2019.

Boyer, Christopher and Emily Wakild. "Social Landscaping in the Forests of Mexico: An Environmental Interpretation of Cardenismo, 1934–1940." *Hispanic American Historical Review* 92:1 (2012): 73–106.

Brown, Karen and Daniel Gilfoyle, eds. *Healing the Herds: Disease, Livestock Economies, and Globalization.* Athens, OH: Ohio University Press, 2010.

Bresalier, Michael. "From Healthy Cows to Healthy Humans: Integrated Approaches to World Hunger, c. 1930–1965." In *Animals and the Shaping of Modern Medicine*, edited by Rachel Mason Dentinger, Angela Cassidy, Michael Bresalier, and Abigail Woods, 119–60. London: Springer International, 2017.

Buchenau, Jürgen. "Ambivalent Neighbor: Mexico and Guatemala's 'Ten Years of Spring,' 1944–1954." *The Latin Americanist* 61: 4 (2017): 458–73.

Buckles, Daniel and Jacques Chevalier. *A Land Without Gods: Process Theory, Maldevelopment and the Mexican Nahua.* London: Zed Books, 1988.

Bulliet, Richard. *Hunters, Herders and Hamburgers: The Past and Future of Human-Animal Relations.* New York: Columbia University Press, 2005.

Butler, James. "Follow the Science." *London Review of Books* 42:8 (16 April 2020).

Cano, Gabriela. "Unconcealable Realities of Desire: Amelio Robles's (Transgender) Masculinity in the Mexican Revolution." In *Sex in Revolution: Gender, Politics and Power in Modern Mexico*, edited by Mary Kay Vaughan, Gabriela Cano, and Jocelyn Olcott, 35–56. Durham, NC: Duke University Press, 2006.

Camou Healy, Ernesto. *De rancheros, poquiteros, orejanos y criollos: los productores ganaderos de Sonora y el mercado international.* Zamora; Hermosillo: El Colegio de Michoacán; Centro de Investigación en Alimentación y Desarrollo, 1998.

Carroll, Michael Christopher. *Lab 257: The Disturbing Story of the Government's Secret Plum Island Germ Laboratory.* New York: Harper Collins, 2004.

Castro Rosales, Víctor Manuel. "La aftosa en Zacatecas, sus efectos en el hato, en la economía y la política local: 1946–1954." PhD diss., Universidad Autónoma de Zacatecas, 2016.

Cervantes Sánchez, Juan Manuel. "Historiografía veterinaria Mexicana (siglos XVI–XX)." *REDVET. Revista Electrónica de Veterinaria* 15:5 (2014): 1–8.

Cervantes Sánchez, Juan Manuel and Ana María Román de Carlos. "Las consecuencias de la epizootia de la fiebre aftosa (1946–1955) sobre la veterinaria y zootecnia mexicanas." *Imágen veterinaria* 1:2 (2001), 17–20.

Cervantes Sánchez, Juan Manuel, Ana María Román de Carlos, Cristián López Montelongo. *La medicina veterinaria mexicana (1853–1985): vista desde sus instituciones.* Mexico City: Universidad Nacional Autónoma de México, 2009.

Chauvet, Michelle. *La ganadería bovina de carne en México: del auge a la crisis.* Mexico City: Universidad Autónoma Metropolitana, 1999.

Collingham, Elizabeth. *The Taste of War: World War Two and the Battle for Food.* London: Allen Lane, 2011.

Corner, George W. *A History of the Rockefeller Institute, 1901–1953.* New York, Rockefeller Institute Press, 1965.

Corrales, Rodolfo. *Hacienda de Atotonilco, Raymond Bell: un ejemplo de explotación racional de los pastos.* Yerbanís, Durango: n.p., 1993.

Cotter, Joseph. *Troubled Harvest: Agronomy and Revolution in Mexico, 1880–2002*. Westport, CT: Praeger, 2003.

Crosby, Alfred W. *Ecological Imperialism: The Biological Expansion of Europe, 900–1900*. Second Edition. Cambridge: University of Cambridge Press, 2004.

Cueto, Marcos. *Cold War, Deadly Fevers: Malaria Eradication in Mexico, 1955–1975*. Baltimore: Johns Hopkins University Press, 2007.

The Value of Health: A History of the Pan American Health Organization. Rochester NY: University of Rochester Press, 2007.

Cueto, Marcos and Steven Palmer. *Medicine and Public Health in Latin America: A History*. Cambridge: Cambridge University Press, 2014.

Dehouve, Danielle. *Entre el caimán y el jaguar: los pueblos indios de Guerrero*. Tlalpan: Centro de Investigaciones y Estudios Superiores en Antropología Social, 1994.

De la Peña, Moisés T. *Guerrero económico*. Mexico City: n.p., 1949.

Delay, Brian. *War of a Thousand Deserts: Indian Raids and the US–Mexican War*. New Haven: Yale University Press, 2008.

De los Reyes Patiño, Reynaldo. "En la frontera: tensiones políticas y económicas de la ganadería bovina del norte de Coahuila, 1947–1982." *America Latina en la Historia Económica* 25:3 (2018): 187–222.

Demuth, Bathsheba. "The Walrus and the Bureaucrat: Energy, Ecology and Making the State in the Russian and American Arctic, 1870–1950." *American Historical Review* 124:2 (2019): 483–510.

Descola, Philippe. *Beyond Nature and Culture*. Chicago: University of Chicago Press, 2013.

Doeppers, Daniel. "Fighting Rinderpest in the Philippines, 1886–1941." In *Healing the Herds: Disease, Livestock Economies, and the Globalization of Veterinary Medicine*, edited by Karen Brown and Daniel Gilfoye, 108–28. Athens, OH: Ohio University Press, 2010.

Dusenberry, William Howard. "Foot and Mouth Disease in Mexico, 1946–1951." *Agricultural History* 29:2 (1955): 82–90.

The Mexican Mesta: The Administration of Ranching in Colonial Mexico. Urbana: University of Illinois Press, 1963.

Dwyer, John J. "Diplomatic Weapons of the Weak: Mexican Policymaking during the US–Mexican Agrarian Dispute, 1934–1941." *Diplomatic History* 26:3 (2002): 375–95.

Ervin, Michael A. "The 1930 Agrarian Census in Mexico: Agronomists, Middle Politics, and the Negotiation of Data Collection." *Hispanic American Historical Review*, 87:3 (2007): 537–70.

Ewing, Sherm. *The Ranch: A Modern History of the North American Cattle Industry*. Missoula, MT: Mountain Press Publishing, 1995.

Fallaw, Ben. "Eulogio Ortíz: The Army and the Antipolitics of Postrevolutionary State Formation, 1920–1935." In *Forced Marches: Soldiers and Military Caciques in Modern Mexico*, edited by B. Fallaw and T. Rugeley, 136–71. Tucson: University of Arizona Press, 2012.

Religion and State Formation in Postrevolutionary Mexico. Durham: Duke University Press, 2013.

Feder, Ernest. *Lean Cows, Fat Ranchers: The International Ramifications of Mexico's Beef Cattle Industry*. London: América Latina, 1980.

"The Odious Competition Between Man and Animal over Agricultural Resources in the Underdeveloped Countries." *Review* 3:3 (1980): 463–500.

Fein, Seth. "Everyday Forms of Transnational Collaboration: US Film Propaganda in Cold War Mexico." In *Close Encounters of Empire: Writing the Cultural History of US-Latin American Relations*, edited by Gilbert Joseph, Catherine Legrande, and Ricardo Salvatore, 400–50. Durham, NC: Duke University Press, 1999.

Few, Martha and Zeb Tortorici, eds. *Centering Animals in Latin American History*. Durham, NC: Duke University Press, 2013.

Fleishman, Thomas. *Communist Pigs: An Animal History of East Germany's Rise and Fall*. Seattle: University of Washington Press, 2020.

Flores, Rubén. *Backroads Pragmatists: Mexico's Melting Pot and Civil Rights in the United States*. College Park, PA: University of Pennsylvania Press, 2014.

Florescano, Enrique. *La bandera mexicana: breve historia de su formación y simbolismo*. Mexico City: Fondo de Cultura Económica, 2014.

Field, Thomas, Stella Krepp, and Vanni Pettinà, eds. *Latin America and the Global Cold War*. Chapel Hill: University of North Carolina Press, 2021.

Figueroa Velázquez, Ana Cecilia. *El tiro de gracia al campo queretano*. Querétaro, Querétaro: Universidad Autónoma de Querétaro, 2011.

Fitzgerald, Deborah. "Exporting American Agriculture: The Rockefeller Foundation in Mexico, 1943–53." *Social Studies of Science* 16:3 (1986): 457–83.

Fox, Kel M. "Aftosa: The Campaign Against Foot-and-Mouth Disease in Mexico, 1946–1951." *Journal of Arizona History* 38:1 (1997): 23–40.

Franklin, Adrian. *Animals and Modern Cultures: A Sociology of Human-Animal Relations in Modernity*. Los Angeles: Sage, 1999.

Freeman Smith, Robert. "The United States and the Revolution, 1921–1950." In *Myths, Misdeeds, and Misunderstandings: The Roots of Conflict in US–Mexican Relations*, edited by Jaime E. Rodríguez and Kathryn Vincent, 181–98. Wilmington, DE: Scholarly Resources, 1997.

Freites, Yajaira. "Relaciones científicas de medicina veterinaria venezolana con sus pares latinoamericanos: México y el Cono Sur (1933–1955)." *História, Ciências, Saúde-Manguinhos* 15:2 (2008): 497–518.

Friedman, Max Paul. "Retiring the Puppets, Bringing Latin America Back In: Recent Scholarship on United States–Latin American Relations." *Diplomatic History* 27:5 (2003): 621–36.

García Maldonado, Alberto. "Regulating Bracero Migration: How National, Regional, and Local Political Considerations Shaped the Bracero Program." *Hispanic American Historical Review* 101:3 (2021): 433–60.

García Garagarza, León. "The Year the People Turned into Cattle: The End of the World in New Spain, 1558." In *Centering Animals in Latin American History*, edited by Martha Few and Zeb Tortorici, 31–61. Durham, NC: Duke University Press.

Gilbert, Jess. *Planning Democracy: Agrarian Intellectuals and the Intended New Deal*. New Haven: Yale University Press, 2015.

Gillingham, Paul. "Maximino's Bulls: Popular Protest after the Mexican Revolution, 1940–1952." *Past and Present* 206: 1 (2010): 175–211.

Unrevolutionary Mexico: The Birth of a Strange Dictatorship. New Haven: Yale University Press, 2021.

"'We Don't Have Arms, But We Do Have Balls': Fraud, Violence, and Popular Agency in Elections." In *Dictablanda: Politics, Work, and Culture in Mexico, 1938–1968*, edited by Paul Gillingham and Benjamin Smith, 147–79. Durham, NC: Duke University Press, 2014.

"Who Killed Crispín Aguilar? Violence and Order in the Post-Revolutionary Countryside.' In *Violence, Insecurity, and the State in Mexico: The Other Half of the Centaur*, edited by Wil Pansters, 91–111. Stanford: Stanford University Press, 2012.

Gillingham, Paul and Benjamin Smith, eds. *Dictablanda: Politics, Work, and Culture in Mexico, 1938–1968*. Durham, NC: Duke University Press, 2014.

"Introduction: The Paradoxes of Revolution." In *Dictablanda: Politics, Work, and Culture in Mexico, 1938–1968*, edited by Paul Gillingham and Benjamin Smith, 1–44. Durham, NC: Duke University Press, 2014.

Gledhill, John. *Casi Nada: A Study of Agrarian Reform in the Homeland of Cardenismo*. New York: State University of New York Press, 1991.

González, Roberto J. *Zapotec Science: Farming and Food in the Northern Sierra of Oaxaca*. Austin: University of Texas Press, 2001.

González Martínez, Laura. "Political Brokers, Ejidos, and State Resources: The Case of Arturo Quiroz Francia, a Peasant Leader from Guanajuato, Mexico." PhD diss., University of California, Santa Barbara, 1996.

González-Montagut, Renée. "Factors That Contributed to the Expansion of Cattle Ranching in Veracruz, Mexico." *Mexican Studies/Estudios Mexicanos* 15:1(1999): 101–30.

Gómez Galvarriato, Aurora. "La construcción del milagro mexicano: el Instituto Mexicano de Investigaciones Tecnológicas, el Banco de México, y la Armour Research Foundation." *Historia Mexicana* 69:3 (2020): 1247–1309.

Graf von Hardenberg, Wilko, Matthew Kelly, Claudia Leal and Emily Wakild, eds. *The Nature State: Rethinking the History of Conservation*. London: Routledge, 2019.

Grijalva Dávila, Miguel Ángel. "El ocaso del latifundio Greene: ilegalidad, política internacional y agrarismo en la frontera Sonora-Arizona, 1954–1958." *Historia Mexicana* 67:3 (2018): 1295–344.

Gutiérrez Núñez, Nezahualcóyotl Luis. "Cambio agrario y revolución verde. Dilemas científicos, políticos y agrarios en la agricultura mexicana del maíz, 1920–1970." PhD diss., Colegio de México, 2017.

Guzmán Urióstegui, Jesús. *Oxtotitlán y el milagro del apóstol señor Santiago*. Mexico City: Editorial Los Reyes, 2016.

Halffter, Gonzalo, Magdalena Cruz, and Carmen Huerta, eds. *Ganadería sustenable en el Golfo de México*. Xalapa: Instituto de Ecología, 2018.

Harmer, Tanya. "The Cold War in Latin America." In *The Routledge Handbook of the Cold War*. London: Routledge, 2014.

"Review of *The Ideological Origins of the Dirty War* by Federico Finchelstein." *Cold War History* 15:3 (2015): 417–20.

Harwood, Jonathan. "Peasant-friendly Plant Breeding and the Early Years of the Green Revolution in Mexico." *Agricultural History* 83:3 (2009): 384–410.

"Whatever Happened to the Mexican Green Revolution?" *Agroecology and Sustainable Food Systems* 44:9 (2020): 1243–52.

Hobsbawm, Eric. "The Machine Breakers." *Past and Present* 1:1 (1952): 57–70.

Hribal, Jason. "'Animals are Part of the Working Class': A Challenge to Labor History." *Labour History* 44:4 (2003) 435–53.

Hunt, Linda. *Secret Agenda: The United States, Nazi Scientists, and Project Paperclip, 1945–1990*. New York: St Martin's Press, 1991.

Jones, Halbert. *The War Has Brought Peace to Mexico: World War II and the Consolidation of the Post-Revolutionary State*. Albuquerque: University of New Mexico Press, 2014.

Joseph, Gilbert M. "Rethinking Mexican Revolutionary Mobilization: Yucatán's Seasons of Upheaval, 1909–1915." In *Everyday Forms of State Formation: Revolution and the Negotiation of Rule in Modern Mexico*, edited by Gilbert M. Joseph and Daniel Nugent, 135–69. Durham, NC: Duke University Press, 1994.

Keller, Renata. *Mexico's Cold War: Cuba, the United States, and the Legacy of the Mexican Revolution*. Cambridge: Cambridge University Press, 2015.

Kheraj, Sean. "The Great Epizootic of 1872–73: Networks of Animal Disease in North American Urban Environments." *Environmental History* 23 (2018): 495–521.

Kean, Hilda and Phillip Howell, eds. *The Routledge Companion to Animal-Human History*. London: Routledge, 2018.

Kloppe-Santamaría, Gema. *In the Vortex of Violence: Lynching, Extrajudicial Justice, and the State in Post-Revolutionary Mexico*. Berkeley: University of California Press, 2020.

Knight, Alan. *The Mexican Revolution*. 2 vols. Cambridge: Cambridge University Press, 1986.

Mexico: Volume 2, The Colonial Era. Cambridge: Cambridge University Press, 2002.

"Popular Culture and the Revolutionary State in Mexico, 1910–1940." *Hispanic American Historical Review* 74:3 (1994): 393–444.

"The Weight of the State in Modern Mexico." In *Studies in the Formation of the Nation State in Latin America*, edited by James Dunkerley, 212–53. London: Institute for the Study of the Americas, 2002.

Krauze, Enrique. *La presidencia imperial: ascenso y caída del sistema político mexicano (1940–1996)*. Mexico City: Tusquets Editores, 1997.

Krige, John and Jessica Wang. "Nation, Knowledge, and Imagined Futures: Science, Technology, and Nation-building, Post-1945." *History and Technology* 31:3 (2015): 171–9.

Kumar, Prakash, Tim Lorek, Tore Olsson, Nichole Sackley, Sigrid Schmalzer, and Gabriela Soto Laveaga. "Roundtable: New Narratives of the Green Revolution." *Agricultural History* 91:3 (2017): 397–422.

Lear, John. *Workers, Neighbors, and Citizens: The Revolution in Mexico City*. Lincoln: University of Nebraska Press, 2001.

Leary, John Patrick. *A Cultural History of Underdevelopment: Latin America in the US Imagination*. Richmond: University of Virginia Press, 2016.

Ledbetter, John. "Fighting Foot-and-Mouth Disease in Mexico: Popular Protest Against Diplomatic Decisions." *Southwest Historical Quarterly* 104: 3 (2001): 386–415.

Léonard, Éric. "Los empresarios de la frontera agraria y la construcción de los territorios de la ganadería: la colonización y la ganaderización del istmo central, 1950–1985." In *El istmo mexicano: una región inasequible: estado, poderes locales y dinámicas espaciales*, edited by Emilia Velázquez, Éric Léonard, Odile Hoffmann, M. F. Prévôt-Shapira. Marseille: IRD Éditions, 2009.

Una historia de vacas y golondrinas: ganaderos y campesinos temporeros del trópico seco mexicano. Mexico City: Fondo de Cultura Económica; El Colegio de Michoacán; ORSTOM, 1995.

Lewis, Oscar. *The Children of Sánchez: Autobiography of a Mexican Family*. New York: Vintage, 1963.

Loaeza, Soledad. "Dos hipótesis sobre el presidencialismo autoritario." *Revista Mexicana de Ciencias Políticas y Sociales* 218 (2013): 53–72.

Lomnitz Adler, Claudio. *Exits From the Labyrinth: Culture and Ideology in the Mexican National Space*. Berkeley: University of California Press, 1993.

Lopes, María-Aparecida and María Cecilia Zuleta, eds. *Mercados en común: estudios sobre conexiones transnacionales, negocios y diplomacia en las Américas*. Mexico City: El Colegio de México, 2016.

Lopes, María-Aparecida and Paolo Riguzzi. "Borders, Trade, and Politics: Exchange between the United States and Mexican Cattle Industries, 1870–1947." *Hispanic American Historical Review* 92:4 (2012): 603–35.

Lopes, María-Aparecida and Reynaldo de los Reyes Patiño. "Institutions and Interest Groups: Meat Provision in Mexico City, 1850–1967." *Mundo Agrario* 21:46 (2020).

López, Rick. *Crafting Mexico: Intellectuals, Artisans, and the State after the Revolution*. Durham, NC: Duke University Press, 2010.

Lorek, Timothy W. and Andra B. Chastain, eds. *Itineraries of Expertise: Science, Technology and the Environment in Latin America*. Pittsburgh: University of Pittsburgh Press, 2020.

Lorenzini, Sara. *Global Development: A Cold War History*. Princeton: Princeton University Press, 2019.

Lurtz, Casey. "Developing the Mexican Countryside: The Department of Fomento's Social Project of Modernization." *Business History Review* 90:3 (2016): 431–55.

Machado, Manuel. *Aftosa: A Historical Survey of Foot-and-Mouth Disease and Interamerican Relations*. Berkeley: University of California Press, 1969.

An Industry in Crisis: Mexican-United States Cooperation in the Control of Foot-and-Mouth Disease. Berkeley: University of California Press, 1968.

Macekura, Stephen and Eric Manela, eds. *The Development Century: A Global History*. Cambridge: Cambridge University Press, 2018.

Macías Cardone, Luis. *México: constantes y variantes de su sistema político, 1968–1976*. Mexico City: Tribuna de la Juventud, 1975.

Maldonado Aranda, S. *Los márgenes del Estado mexicano. Territorios ilegales, desarrollo y violencia en Michoacán*. Zamora: COLMICH, 2010.

Mayer, Leticia and Larissa Adler de Lomnitz. *La nueva clase: desarrollo de una profesión en México*. Mexico City: Universidad Nacional Autónoma de México, 1988.

McCrea, Heather. "Pest to Vector: Disease, Public Health, and the Challenges of State-Building in Yucatán, Mexico, 1833–1922." In *Centering Animals in Latin American History*, edited by Martha Few and Zeb Tortorici, 149–79. Durham, NC: Duke University Press, 2013.

McDonald, Bryan. *Food Power: The Rise and Fall of the Postwar American Food System*. New York: Oxford University Press, 2017.

McNeill, John R. and Corinna R. Unger. "Introduction: The Big Picture." In *Environmental Histories of the Cold War*, edited by John R. McNeill and Corinna Unger, 1–18. Cambridge: Cambridge University Press, 2013.

McVety, Amanda Kay. *The Rinderpest Campaigns: A Virus, Its Vaccines, and Global Development in the Twentieth Century*. Cambridge: Cambridge University Press, 2018.

Melville, Elinor. *A Plague of Sheep: Environmental Consequences of the Conquest of Mexico*. Cambridge: Cambridge University Press, 1994.

Mendoza, Mary. "Battling Aftosa: North to South Migration Across the US–Mexico Border, 1947–1954." *Journal of the West* 54:1 (2015): 39–50.

Meyer, Jean. *El sinarquismo, el cardenismo y la iglesia: 1937–1947*. Mexico City: Tusquets, 2003.

Mikhail, Alan. *The Animal in Ottoman Egypt*. Oxford: Oxford University Press, 2013.

Millet, Piers. "Anti-Animal Biological Weapons Programs." In *Deadly Cultures: Biological Weapons since 1945*, edited by Malcolm Dando, Mark Wheelis, and Lajos Rózsa, 224–35. London: Harvard University Press, 2006.

Mitchell, Timothy. "The Limits of the State: Beyond Statist Approaches and Their Critics." *American Political Science Review* 85:1 (1991): 77–96.
The Rule of Experts: Egypt, Techno-Politics, Modernity. Berkeley: University of California Press, 2002.

Mociño, José Mariano. *Real expedición botánica a Nueva España*. Volumes XII, XIII. Mexico City: Siglo XXI; Universidad Nacional Autónoma de México; El Colegio de Sinaloa, 2010.

Moreno, Julio. *Yankee Don't Go Home! Mexican Nationalism, American Business Culture, and the Shaping of Modern Mexico, 1920–1950*. Chapel Hill: University of North Carolina Press, 2004.

Morris, Nathaniel. "Serrano Communities and Subaltern Negotiation Strategies: The Local Politics of Opium Production in Mexico, 1940–2020." *The Social History of Alcohol and Drugs* 34:1 (2020): 48–81.

Mújica Vélez, Rubén. *Los condenados en su tierra*. Mexico City: Plaza y Valdés, 2001.

Nash Carter, Craig. *One Man, One Medicine, One Health: The James H. Steele Story*. n.p, 2009.

Niblo, Stephen. *War, Diplomacy, and Development: The United States and Mexico, 1938–1954*. Wilmington, DE: Scholarly Resources, 1995.

Norton, Marcy. "The Chicken and the Iegue: Human-Animal Relationships and the Colombian Exchange." *American Historical Review* 120:1 (2015): 28–60.

Ochoa, Enrique C. "Reappraising State Intervention and Social Policy in Mexico: The Case of Milk in the Distrito Federal during the Twentieth Century." *Mexican Studies/Estudios Mexicanos* 15:1 (1999): 73–99.

Olea-Franco, Adolfo. "One Century of Higher Agricultural Education and Research in Mexico (1850s–1960s), with a Preliminary Survey on the Same Subjects in the United States." PhD diss., Harvard University, 2001.

Olmstead, Alan. L. and Paul Rhode, *Arresting Contagion: Science, Policy and Conflicts over Animal Disease Control.* Cambridge, MA: Harvard University Press, 2015.

"Not on my Farm! Resistance to Bovine Tuberculosis Eradication in the United States." *The Journal of Economic History* 67:3 (2007): 768–809.

Olsson, Tore C. *Agrarian Crossings: Reformers and the Remaking of the US and Mexican Countryside.* Princeton: Princeton University Press, 2020.

Padilla, Tanalís. *Rural Resistance in the Land of Zapata: The Jaramillista Movement and the Myth of the Pax PRIísta, 1940–1962.* Durham, NC: Duke University Press, 2008.

Palacios, Carlos and Edgardo Seoane. *Informe sobre la aftosa, problema presente y future del continente americano y la importancia del centro Panamericano de fiebre aftosa.* Washington, DC: Unión Panamericana, 1967.

Parry, Tyler D., and Charlton Yingling. "Slave Hounds and Abolition in the Americas." *Past and Present* 246:1 (2020): 69–108.

Pavia Guzmán, Edgar. *Acciones políticas ganaderas en Guerrero.* Chilpancingo: Asociación de Historiadores de Guerrero, 1997.

Piccato, Pablo. *Historia mínima de la violencia en México.* Mexico City: El Colegio de México, forthcoming.

Pensado, Jaime and Enrique Ochoa. "Introduction." In *México Beyond 1968: Revolutionaries, Radicals, and Repression During the Global Sixties and Subversive Seventies,* edited by Jaime Pensado and Enrique Ochoa, 3–18. Tucson: University of Arizona Press, 2018.

Pérez Escutia, Ramón Alonso. *Senguio, Michoacán: una historia de haciendas, pueblos y ejidos.* Morelia: Universidad Michoacana de San Nicolás de Hidalgo, 2006.

Pérez Espejo, Rosario. *Granjas porcinas y medio ambiente. Contaminación del agua en La Piedad, Michoacán.* Mexico City: Plaza y Valdés, 2006.

Perezgrovas Garza, Raúl. *Antología sobre etnoveterinaria: origin y evolución en Chiapas.* San Cristóbal de las Casas, Chiapas: Instituto de Estudios Indígenas, Universidad de Chiapas, 2014.

Pérez Ricart, Carlos A. "U.S. Pressure and Mexican Anti-drug Efforts from 1940 to 1980: Importing the War on Drugs?" In *Beyond the Drug War in Mexico: Human Rights, the Public Sphere and Justice,* edited by Wil Pansters, Benjamin T. Smith, and Peter Watt, 33–52. Oxford: Routledge, 2018.

Pettinà, Vanni. "Adapting to the New World: Mexico's International Strategy of Economic Development at the Outset of the Cold War, 1946–1952." *Culture and History Digital Journal* 4:1 (2015).

Pilcher, Jeffrey. *The Sausage Rebellion: Public Health, Private Enterprise, and Meat in Mexico City, 1890–1917.* Albuquerque: University of New Mexico Press, 2006.

Proctor, Frank "Trey." "*Amores perritos*: Puppies, Laughter, and Popular Catholicism in Bourbon Mexico." *Journal of Latin American Studies* 46:1 (2014): 1–28.

Quezada, J. Gilberto. *Border Boss: Manuel B. Bravo and Zapata County.* College Station: Texas A & M University Press, 2001.

Quintana, Alejandro. *Maximino Ávila Camacho and the One-Party State: The Taming of Caudillismo and Caciquismo in Post-Revolutionary Mexico.* Boulder: Lexington Books, 2010.

Quintana Rodríguez, Benito. ¡*Ellos fueron!* Mexico City: Palabros Palibros, 2012.

Ramírez, Paul. *Enlightened Immunity: Mexico's Experiments with Disease Prevention in the Age of Reason.* Stanford: Stanford University Press, 2018.

Rath, Thomas. "Burning the Archive, Building the State? Politics, Paper, and US Power in Postwar Mexico." *Journal of Contemporary History* 55:4 (2020): 764–92.

"Modernizing Military Patriarchy: Gender and State-Building in Postrevolutionary Mexico." *Journal of Social History* 52:3 (2019): 807–30.

Myths of Demilitarization in Postrevolutionary Mexico, 1920–1960. Chapel Hill: University of North Carolina Press, 2013.

Rodríguez, María J. and Robert D. Shadow. "Religión, economía y política en la rebelión cristera: el caso de los gobiernistas de Villa Guerrero, Jalisco." *Historia Mexicana* 43:4 (1994): 657–700.

Romanucci Ross, Lola. *Conflict, Violence, and Morality in a Mexican Village.* Chicago: University of Chicago Press, 1973.

Rosenberg, Charles E. "What is an Epidemic? AIDS in Historical Perspective." *Daedalus* 118:2 (1989): 1–17.

Rosemblatt, Karin A. "Other Americas: Transnationalism, Scholarship, and the Culture of Poverty in Mexico and the United States." *Hispanic American Historical Review* 89:4 (2009): 603–41.

Ross, Eric B. "A Critic Unfettered: The Legacy of Ernest Feder." *Development and Change* 42:1 (2011): 330–48.

Ritvo, Harriet. "On the Animal Turn." *Daedalus* 136:4 (2007): 118–22.

Russell, Edmund. "Can Organisms be Technology?" In *The Illusory Boundary: Environment and Technology in History*, edited by Martin Reuss, 249–62. Richmond: University of Virginia Press, 2010.

Salas Landa, Mónica. "Enacting Agrarian Law: The Effects of Legal Failure in Postrevolutionary Mexico." *Journal of Latin American Studies* 47:4 (2015): 685–715.

Sanderson, Steven E. *Agrarian Populism and the Mexican State: The Struggle for Land in Sonora.* Berkeley: University of California Press, 1981.

The Transformation of Mexican Agriculture: International Structure and the Politics of Rural Change. Princeton: Princeton University Press, 1986.

Saragoza, Alex. *The Monterrey Elite and the Mexican State, 1880–1940.* Austin: University of Texas Press, 1988.

Saucedo Montemayor, Pedro. *Historia de la ganadería en México.* Mexico City: Universidad Nacional Autónoma de México, 1984.

Schmidt, Arthur C. "Making it Real Compared to What? Reconceptualizing Mexican History Since 1940." In *Fragments of a Golden Age: The Politics of Culture in Mexico Since 1940*, edited by Gilbert Joseph, Anne Rubenstein, and Eric Zolov, 23–68. Durham, NC: Duke University Press, 2001.

Schryer, Franz. *Ethnicity and Class in Rural Mexico.* Princeton: Princeton University Press, 1990.

Scott, James C. *Seeing Like a State: How Certain Schemes to Improve the Human Condition Have Failed.* New Haven: Yale University Press, 2001.

Weapons of the Weak: Everyday Forms of Peasant Resistance. New Haven: Yale University Press, 1985.

Scruggs, Charles G. *The Peaceful Atom and the Deadly Fly.* Austin: Jenkins, 1975.

Serrano Álvarez, Pablo. *La batalla del espíritu: el movimiento sinarquista en el Bajío (1932–1951).* 2 vols. Mexico City: Consejo Nacional para la Cultura y las Artes, 1992.

Shepard, Todd. "Algeria, France, Mexico, UNESCO: A transnational history of anti-racism and decolonization, 1932–1962." *Journal of Global History* 6:2 (2011): 273–97.

Sigsworth, Grant Wilkins. "The Mexican Epizootic of Foot-and-Mouth Disease: A Study in the Spread, Eradication and Impact of Infectious Livestock Disease, and Associated Modernization of the Cattle Industry." PhD diss., University of Illinois at Urbana-Champaign, 1975.

Sluyter, Andrew. *Colonialism and Landscape: Postcolonial Theory and Applications.* London: Rowman and Littlefield, 2002.

Smith, Benjamin T. "The Paradoxes of the Public Sphere: Journalism, Gender, and Corruption in Mexico, 1940–70." *Journal of Social History* 52:4 (2019): 1330–54.

The Roots of Conservatism in Mexico: Catholicism, Society, and Politics in the Mixteca Baja, 1750–1962. Albuquerque: University of New Mexico Press, 2012.

Soluri, John. "Home Cooking: Campesinos, Cuisine, and Agrodiversity." In *A Living Past: Environmental Histories of Modern Latin America*, edited by Claudia Leal, José Augusto Pádua, and John Soluri, 163–82. New York: Berghahn Books, 2018.

Sonnenfeld, David A. "Mexico's 'Green Revolution,' 1940–1980: Towards an Environmental History." *Environmental History Review*, 16:4 (1992): 29–52.

Soto Correa, José Carmen. *El rifle sanitario, la fiebre aftosa y la rebelión campesina: guerra fría, guerra caliente.* Mexico City: Instituto Politécnico Nacional, 2009.

Soto Laveaga, Gabriela. *Jungle Laboratories: Mexican Peasants, National Projects, and the Making of the Pill.* Durham, NC: Duke University Press, 2009.

"The Socialist Origins of the Green Revolution: Pandurang Khankhoje and Domestic 'Technical Assistance.'" *History and Technology* 36:3–4 (2020): 337–59.

Sowell, David. *Medicine on the Periphery: Public Health in the Yucatán, Mexico, 1870–1960.* Lanham: Lexington Books, 2015.

Specht, Joshua. *Red Meat Republic: A Hoof-to-Table History of How Beef Changed America.* Princeton: Princeton University Press, 2019.

Stakman, E. C., Richard Bradfield, Paul C. Mangelsdorf. *Campaigns Against Hunger*. Cambridge, MA: The Belknap Press of Harvard University Press, 1967.

Strom, Claire. *Making Catfish Bait Out of Government Boys: The Fight Against Cattle Ticks and the Transformation of the Yeoman South*. Athens: University of Georgia Press, 2010.

Swabe, Joanna. *Animals, Disease and Human Society: Human-animal relations and the Rise of Veterinary Medicine*. London: Routledge, 1998.

Taracena, Alfonso. *La vida en México bajo Miguel Alemán*. Mexico City: Jus, 1979.

Taylor, William B. *Drinking, Homicide and Rebellion in Colonial Mexican Villages*. Stanford: Stanford University Press, 1979.

Téllez Reyes-Retana, Eduardo. "Cuando la fiebre aftosa apareció en México." *Imágen Veterinaria* (2001): 5–8.

Tenorio Trillo, Mauricio. *Latin America: The Allure and Power of an Idea*. Chicago: University of Chicago Press, 2017.

"Stereophonic Scientific Modernisms: Social Science between Mexico and the United States, 1880s–1930s." *Journal of American History* 86:3 (1999): 1156–87.

Thornton, Christy. "Review." In H-Net Roundtable XXII–33 on Eric Zolov, *The Last Good Neighbour: Mexico in the Global 1960s*, March 2021. https://hdiplo.org/to/RT22–33.

Revolution in Development: Mexico and the Governance of the Global Economy. Berkeley: University of California Press, 2021.

Torres Ramírez, Blanca. *México en la segunda guerra mundial: historia de la Revolución Mexicana, periodo 1940–1952*. Mexico City: Colegio de México 1979.

Tortorici, Zeb. *Sins Against Nature: Sex and Archives in Colonial New Spain*. Durham, NC: Duke University Press, 2018.

Tutino, John. *The Mexican Heartland: How Communities Shaped Capitalism, A Nation, and World History, 1500–2000*. Princeton: Princeton University Press, 2018.

Ulloa Bornemann, Alberto. *Surviving Mexico's Dirty War: A Political Prisoner's Memoir*. Philadelphia: Temple University Press, 2007.

Uribe Mendoza, Blanca Irais. "La invención de los animales: una historia de la veterinaria mexicana, siglo XIX." *História, Ciências, Saúde-Manguinhos* 22:4 (2015): 1391–1409.

Vargas-Terán, Moisés. "The New World Screwworm in Mexico and Central America." *World Animal Review*, Special Issue on screwworm, 1991.

Vaughan, Mary Kay. *Cultural Politics in Revolution: Teachers, Peasants, and Schools in Mexico*. Tucson: University of Arizona Press, 1997.

Viqueira Albán, Juan Pedro. *Propriety and Permissiveness in Bourbon Mexico*. Wilmington, DE: Scholarly Resources, 1999.

Wald, Patricia. *Contagious: Cultures, Carriers, and the Outbreak Narrative*. Durham, NC: Duke University Press, 2007.

Warman, Arturo. *El campo mexicano en el siglo XX*. Mexico City: Fondo de Cultura Económica, 2001.

Wiarda, Howard. "Beyond the Pale: The Bureaucratic Politics of United States Policy in Mexico." *World Affairs* 162:4 (2000): 174–90.

Williams, Ben F. and Teresa Williams Irvin. *Let the Tail Go with the Hide: The Story of Ben F. Williams as told to Teresa Williams Irvin*. Bloomington: Unlimited Pub, 2001.

Wilcox, Robert W. *Cattle in the Backlands: Mato Grosso and the Evolution of Ranching in the Brazilian Tropics*. Austin: University of Texas Press, 2017.

Wilcox, Robert W. and Shaun Van Ausdal. "Hoofprints: Ranching and Landscape Transformation." In *A Living Past: Environmental Histories of Modern Latin America*, edited by Claudia Leal, José Augusto Pádua, and John Soluri, 183–204. New York: Berghahn Books, 2018.

Woods, Abigail. *A Manufactured Plague: The History of Foot-and-Mouth Disease in Britain*. London: Earthscan, 2004.

"Patterns of Animal Disease." In *The Routledge History of Disease*, edited by Mark Jackson, 147–64. London: Routledge, 2017.

"Why Slaughter? Cultural Dimensions of Britain's Foot-and-Mouth Disease Control Policy, 1892–2001." *Journal of Agricultural and Environmental Ethics* 17:4 (2004): 341–62.

Wright, Angus. *The Death of Ramón González: The Modern Agricultural Dilemma*. Austin: University of Texas Press, 1990.

Yates, Paul L. *Mexico's Agricultural Dilemma*. Tucson: University of Arizona Press, 1981.

Zazueta, Pilar. "Milk Against Poverty: Nutrition and the Politics of Consumption in Twentieth-Century Mexico." PhD diss., Columbia University, 2011.

Zhang, Sarah. "America's Never-Ending Battle Against Flesh-Eating Worms." *The Atlantic*, May 26, 2020.

Zolov, Eric. *The Last Good Neighbour: Mexico in the Global Sixties*. Durham, NC: Duke University Press, 2020.

Zuleta, María Cecilia. "Laboratorios de cambio agrario: tecnología y ciencia en el campo." *Historia Mexicana* 70:1 (2020): 61–97.

Index